ANOTHER SPRING

A Year of Self Therapy & Spiritual Practices for Every Woman

TERRY FOLKS
Spiritual Integrated Psychotherapist

CLIPSTON PUBLISHING
Vancouver, British Columbia

Another Spring: A Year of Self Therapy and Spiritual Practices
by Terry Folks

Quotation, Fair Use & Permissions Notice

General Disclaimer

Publisher: Clipston Publishing • Edited by: Jessica Kirby • Cover Design: Teena Clipston
Cover Artwork: Joyce Olson and Cathy Gunter, created using DALL·E 3 on the RUBI Virtual Studio. Special thanks to Erika Tafel.

• ISBN (Hardcover): 978-1-7381705-8-6 • ISBN (Paperback): 978-1-7381705-6-2
• ISBN (eBook): 978-1-7381705-7-9

Requests for permission, inquiries, or corrections:
Clipston Publishing via www.clipstonpublishing.com

“Every human is born of Woman.

Revere Her.”

For my daughter Somer
who taught me what it means to let go

For Marge Folks,
my earthly mother, whose Spirit still shines
brighter than anyone I know

and

For the individuals I have had the privilege
of serving and witnessing empower themselves

I am grateful to live, work, and play on the unceded lands of the K'omoks First Nation.

Contents

Preface

I approach my altar. Lighting a candle, I greet my Deep Self with reverence. When I recognize myself this way, I am also communing with Source who enlivens me and is the ground of my being. Standing eye level with the mirror just above my altar, I smile sleepily. I raise my arms above my head and give thanks for waking alive, for being incarnated in human form to do good work for the world, and for earth, air, fire, and water. Without these elements we would not exist, and I am profoundly grateful. I set my intention for the day. Today my intention is to provide a safe, healing space for the women I serve. I am honoured to do this work. I ask for the grace to receive assistance from Source, my inner teacher, guides, ancestors, and my intuitive gifts. With my own *mudras* (gestures) for balance, I awaken and enliven my crown chakra, third eye, throat, heart, solar plexus, sacral, and root chakra. I strike my gong gently, blow out my candle, and step away.

Following morning ablutions, I journal. I trace the trajectory of my feelings over the course of yesterday, how they have resolved themselves, and what is left to dissolve. I then contemplate who I am serving today, and each woman's energy surfaces as I consider her process. I am privileged to be invited into each woman's universe. I bring my intention to my thoughts about each and wonder how I will be a healing container today. I turn to my daily readers and reflect on the offerings. I am using two readers these days—a boundary reader and a Goddess Spirituality reader. Finally, I repeat today's abundance affirmation and sit with it awhile.

Forest beckons today. Sometimes it is the river, or the sea, or the garden, or the park down the street. Today it is the forest. As I approach the treed opening, I cannot help smiling. The trail head always makes me feel this way, anticipatory and happy, as though greeting me with love, inviting me further in to shower me with healing aerosols. After an hour I am feeling grounded, balanced, centred, enlivened. I intentionally build my qi, my resilience, my readiness and capacity to be of good service. Throughout the day and between clients I gather in and recentre, reground, rebalance. After visiting the last woman's universe, I rest.

Due to the nature of my work, sleep is important for me, so my rituals begin mid-evening. I sit in silence, contemplating the words of one of my many great spiritual teachers, and I am moved to tears by the great love from Source flowing through them. I approach my altar. Lighting a candle, I greet my Deep Self again with reverence. I raise my arms above my head and give thanks for delicious sleep, for healing dreams, and for the opportunity to have done good work today. As I lie in bed, I rebalance my vagus nerve and practise presence through one of the many portals offered. I drift off to sleep.

All roads lead here...

My five year old self, please hear me when I tell you

we made it through to the other side.

For sixty years you were guided in your search for unconditional love.

It was hard for you to hear the guidance.

Your trauma combined with free will, Little Terry, so it got complicated.

You didn't know me yet

(your spiritual mom, your inner being... call me what you want now)

and you were... a little headstrong.

I'm sorry the path wasn't straightforward, my darling one.

Yet...

all roads would have led you here anyway

because I have always loved you.

Welcome home, dear one. Welcome home.

- Terry Folks, 2026

Introduction

As a spiritually integrated psychotherapist with a thriving private practice, I model what I teach. The word psychotherapy comes from the Greek roots *psyche*, meaning soul or breath of life, and *therapeia,* meaning to serve or attend. In this sense, my work is a form of service to the soul. I love being part of journeys where women discover their own power. The book you are holding in your hands is meant to empower you by demystifying spiritual practices and therapy strategies and introducing you to your inner teacher. I see myself as your sacred escort.

The 'outer' teacher who has had the most influence on my conscious evolution is Eckhart Tolle with his beautiful book *The Power of Now*. I use this seminal reference every day in my personal and professional life. The other influential person in my life was, and still is, Oprah Winfrey. During the most difficult periods of my life as a single mom, I found comfort in her steadfast presence on television. Finally, I am indebted to Starhawk who may never know how her rational yet reverent approach to Earth-based Spirituality has so deeply influenced my spiritual evolution from my baptism, catechism, and confirmation in the Anglican faith (Church of England), through my marriage and my position as a Lay Minister in the

United Church of Canada (Progressive Protestant), to my current identification as Gaian (Earth revering), gynocentric (woman honouring), and syncretic (many paths to consciousness).

My first empowerment gift to you is some demystification of therapy. *Common Factors* research has revealed that we can predict successful therapy regardless of the counsellor's technique or any theory underpinning her work. In other words, we know what good therapy is and what it looks like. When they broke it all down for us way back in 1997, researchers Scott Miller, Barry Duncan, and Mark Hubble found that you, the clients, are the most important contributors to successful therapy[1]. This may seem obvious, but many clients and therapists think the therapist holds the most power. This is simply not true. The order of influence, from greatest to least, are events outside the therapy room, the quality of the relationship between clients and counsellors, and then the therapist's framework and techniques. Miller, Duncan, and Hubble also noted that hope or expectancy (otherwise known as the placebo effect[2]) also had an influence.

What this means in plain language is that even if a therapist had the egotistical gall to think they were responsible for your success, the research shows otherwise. You, the client, hold the most power in your healing. You are empowered in therapy, whether you do it yourself using a book like this, or with a qualified professional.

The second most important contributing factor is a strong match between you and your counsellor. This, of course, begs the question: what is a good match? It's when you feel genuine positive regard from the counsellor and experience the counsellor as authentic, real, and congruent. As a young graduate student, I was captivated by *On Becoming a Person* (1961), by Carl Rogers, wherein he taught me that it is quite possible to do excellent therapy without pathologizing people. Rather than using a medical model, I choose to believe that each person I serve has a reason for their behaviour. Every behaviour serves a function. Yes, I memorized the

DSM—the *Diagnostic and Statistical Manual of Mental Disorders*—in its various editions during my rigorous training. While diagnosis has its place, Rogers taught me that self-acceptance is the key to change. Once a person can accept who they are, both shadow and light, we are underway. Therefore, an important focus of this book is your feeling that I am authentic, real, and congruent. I welcome you, celebrate your courage, and validate your progress.

This book is all about you. Yet, to affirm that I truly know where you are, I offer some of my personal experiences with each strategy and topic. Look to me as your guide. Learn with me how to listen to your inner teacher. Believe in our relationship as a motivating force. Work on and believe in the strategies I offer. Your chances of success are high. If I am not your personal therapist in life, we can build a relationship based on hope and trust through the strategies in this book. As you grow your comfort with mystery, making spirituality and spiritual practices accessible and practical will deepen your reverence for that mystery.

Maintaining a Solid Support System

Working through these chapters will be fruitful, but it can be destabilizing at first. It is important to build and maintain a solid support system in your daily life. If you choose to work with a therapist, too, please go to ***Appendix: How to Choose a Therapist***. If you choose to work through this book without a therapist, then please make sure that you have a safe adult, group, friend, or peer counsellor with whom you feel comfortable discussing your personal work. On the other hand, if these friends are not professionally trained therapists, you will want to measure their well-intentioned feedback against your own internal or intuitive sense of the best way to proceed. It is your life, after all.

That said, connection with others is crucial. I challenge you to get vulnerable and get real. We are all human. We have all experienced pain and shame. If you want to bond, get intimate, or deepen a relationship, take a risk and tell a safe person the truth about your pain. We really are all connected. We really are all in this together. In ***Chapter Eleven: Partnerships, Trust, and Anxiety***, I offer a strategy for discerning the best Circle of Support for yourself, the circle of supportive people you want in your orbit.

A Note on Appropriation, Biases, and Language

My first culture is human. Equally important in my worldview and spirituality is my membership in the culture of women. My heritage is Irish and Scottish so there are aspects of the Old Religions embedded in my make up: Celtic and Pagan, Earth-based Spirituality. Drawing on the worldview articulated by Robin Wall Kimmerer in *Braiding Sweetgrass*, and combined with the honour of being able to live, work, and play on the unceded Territory of the K'omox First Nation, I have come to understand that all of us originate from ancestral peoples who were once deeply rooted in place and land. I have become naturalized[3] to place with the understanding that every one of us has come from somewhere. Starhawk captures this idea beautifully in her book *The Earth Path* when she lovingly documents her intimate connection to the land on which she resides in northern California. I am not indigenous to Vancouver Island, but I can still be a guardian of this land and its future. I feel like I belong to the land I walk on every day. It does not belong to me. I have been colonized, but I relate to marginalized women, as a woman in exile, like women everywhere, regardless of race. So, I cherish the earth as Mother, as a Great Woman in need of guardianship and respect.

Using a term I first encountered by Riane Eisler in *The Chalice and the Blade*, I currently identify as "gynocentric (or Goddess-based)"[4] because I believe this position, if taken up by the majority of human beings, will save the Earth. By the way, Eisler's *The Chalice and the Blade* should be required reading for anyone who considers themselves educated on this planet. I believe that when *any* woman or female-identified-person—regardless of age, race, ethnicity, economic status, size, intellect, or any other attribute you give her—can safely, comfortably, and freely walk down *any* street in the world at 2 am, we will have evolved as a species.

The spiritual practices in this book are shared mainly from Earth-based Spirituality, Celtic traditions, Paganism, Goddess Spirituality, liberation theology, logotherapy, existential philosophy, transpersonal psychology, Buddhism, Taoism, Vedism (forerunner of Hinduism), and Unitarian principles, with the theoretical underpinnings of Carl Rogers and Carl Jung (except, of course, for any androcentric or androcratic assumptions they make). Further, I identify as syncretic—a spiritual position that acknowledges that all spiritual traditions and many religions have something to teach us. Love is the common ground that I look for. I have no patience for hate crimes disguised as doctrine, and no tolerance for accusations of appropriation from non-practising 'religious' individuals. I believe human rights and the health of Mother Earth take precedence over religious privilege. The Elders, gurus, practitioners, and mentors who have generously taught me have asked me to share these strategies with you. I have their blessings. I will respectfully enter a dialogue around appropriation with those who practise a particular religion or spiritual tradition. Fair warning: I will constantly return to what we share, not how we differ.

I also identify as non-dualistic. One of my teachers, Anandamayi Ma, helped me learn that the One appears as many because each person needs a different way of accessing the Divine within and without. Non-dualism has important implications for how I approach Spiritually Integrated psychotherapy. First, I accept whatever path has led you to understand yourself as more than your Ego (far more!). I understand that dualistic thinking helps people organize reality when it all feels a bit overwhelming. Our culture tends toward "us" versus "them" or "this" but not "that". However, life is much more complicated than this form of black and white thinking. Non-duality teaches that all is one, we are all interconnected, and any sense of our separateness from each other is just a fear-based strategy of the Ego, which wants to be "special". I look for the Tao, or the middle way. I encourage clients to use "both/and" language and thinking instead of "either/or". The logo for my practice, and one of my tattoos, is the Yin Yang symbol: a reminder that non-duality does *not* mean a muddy, milky, merged grey position. Rather, I believe we are capable of holding two positions (sometimes more) at the same time.

"Both/and" thinking is also the language of feminism, and I encourage my clients to practise this kind of thinking. "Both/and" language and context are much more helpful and productive than "either/or" or "us/them" or "black/white" thinking. The ability to live with mystery, ambiguity, contradiction, and paradox is a natural part of the healing process that our culture has all but colonized out of us.

My position on non-duality is also integral to my holistic psychotherapeutic approach. I reference the "Big Brain" as from the neck down, considering your body's intelligent attempts to communicate with you as stories of embodied cognition. The nonverbal communication of your Big Brain (your body) is in the form of symptoms, and if you choose not to listen, your body loves you so much that it will up the ante until you must pay attention to it. Non-duality in this context suggests our mind, body, and Spirit are inextricably connected.

Finally, all my spiritual training and personal experiences have led me to understand that Source, Divine Mind, Universal Intelligence, the Creator, or Higher Power is both immanent and transcendent (both/and). In my journey toward self-realization, the Divine is both within and without, as close as my breath and at the same time beyond time and form, manifest and unmanifest. Whatever you choose to call your Higher Self, or True Self, or Soul, it longs to make itself known and to guide your journey. Listen. Stillness, deep listening, courage, dream reflections, and consciously seeking images from your imagination will allow your Soul or Inner Essence to speak to you. I felt this when I was a child, when I did not have words for it. I feel this truth even more profoundly now. I have an expression, a *Terry'ism*, "Your soul gets to look out through your eyes, use your hands, speak your words". My Reiki Master teacher, Sister Eileen Curteis, also instilled in me that I am a conduit for consciousness to express itself. I am helping to formulate new myths, creating new symbols within our collective psyche as we co-create the healing of our planet. I theorize that these new symbols come from nature and from our active imaginations, yes, but I also believe that as we heal ourselves, we heal the planet.

For my master's dissertation/thesis, I chose to remedy what I thought was a gaping hole in most psychotherapy training programs: few if any courses in Spiritually Integrated psychotherapy. I could not fathom claiming to help people with life transitions while avoiding their spirituality. So, I created a master's level course for counsellor-trainees in Spiritually Integrated Psychotherapy and Spiritual Competencies.[5] My work is syncretic, ecumenical, non-denominational, multi-faith, and global. I respect and acknowledge that spirituality may not be salient for individual clients, and my rigorous training in a variety of psychotherapy modalities allows for other avenues for healing.

My experience with clients over the years has shown that the key to successful self therapy, or formal therapy with a competent qualified professional, or enlightenment, or spiritual evolution, is your willingness to accept *what is*. This may sound so simple as to be overlooked. You may want to skip the next few sentences and just get on with it. However, I want you to stop for a moment here.

Think about this: what causes suffering is resisting *what is*. Choosing to undergo therapy or to seek help or to read this book is an amazing first step because you are acknowledging that maybe there is something about *what is* that can be looked at and possibly healed. Ask yourself, "What is the one thing that I am having the most difficulty accepting?" Your answer brings you to the edge of seeing *what is*. The people I serve often tell me that they never expected therapy to be so hope-filled and tender. When together we find meaning in your struggles, it changes the challenge you are facing. We seek meaning together, and that gives purpose to life.

Terry'ism: The moment you commit to yourself and your evolution is the moment the universe supports you in real and surprising ways. Mean it, really mean it, then watch for miracles.

How to Use This Book

If you are committed to your self therapy, get a binder with pockets and dividers, or some beautiful flat boxes wide enough to hold papers you collect, or a stack of inexpensive coil scribblers for various topics, practices, and strategies. You will also want materials like a candle or gong. Expect rituals and ceremonies, spiritual inspirational pieces to work and play with, and authors to explore on your own.

Attempt to carve out at least an hour a day to work and play with a strategy, to read and reflect on the questions, to journal using the journal stems and prompts, or to walk in the forest, a park, by the ocean, or somewhere outside. Therapy can be interesting and even joyful. Yes, it is hard work and grief is not pleasant, but hope is embedded in every session. We cry and laugh from the belly. Hope allows joy to enter, even if just a little.

Since I have been writing, teaching, and speaking about the Archetypal Human Year for over thirty years, it made sense to me to organize this book using archetypal seasons. The book is divided into the four seasons—winter, spring, summer, and fall—to guide you through a year of self therapy. Each season can represent life stages and tasks that echo the course of human life on a macro level but also trace the trajectory of any profound learning experience on the micro level. You may want to return to each season the following year and go deeper into the spiral of personal evolution and self-realization.

At the end of each season is a section titled ***Risking Vulnerability, Walking the Talk, and Keeping it Real – This Therapist Shares Her Experience***. I never ask a woman I am serving to attempt something I have not experimented with myself. My mentor, Carl Rogers, insisted on congruence as a required element in our therapeutic relationship. Congruence makes me authentic and real; you can tell that I practise what I preach. I am very cautious with the sharing of my personal experiences in my practice—after all, the session is about you and only you—but occasionally, if it feels appropriate, I will share a similar challenge I have faced in my own past. At the end of each season in this book, I offer personal rituals, practices, and ceremonies from my home. You may wish to incorporate some into your own self therapy.

The day after Samhain (Hallowe'en) is experienced by many in Earth-based Spiritual traditions as New Year, so the book opens in early Winter. However, you do not have to wait until then to start! Early winter can mean late harvesting, early preparations for winter's drawing inward, and the end of cycles. Midwinter energy is also often felt as suspended animation, dormancy, pregnancy, and potentiality so, in the first three chapters, strategies and practices relate to ***Reverence, Stillness, and Spirituality***.

Spring imagery is often associated with birth, rebirth, fresh starts, germination, and fertility. Spring chapters help you to prepare your personal plan of action with strategies and activities to achieve ***Balance, Freedom, and Recovery from being Overly Responsive to Others' Needs (Codependence)***.

Summer represents heroism, maturation, growth, coming of age, and the loss of innocence. Here, you'll find spiritual practices and strategies related to ***Feeling and Emotional Regulation, Addiction, and Compulsion,*** and ***Abundance and Gratitude (Reciprocity)***.

Autumn energy is often felt as preparations for endings, but paradoxically there is often a sense of new beginnings in autumn, as well. This unusual combination may be experienced as nostalgia because of its bitter sweetness. Remember that all endings mean new beginnings, so to bring the book and the year to a close, the final three Autumn chapters cover ***Grief, Change, and Loss; Partnerships, Trust, and Anxiety,*** and ***Guidance and Intuition***. At this point you may choose to begin again and cycle through another year, going deeper into the spiral of personal work.

Each chapter opens with a personal letter from a client asking for guidance with a particular issue. Through forty years of formal and informal counselling, I have noticed women's issues have common themes. The personal letters that begin each chapter are fictional composites from women over these decades. All names and identifying characteristics have been carefully removed but when you read the letter that opens each chapter, you might see yourself in this woman's struggle. Join me in my intuitive response to this letter writer's life challenge. Perhaps we will agree on what might be at the bottom of this person's struggles.

After the opening letter, each chapter begins with ***Nuts and Bolts,*** a bare bones description of what you will need to help you with the challenge expressed in the letter. ***Spiritual Practice*** guides you through a Spiritually Integrated therapeutic strategy. Make any adjustments that feel right for you. ***Soul Work (Homework or Heartwork)*** is an opportunity to reflect on the strategy or an alternate one as you incorporate it into your daily life. ***Spiritual Journal Stems or Prompts*** challenge you to examine any resistance and your personal goals. ***Spiritual Inspiration*** offers quotes and ideas from spiritual teachers (including me), poets, and thinkers within a variety of global spiritual traditions, which may compel you to go deeper or inspire you to move forward.

In the last half of each chapter, I offer strategies for ***Dismantling Social Constructions and Unlearning Familial Patterns***. Here is an opportunity to celebrate your courage as you dare to question what you have been taught or told is true. Many teachings from families, schools, workplaces, religious communities, and media are designed to keep you conforming to ideals that are not actually your own. Becoming responsible for your own truths and living out these truths can be a scary proposition. You are altering the very structures that underlie the way you live your life. I encourage you to always ask, "Who decides?" Deepen your practice with ***Self Therapy Tools, Rituals, and Practices*** and a ***Biblio-Therapy*** section where you can explore books and other resources.

Closing each chapter are ideas for ***Service to the Planet and Connecting with Others***. The whole point of becoming an evolved being is to save our planet, connect with like-minded conscious people, and model compassionate, loving behaviour whenever possible. You have more power than you may realize to be of service to the planet. You decide. Finally, we ***Follow Up*** on the individual who wrote the opening letter.

Each chapter will have journal prompts and questions, but there may also be visualizations, rituals, and ceremonies, *gathas* and mantras, drumming, prayers, meditations, chants, interactions with the natural world, dialogues, scripts, therapeutic letters, and narration.

I am humbled and honoured that you have chosen to read this book. Thank you. You may choose to see me as one of your spiritual guides—your sacred escort—but always remember... you are your own guru.

I hope the healing and freedom you experience feels empowering and hopeful.

Namaste.

Terry Folks,

Spring 2026

Winter

Reverence, Stillness, Spirituality

Chapter One

reverence

Dear Ms. Terry,

I have a good life. I've made some excellent decisions, and some not-so-great ones. I have friends and family, and I'm active. My work is semi-fulfilling. I'm able to buy pretty much what I need or want. Despite this fairly decent life, I feel like something is missing. Something stirs in me on a windy day, and I have this longing that I can't quite name. I think that it might have something to do with sensing something bigger than me but not quite knowing how to access this... whatever it is. I just feel like there's got to be more. I also feel like I would like to have some kind of bigger effect on the world than my job allows me to.

- At a Bit of a Loss, Chloe

Chloe's brief message was poignant, expressing what I call *divine discontent.* In Spiritually Integrated practice, feeling unsatisfied with your current life is a cue to look for something more. That something more is Reverence: honouring that part of you beyond the superficial labels that our culture convinces us are important. Chloe yearned for reverence. She was like a fish that cannot see it is in the ocean, indeed part of the ocean. If Chloe could tune in to Spirit's perpetual presence, she might reclaim her connection with her True Self, her Spirit. If she reconnected with this part of herself, she could change *her* world, then perhaps *the* world.

The metaphor for our work together could be an antique radio, the kind that requires listening carefully for breaks in the static as she tunes in to a bandwidth. Through our work together, Chloe may reconnect with that part of herself that had not been accessed in a long while: reverence. Perhaps, like Chloe, you, dear reader, are sensing a disconnect from Spirit. Perhaps you too can benefit from our work.

Nuts and Bolts

There are many ways to tune in to Spirit, your Deep Self, or Soul Essence. Our goal here is to see what is always already there beneath the roles and labels imposed or acquired from family or society. A time-honoured strategy for bringing what is deep inside to the surface is through ritual. As within, so without. As above, so below. A ritual feels special because it is. There is a reverent feeling about it, after you get past the self-consciousness of doing something unusual.

Setting yourself up for an uncomplicated ritual is as easy as creating a simple altar, element or earth tray, or holy table. Start with a tray of items representing the four elements—earth, air, fire, and water. Earth (north) can be represented by a small bowl of dirt or a special rock, a crystal, a plant, or a tree branch. A feather or incense burner can symbolize air (east), and fire (south) can simply be a candle or a piece of lava rock. Water (west) can be a small vessel of salt water or a seashell.

These items are special because you decide they are. You imbue the items with energy because you can. Often an item becomes sacred or sanctified because it was a gift from someone special or it landed at your feet at a particular time in your life. Think of a child who decides that a particular rock or seashell is special for whatever reason. The practice of declaring something sacred is called sanctifying it. Hold the object in your hand and declare it so. In ***Self Therapy Tools, Rituals, and Practices for Reverence,*** later in this chapter, you'll find suggestions to deepen your practice with the four directions.

Over time, you'll add other pieces to your altar or earth tray that heighten reverence for the Deep Self, your Essence, Soul, or Spirit. A small gong or chime can serve to signify to yourself (and your helpers) the beginning and/or end of your brief practice. The sound acts as an auditory anchor and can eventually condition you to feel reverence whenever you hear it.

Without a designated She Space, many women need a portable tray they can move up high from little hands. If you are fortunate enough to have a private space, or even a corner of your bedroom that is exclusively yours, you can honour your Spirit daily here so your altar may be on a bench, bureau top, or shelf. If you have acquired a journal as discussed under ***How to Use This Book*** in the ***Introduction***, leave it by your altar. Remember this journal can be a binder with lined paper, a coiled notebook, or a fancy leather bound journal. Finally, place a mirror above your altar at eye level. You will be addressing your imminent divinity (your inner divine nature) as it connects to transcendence (whatever divinity you determine is outside yourself) as part of your spiritual practice, and a mirror will aid with these strategies.

Practically speaking, schedule some attending time to your earth tray so you can dust or move items. You may decide to return some pieces back to the Earth when you do this, as gifts or compost. Remember that children also teach us the art of letting go, or non-attachment, as they decide in a wee moment that a special rock or shell is no longer important. They easily return pieces to the Earth or give them away. We can learn from the children.

Spiritual Practice – Approaching an Altar

Approach your altar or earth tray at the same time every day until it becomes a habit to acknowledge your Spirit, Essence, Higher Self, the great "I Am", the one who knows, your life companion, or whatever words you choose to use to describe this deep, eternal part of yourself. When teaching habit formation or helping someone dismantle a negative or limiting belief, I recommend one hundred days of consistent practice. At first it may feel awkward, contrived, and a little bit like pretend. Be humble with this reality and do it anyway. You are creating space for reverence.

Throughout this book are comprehensive yet simple instructions for your own ritual design. Start with a simple ritual to which you can add a mantra, chant, prayer, or song. Ritual can be understood as a way of communicating intention across layers of awareness, allowing what we know consciously to be received and integrated more deeply within us.

Here is an easy daily ritual, which you may choose to embellish over time:

1. Light a candle.
2. Express gratitude for your incarnation in this body or simply give thanks that you woke up alive.
3. Cleanse by symbolically brushing yourself off or brushing up and down your arms.
4. Ground yourself by imagining roots growing out of the bottom of your feet deep into our Mother Earth and drawing her energy up through your body.
5. Visualize yourself standing at the centre of the four directions. This is your Spirit position, from which you now give thanks for the four elements without which none of us would be here. You may wish to turn and face each of the four directions as you do this.
6. The Spirit position at the centre of the four directions is the point

of transformation and change, so now would be the time to set your intention for the day. Your intention is simply a desire you have for yourself on this particular day, but it might be part of an ongoing transformational undertaking. For example, you may be in the middle of a difficult project, a personal challenge, or attempting to repair a relationship tear. Your intention may be to focus on the positive today, or to remember your worth, or to think before speaking. Some women choose a mantra or an affirmation at this time to guide them through their day.

7. After determining your focus for the day, you may want to request supernatural assistance with your intention. Spirit is both imminent and transcendent, as close as our breath and part of all that is. Some people petition Goddess or God; Divine Mind; pure Consciousness; a Higher Power, or the Source; the unified field or universal intelligence; the Creator or Gaia. Others have specific guides, saints, angels, or ancestors they call upon for assistance. Myself? I ask my Soul (my Inner Eternal Friend, my True Self) to guide me, to help me remember that I am not my Ego, and for the quiet stillness to hear this guidance.

8. Bless yourself, ground yourself, give thanks again, tap your gong if you have one, and blow out your candle.

Soul Work (Homework or Heartwork)

Gratitude Practice

Gratitude is always the primary prayer and the first of many spiritual practices that I teach because giving thanks is a guaranteed connection to Spirit.

Your Soul Work for this chapter is to make one or more of the following gratitude practices a regular part of your day. I first learned the miraculous power of gratitude when I was a single mother with a four-year-old daughter. The divine Ms. Oprah spoke of an "attitude of gratitude." I learned to watch for the magical effects of gratitude in my daily life. I am constantly looking for reasons to be grateful, and this makes me more mindful of everything around me as I move through my day: people, situations, animals, plants, images, and experiences. Surprise! I experience more of what I notice. Remember, what you pay attention to multiplies.

Gratitude was also the first prayer form that I taught my little girl. Some quick and easy examples are to light a candle to sanctify the food on your table and to give thanks for the food before you. Some people thank those who are responsible for this food beginning with our Mother Earth, which provides all the resources we need for food. They might thank the farmers, ranchers, gardeners, and producers who are responsible for tending and harvesting this food. Hunters in the Old Religion might give thanks to the animal that gave its life for the food that would serve the hunter's family. Harvesters might give thanks to the grain, the fruit trees, the vegetables, and other produce that would feed many. This reverence for the gifts of Earth teaches your little ones (and reminds you) that we must protect Earth and her resources because She is life sustaining.

Another simple gratitude practice is to give thanks for people, animals, and experiences in our lives. You will notice objects are not in this list. Some objects are suitable for thanking if they have symbolic significance or if they are sanctified objects on your altar, but this practice is meant to normalize appreciation for living beings and activities, not material possessions. In this particular gratitude practice, rather than simply reciting a list of 'stuff' every day, try saying *why* you are thankful for particular people, animals, or experiences.

One way to express why you are grateful, which also deepens your mindfulness, is to imagine the smell, taste, sound, sight, and texture of each being or activity you are grateful for. This is more deliberately grateful than simply giving a list. We shall deepen this particular gratitude practice in ***Chapter Nine: Abundance and Gratitude (Reciprocity)***.

Over the years, my gratitude practice has grown with help from other teachers. Many have invited me to have a "conversation" with organisms, even if what I am thanking is not human. For example, when I give thanks to the begonia blooming on one of my plants, I consider how the blossom might respond. The warm feeling in my chest from this interaction feels like grace. Grace is also found in the continued expression of abundance in my life as a result of giving thanks this way. Once again, we experience the alchemy of inviting into our lives that which we pay most attention to. Try this form of gratitude on your own and record what you discover in your journal.

Courageous Investigation

If you were raised in a particular religious tradition and whether you still practise it or not, another important piece of ***Soul Work (Homework or Heartwork)*** is an investigation into the inclusiveness or exclusiveness of your religious tradition. This takes tremendous courage, especially if you have been taught not to question.

Ask yourself, "Who decides?" Examine the religious or spiritual tradition that you were raised in, or are currently practising, for any "rules" that are disguised hate crimes, rules or doctrine that lack reverence, or doctrine that encourages superiority over Mother Earth. Remember, reverence is found in what people do, not what they say. You may have to dig a little or ask pointed questions of your organizational leaders.

Any rule or doctrine that promotes exclusivity, self-righteousness, judgment, exploitation of our planet, racism, hate crimes, homophobia, misogyny, sexism, ableism, ageism, or intellectual elitism is now your right to reject, or at the very least question. These constructs are not acts of reverence. Does the faith have reverence for women? For the Earth?

Print any teachings against humanity and the environment on slips of paper, put them in a box, and visualize giving the box back to the institution, organization, or community that promotes them. Some people ritualistically burn these pieces. However you find the courage to reject your further participation in hate crimes, do so with environmental sensitivity and with compassion for those who are still blindly following unexamined doctrine.

Chloe, the woman from the letter at the beginning of this chapter, was hesitant about creating an altar because it felt too 'woo woo'. She wondered if she would be "punished" by God or her elderly parents for doing something against her fundamentalist religious upbringing. Even though she no longer practised her childhood religion, she still felt influenced by it. Spiritual fear is very real. Some religions emphasize fear and punishment if their doctrines are not followed to the letter. The instillation of fear allows for compliance within the community. Unfortunately, it can have a pronounced negative effect on mental health or, as in Chloe's case, inhibit her deepening faith, especially her faith in herself. The reward and punishment mindset is an ingrained part of our human evolution, and the cause of much personal anguish and historical bloodshed. You will see this mindset questioned throughout this book. For now, it is enough to ask, "Who decides?"

If a client is experiencing spiritual fear like Chloe is, we can use the altar or earth tray to bridge spirituality—which is highly personal—to religion, which can be more communal in focus. Creating a simple altar would give Chloe something concrete to approach each morning for tuning in, to give thanks for life through the four elements, and to acknowledge her Spirit each day. When I wondered with Chloe if deepening her reverence for her inner Spirit might actually enhance her faith, she agreed to try greeting her Deep Self at an altar each day. In my experience, when people deepen their reverence for their inner Spirit, they often rediscover meaning and depth within the spiritual tradition they already know, while also coming into a deeper relationship with themselves. She chose the word 'soul' to describe her Deep Self and insisted on connecting this part of herself to the 'Holy Spirit', which had special meaning in her particular religion. I invited Chloe to include objects and images that reflected the parts of her childhood faith that felt most personal. She chose a crucifix and a rosary.

Spiritual Journal Stems and Prompts

What archetype, symbol, landscape, journey, or image would best reflect your initial explorations of your early religious or spiritual upbringing? Some people choose the image of a cave and don a headlamp. It might be a landscape, like crossing a desert, or a hike alongside a river, or a trek up a mountain. The old radio metaphor I offered Chloe near the beginning of this chapter might work for you. You might be drawn to tuning into the spiritual channel that is always present and just waiting for you. Some people like the idea of awakening to the fact that they are already a part of the ocean they inhabit. Choose an image for this month's work and write about it in your Spiritual Journal. Return to your journal as the month unfolds to explore your progress. Is your daily altar practice becoming a habit? Is it helping you to feel connected to Spirit?

Use the following prompts to explore your thoughts and feelings in your Spiritual Journal:

- *"If I treat the altar experience as an investigation, I can track my feelings over time. For example, on the first day I noticed..."*
- *"I have a mixture of curiosity and fear around exploring the inclusiveness and exclusiveness of various major global religions. This is because..."*
- *"What I have noticed about incorporating a gratitude practice into my life, and with my family, is..."*

Spiritual Inspiration

Consider the following ideas I hope inspire you as you work through this chapter. Note your reflections in your journal.

Divine discontent can ironically point to your deepest desire to connect with Spirit. She is calling to you. Tell Her you hear Her and want to join Her.

Take to heart your responsibility for staying in the here and now, and return to conscious awareness whenever you notice you are drifting into the past or considering the future. Protect your sacred self in her awareness.

See your dedication to your spiritual practices as necessary as water. This is a noble and courageous commitment to yourself.

Dismantling Social Constructions and Unlearning Familial Patterns

In addition to spiritual fear, Chloe was still trapped in the prison of judgment or approval by others. She worried what people would think if they found out she was honouring herself at an altar each day. Deliberately and with intention bringing reverence into your life defies the common social construction that we must work daily, vigilantly, at acquiring more money, more attention, more approval, more, more, and more. If you find yourself yearning to free yourself from imprisonment in others' approval, you may find ideas for your evolution in ***Chapter Six: Overly Responsive to Others' Needs (Codependence)***. If you are caught up in consumerism or materialism, and wish to change that, have a look at ***Chapter Nine: Abundance and Gratitude (Reciprocity)***.

With the decreasing relevance of organized religion, how do we then remember Spirit?

Daring to create your own ritual where you acknowledge your Source, Soul, Spirit, Higher Self, True Self, "I Am", or Inner Divine is a radical act. You are liberating yourself from the restrictions of a social construct that keeps you in your place, makes you forget that you are Spirit First.

The freedom you give yourself through this empowering practice is stunning to behold.

Any ceremony or ritual that you dare to create and humbly experiment with is an act of courage. No one is telling you what to do or how to do it. This book is only offering ideas and suggestions. In my work co-designing rituals and ceremonies with people, we feel the power of declaring a life experience as sacred or spiritual through the ritual itself. We know we are touching something primal and extraordinary when we set our intention to be changed by the acts we design. The rituals you design for yourself, or with others, become part of your treatment plan for what is troubling you. The healing that comes through the act of creating rituals, as well as your participation in your daily practices, is what makes them both sacred and pragmatic.

Initiation is a term used to describe a ritual wherein you become a member of a particular belief community, not only spiritual or religious groups. However, you can use ritual to *initiate yourself* into your own evolving spirituality, and to bless yourself. While many groups and individuals offer initiation as a service, often at great cost, initiation itself cannot be given by another. It arises from your own willingness, openness, and participation. When your heart is receptive, ordinary experiences can become initiatory; without that openness, no ceremony can do the work for you.

Consider this as you proceed. It might feel strange to take your own desire for reverence into your own hands. However, when you feel brave enough to share what you are doing with others, you may be surprised how many individuals on our planet are ready to take the next step in evolving consciousness, for their own sakes, yes, but also for the evolving consciousness of humanity.

Self Therapy Tools, Rituals, and Practices for Reverence

Mantras and Chakra Work

When you start your day by approaching your personal altar, you create a body memory or a sensation/feeling memory that re-surfaces throughout your day. Continue with your initial ritual, then consider adding pieces that have meaning for you.

If you find yourself particularly sensitive to energy, try the following affirmations from my personal morning, midday, and evening altar practice as a way to shield yourself. These affirmations remind me to keep myself centred in Spirit and not to be negatively affected by those who want me to participate in Ego drama with them. The mantras also serve as a way for me to bless myself. You can decide for yourself how porous you would like your shields to be. You may also choose to put a mirror at eye level for your practice.

- I look in the mirror above my altar and maintain eye contact until my inner being emerges, and all else falls away from my attention.
- I hold my hands to the sides of my head. "I shield my mind from negativity, but I allow positive thoughts in."
- I hold my hand over my heart. "I shield my heart from hate, but I allow love in."
- I run my hands up and down the sides of my body. "I shield my body from hurt, but I invite health and warm affection."
- With my hands facing outward, I move them up and down a few inches from my body. "I shield my aura from unseen negative forces, but I allow supernatural goodness and light to enter."
- One arm lifts above my head, and one hand pushes down toward the floor. "I invite my inner being, my soul, my higher self, my Light to penetrate my shields, offering positive energy outward to those around me."

I designed my own affirmations and *mudras* for each of the seven major chakras. Please feel free to adopt and adapt as you feel comfortable.

1. **Crown** - *"I am Divine"* - I fold my hands in the prayer position above my head.
2. **Third Eye** - *"I am Intuitive and Wise"* - I fold my hands in the prayer position then open them like a door in front of my forehead.
3. **Throat** - *"I listen to my Inner guidance then I listen more than I speak"* - I fold my hands in the prayer position then open them in an offering gesture like a drawbridge in front of my throat.
4. **Heart** - *"I am Love"* - I hold a large imaginary bowl or vessel in front of my heart and offer it first to the woman in the mirror, and then to all the people I will encounter this day, then to those who have yet to make themselves known.
5. **Solar Plexus** - *"My Power comes from Source through me effectively"* - I imagine energy running up through the soles of my feet, up my body, through my heart and head, then cascading down around me like a waterfall.
6. **Sacral** - *"I am creative, magnetic, passionate, and constantly birthing"* - I attempt to bring my breath to my sacral area, hold it there for five seconds, then release it slowly through my mouth. Do two or three kegels to bring your mind/body attention to this area.
7. **Root** - *"I am grounded, rooted, balanced, and safe"* - I put my hands on my hips and send energy down through the soles of my feet to the centre of our Mother, then draw energy back up through my feet. Sometimes I imagine roots growing out of the arches of my feet down into the Earth, holding me steady like I am planted. More practices with the seven chakras appear in **Chapter Four – Balance**.

Mirror Work

The renowned Louise Hay first introduced me to mirror work in her seminal, *You Can Heal Your Life*[1], long before I became a therapist. My own mirror practice and teaching deepened when her book *Mirror Work*[2] was published in 2016. Keep the altar ritual you have created, then consider deepening your practice with mirror work. You may choose to do mirror work daily, throughout the day, or as a special practice on a specific day.

If you have not already done so, hang or affix a mirror above your altar where you can see your beautiful eyes. Add to your altar ritual at any point the words, "I see you" as you look in the mirror. Louise Hay's invitation to look in the mirror and say, "I love you" was a breakthrough practice in my own personal journey. It may feel contrived and a little awkward at the beginning but please do not give up on yourself. You can deepen this reverence by whispering to yourself, "I see you as a fellow sacred being" as you approach each person and living being. Watch how the energy shifts in your interactions when you do this. You will be astonished.

Inner Child Work

Repairing childhood wounds by loving your little self beyond reason here and now has assisted the healing of many clients over the years. If you are doing inner child work with me or another qualified therapist, congratulations. I will discuss this important work in greater detail in ***Chapter Six: Overly Responsive to Others' Needs (Codependence)*** and in ***Chapter Seven: Feeling and Emotional Self-regulation***. For now, simply add to your altar a framed photo of yourself before the age of nine. Your commitment to caring for your little self becomes part of your daily intention no matter what other daily intentions you may have formulated. Consistency for this important personal work is key.

An important note is appropriate here. I caution each of my clients to take great care not to let her little self drive the bus. She is too small for the driver's seat, her feet cannot reach the pedals, and she cannot see over the dashboard. She simply does not have the strategies that you, as an evolved Spiritual adult, have. As her Spiritual Mom, tell her that you've got this. Her job is to play, to receive unconditional love from you, to teach you how to be spontaneous, and to create from a clear, innocent place. You can be her Spiritual Mom and teach her how powerful she is becoming. You can teach your little self things now that your own mother may not have had the capacity to do. Your little self can also teach you, if you let her. Aside from spontaneity and pure creativity, your little one can also teach you how to be exquisitely present in each moment. Again, it is important to note and worth repeating here that she is not in charge and it is unfair to her, to yourself, and to those around you to put her there.

We do not blame mothers (or fathers or spouses or siblings) in my practice. We acknowledge what happened, sometimes with great pain, grief, anger, and sadness. We find the courage to look at the facts of your upbringing together. However, continuing to blame, or to expect an apology, or to seek revenge will never serve you at the end of the day. This other-focused behaviour only perpetuates avoidance strategies that deflect from looking at yourself and experiencing mature spiritual evolution. It may be a fact that you were not treated the way you should have been. Now it is *your turn* to parent yourself the way you want.

Be kind, patient, consistent, and loving with your little self. When you approach your altar, pick up or meditate on the framed image of your younger self. Set your intention to develop a loving relationship with her. If you find this work fascinating, go to ***Chapter Seven: Feeling and Emotional Self-regulation*** for a more detailed description of my ***Parts and Positions*** strategy. This activity will deepen your healing.

Deepening Your Understanding of the Four Directions

Acknowledging the four directions as reverence for Earth, as an ongoing daily practice, as a way of sanctifying any ceremonial space, or as an automatic balancing exercise, goes back millenniums. We have no way of knowing when it was first used by our ancestors, but I remember it in my cells. It is a practice that has not been colonized out of me. I was first invited to remember the practice during Earth-based Spiritual rituals. The tradition varies from group to group, but I was shown how to stand, face, welcome, and thank each direction, meditate on the ancient psycho-spiritual associations with each direction, sometimes speak or enact these associations out loud, and invite their healing qualities to inform my personal work in the ceremony or in the work of the community.

Here is one way to deepen your work with Reverence at your altar or earth tray:

Face north. North is sometimes associated with the element earth, and the gifts of Earth for which we now hold with reverence and give thanks. This would include all that we receive from Her. The psycho-spiritual qualities of the north are foundational in nature, giving us a sense of being grounded, balanced, rooted, safe, home. Some people drum, stomp their feet, or use their bodies in a way that makes them feel connected to Earth and welcomes Her gifts into the ceremony or practice. You may have dirt in a bowl, a crystal, stones, or plants on your altar as a way of honouring Earth.

Face east. It may seem obvious that the rising sun and new beginnings are associated with the east. East has also traditionally been connected with the element air, and Her gifts are those that are received on the wind, the breath of Gaia. Psycho-spiritually, we welcome all the gifts that come from intuition, thinking, cognition, the intellect, ideas, and connections between those ideas. If you are looking for inspiration, meditate on the qualities of the East. Some people wave a feather, or make wind sounds with their lips, or move into deep breath work when they face east.

Face south. South is usually connected to the fire element. The spiritual qualities of fire are passion, creativity, sensuality, warmth, light, and action. Some people light candles or incense as they do their daily ritual, or when they are creating a community circle and acknowledging fire. Give thanks for fire and invite the qualities of fire into your ritual. Imagine discovering fire and all that might have meant for our ancestors. It is difficult to take warmth and light for granted when you are thanking fire.

Face west. The west is associated with the setting sun, the sweet tiredness at the end of a day of meaningful work. West is watery. Water as an element is cleansing and stepping into the flow, but it is also the carrier of the unconscious realm, often associated with our emotional self. Without introspection, self-reflection, and emotional awareness, we'd be unable to metabolize emotions' impact on our bodies. You may want a favourite shell, a tiny flask of water, or beach glass on your altar to acknowledge the west.

Notice where you are standing. You are the centre, and the directions are all around you. The centre is your Spirit position. Draw into yourself all the energies of the four directions, set your intention, and allow yourself to receive. Over time, as you deepen your relationship with your Deep Self (True Self, Essence, Inner Beloved, Soul, or Spirit), you will find that this part of you is inextricably connected to Nature, Gaia, Mother Earth—both imminent and transcendent. The four directions work will take on enhanced meaning for you.

Always ground yourself before and after any ritual. Grounding simply means you deliberately visualize yourself connected to the Earth in some specific way. I usually ground by imagining roots growing out of the bottom of my feet, or I do two or three sun salutations with the intention of connecting with Mother Earth.

Nature teaches us how to be resilient without retribution. Wind inspires, water flows, soil grounds, and fire stirs. In her book *The Earth Path,* Starhawk shows how our responding patterns can shift once we notice how we work with, and against, energy from our Spirit centre in our Four Directions work.[3]

Service to the Planet and Connecting with Others

Plant a tree. Plant a garden. Honour Earth. In the thought-provoking book *Braiding Sweetgrass*, Robin Wall Kimmerer uses the term *more-than-human* to describe the trees, plants, birds, fish, animals, and other sentient beings who give us life. We owe them not only gratitude but as much restorative work as we can find energy for. As you practise recognizing your own divinity, it becomes easier and naturally more comfortable for you to acknowledge and respect the divinity in others and in our *more-than-human* relatives on this generous, loving planet.

You may find yourself more compelled to work with stream-keepers, forest stewardship, or ocean restoration initiatives as you evolve and heal yourself. I like Kimmerer's term "practical reverence"[4] as she invites her readers to plant gardens to deepen their bonds with Mother Earth. I use practical reverence in my work since women are often faced with the dirty nitty gritty of daily life. Our spirituality and reverence must always be grounded in reality. If you do not have a garden area, grow some micro greens or herbs on your windowsill or contribute your time and energy to a community garden.

When you begin and maintain a spiritual practice, you'll notice opportunities for connecting with like-minded others. They will surface automatically but softly, so pay attention. You will notice in your volunteer work many opportunities to connect. In terms of support, you may wish to connect with a Spiritually Integrated psychotherapist like me to discuss your ongoing reflections, obstacles, and evolution. You may also wish to initiate a support group or join an existing one.

Follow Up with Chloe

Perhaps you, dear reader, have grown in your understanding of yourself by working through this first chapter alongside Chloe. As she began to understand her altar as a bridge between her personal spirituality and the religion she grew up with but no longer practised, Chloe felt permission to acknowledge her Spirit's perpetual presence. For her, it became a matter of tuning in to Source, to what was already and would always be there. She is fortunate in that she was raised in organized religion, so she had some sense of what belief in something outside herself felt like. Not so fortunate was what she discovered when she found the courage to delve more deeply into the tenets of her religion. To her dismay, the original founding principles of love and inclusiveness were missing in the contemporary re-interpretation of these principles. Chloe began the journey into reverence for herself and for the planet with some trepidation, but for her there was no turning back. She was excited to awaken to her life's purpose.

Biblio-Therapy for Chapter One

Books and Resources to Support Your Work with Reverence

- *Braiding Sweetgrass: Indigenous Wisdom, Scientific Knowledge, and the Teachings of Plants,* Robin Wall Kimmerer
- *The Spiral Dance,* Starhawk
- *The Earth Path,* Starhawk
- *The Book of Ceremony,* Sandra Ingerman
- *Homecoming,* John Bradshaw
- *Mirror Work,* Louise Hay
- *A Goddess Among Us: The Divine Life of Anandamayi Ma* by Swami Mangalananda
- *Avatar* (2009); *Avatar: The Way of Water* (2022)
- *A New Earth,* Eckhart Tolle.

Chapter Two

stillness

Dear Ms. Terry,

I'm agitated when I have nothing to do. I hate boredom. I tried meditating and I even downloaded some mindfulness and meditation apps. I keep thinking I suck at this meditating stuff. I last maybe a minute before I start shaking my knee, tapping my fingers on my leg, or planning the rest of my day. I really want to feel serene and tranquil sometimes, but I just don't know if I'm cut out for it. So, do you think there are just some people who can't do this meditating stuff?

- Craving Calm, Vera

Vera was feeling overwhelmed by life, she told me. She could not narrow this feeling of *overwhelm* down to one specific responsibility at home or at work, not to one daily task among many chores, nor could she specify one incident or one person in her family or circle of friends who *made* her feel this way. My felt sense of Vera's universe, of her typical daily routine, was that she spent most moments 'other' focused and in perpetual motion.

We began our work together by intentionally connecting with a memory of natural stillness somewhere in her history.

Such a memory could be the morning after an overnight snowfall. The air is still, muffled, silent. The whiteness unmarked yet, the final snowflakes few. Stay there, in that memory, for a moment. That is stillness.

Or think about a waterfall you visited, a river you sat beside, a great tree you touched, or a mountain you ascended. Be in this present moment while thinking about that natural phenomenon as it is right now, however far away. That water still flows although you are not there. Think about this. That river still moves. That majestic tree has not moved. Stay in this natural memory. This is stillness. Fellow traveller, might a memory of natural stillness also help you?

Nuts and Bolts

A *stillness-in-solitude* event means no movement, no phone, no tablet, no person, no food, no distraction for at least twelve minutes. Keep your eyes open. Be present in the moment: note the smells, tastes in the air, the sounds and sights in your line of vision, the textures or sensations around you in this moment, right now. Draw energy up from the Earth through your feet by pretending to breath through your soles, then notice sensations in the rest of your body. Try this at your altar, on your front porch, on a park bench, under a favourite tree in the forest, sitting by the sea, or while soaking in the tub.

Start with one stillness-in-solitude event per day. Add more as you become familiar with the sensation. At first your mind might race, memories of an earlier moment in the day might surface, or you might start composing future 'to-do' lists in your head. Give your head a wee shake and begin again. Bring yourself back to the present moment and start noting whatever your five senses are picking up in this moment. Say (out loud or to yourself) what you notice. Take it to the next level by paying very close attention to what is in the air between you and the closest object. That space between holds energy. Where does your personal and psychic space end and the other's begin? Do they overlap? When your mind wanders, bring it back to the present by counting to five on the inhale, hold for three, then count to seven on the exhale. Repeat the breath count until you are back in your body. Begin again. I have been told and have experienced it for myself that it takes at least twelve minutes of stillness in the forest for the creatures, trees, birds, and other wildlife to accept your presence and resume natural activity. Watch for this shift in energy.

Make a note in your Spiritual Journal on the day that you can bring that body memory of stillness into your body at will, and at random. For me, it feels like an infusion or a warmth that spreads from the top of my head down the back of my neck, over my shoulders, down my arms, into my hands then spreads across my chest, torso, pelvis, thighs, and calves then into my feet and down into the Earth. Sometimes I play and bring it back up from the core of our Mother, then up through my body and release it back to the cosmos through my crown. What an infusion!

Spiritual Practice – Practising Presence

Eckhart Tolle invites us to acknowledge Ego-generated thoughts and then to deliberately move beyond thought to a position of pure awareness. When we notice Ego-generated thoughts without identifying with them, we can step into a state of presence that exists beyond habitual thinking. While we need our Ego in order to get up every morning and put on clothes, remember that Ego is fed by thoughts of the future or memories of the past while our Deeper Self or Essence loves its position in the present moment. The present moment is ultimately the only thing that we can actually say is real.

Some Portals to Presence

1. Consider the five senses. What do you smell, taste, see, hear, and touch in your present moment?

2. Concentrate on breath moving through your nostrils. Follow its passage to the lungs. Note the expansion of your diaphragm. Again, follow the breath up and out on the exhale.

3. Look around your environment, noticing the space between objects rather than the objects themselves.

4. Imagine light or liquid energy filling your entire body, a flooding sensation like the infusion I described earlier.

5. Immerse yourself in a memory of natural stillness. Call up a memory of ocean waves, a forest creek meandering, or a waterfall... and consider that it is still flowing even when you are not there. Smile inwardly to remember the age-old question, "If a tree falls in a forest, does anybody hear?" This knowing that nature continues its *being-ness* in our absence is a beautiful portal to presence.

When I move through these portals in my sleep preparations, Ego stops nattering away and my mind relaxes. I drift off.

For your spiritual practice this month, try out the strategies described under ***Nuts and Bolts*** and then try the different portals to presence described above. Note especially how your body feels when you do this and try to replicate that sensation throughout the day. You will notice that paying attention is like a little energy exchange between yourself and what you are attending to.

Soul Work (Homework or Heartwork)

Schedule one stillness-in-solitude event for twelve minutes at any point in your day. You can do this at your altar, sitting quietly anywhere, or outside at a safe space. In her stunning book *The Earth Path*, Starhawk recommends you choose a "home base," a place preferably outside that you return to time and again for stillness and observation.[1] Vera could not imagine how she could fit a stillness event into her daily round. She felt she lacked time to do everything she had to in a day, never mind adding one more task. The alchemy of stillness has to be experienced to be appreciated, so treat the stillness-in-solitude moment as an investigation, paying attention to how the practice impacts your energy in interactions with others, in your daily tasks, and in your mood throughout the day.

The time spent in pure presence alters the course of your day. Rather than being yet another task, the moments spent in pure presence are rejuvenating yet calming at the same time. We return to the daily round with renewed perspective and deliberation. An absolute stillness-in-solitude event often makes my clients more efficient as they continue with their day. If efficiency is important to you, you will be surprised. In addition, many of my clients practise pure presence awareness as part of their sleep hygiene as they come to appreciate its calming effect.

Demystifying Meditation

As part of your Soul Work for this month, try out some of the following forms of meditation. There are as many kinds of meditation as there are people. Common threads include attending to your breath and invitations to inner stillness, even in a group meditation or when practising a walking forest meditation. I teach several forms in my practice and in my groups.

When I teach meditation, the first obstacle to overcome is the person's previously held stories about what meditation actually is. A common story includes an image of a person sitting blissfully in meditation for hours and hours, becoming more enlightened every second. Another hurdle to challenge when learning and practising a meditation or mindfulness practice is Ego's constant attempts to move you out of the present moment and into a story, either past or future. The more drama, the better. Ego will even make up a story about how hard meditation is!

To help the people I serve, I practice and teach a form of mindfulness that I call Dual Process. It is a unique doorway to meditation. As you are participating in an activity, talk to yourself about why you are doing this activity. What is your intention? I call it Dual Process because you are involved in two processes at once: you are doing an activity, and you are narrating it at the same time.

"I am doing this cold water plunge to wake myself up to being fully present in this moment and to invigorate my nervous system. I know I will sleep like a baby tonight if I do this."

While my Dual Process strategy is not meditation per se, it is excellent training for observing the self, a key component of many forms of meditation.

A lovely way to try meditation without feeling pressured is to follow a guided meditation. There are many excellent guides, but one of my favourite guides is Tara Brach. She offers online samples of her meditations. Listen to a Meditation Moment offering on my website. Here, when I talk about spaciousness, the pineal gland, breathing love in, balance, expansion and contraction, concentrated breath work, and gratitude—what comes up for you? You can find this meditation at *spiritfirstcounselling.ca.* Following the guided meditations, note your reflections in your journal.

Try Contemplative Prayer, sometimes called Centring Prayer. Acclaimed modern mystic Cynthia Bourgeault taught me contemplative prayer in the Benedictine tradition. leading to my first formal immersions into stillness. At various retreats, we would alternate silent centring prayer with Cynthia's gentle teaching. Her silent retreats lasted for days. Cooking together in silence is a very interesting experience!

Contemplative (or centring) prayer comes out of the beautiful interfaith teachings of Trappist monk Thomas Keating. Its goal is to achieve a state of interior stillness and receptivity to the presence of Source (God in the Christian tradition). We choose a word—*love*, for example—or a short phrase like *let go* as an anchor to return to when our thoughts inevitably stray. In contemplative prayer you can *expect* your mind to wonder. Your word or phrase is a tool. S*peak it silently* inside your mind to draw you back to silence again and again. Cynthia advised that, rather than berate ourselves when our minds wander, we accept this normal experience of mind wandering as an opportunity to practise our return to the present.

Another of Bourgeault's teachings is a form of meditation called *lectio divina*. Although originally taught in the Christian tradition, I modified it for interfaith or personal spirituality adherents. Lectio devina allows you to reflect ever more deeply on the layers of meaning in a piece of scripture from the sacred text of your choice. You could use a piece from your tradition, or a *koan* in the Zen Buddhist tradition (a koan is a thought that gives you pause or 'doubt' like the possibly familiar, "Two hands clap and there is a sound. What is the sound of one hand clapping?"). I often draw my text choices for *lectio divina* from my favourite mystic, Rumi, or from one of my treasured contemporary Hindu saints, Anandamayi Ma, or from poetry by my personal favourites, Mary Oliver or Steve Taylor.

The steps in *lectio devina* are simple in outline but often insightful:

1. Drop into stillness and silence.
2. Read the piece slowly.
3. Think about its surface meaning.
4. Ask for guidance from Source.
5. Read the selection again then close your eyes with a desire to allow insight or subtext to surface.
6. Rest in the deeper meaning.
7. Let it go, or release it, knowing you can return to it as many times as you like.

8. Some people love to hear their text over and over again, so they find an audible version.

If you would like to try *lectio divina*, set a time for yourself, and reflect on these words: *I have a centre that vibrates even when I am alone.*

Two other meditation teachers are Jack Kornfield in the Theravada Buddhist tradition and mindfulness pioneer Jon Kabat-Zinn in the Zen Buddhist practice. Their forms involve stillness either outwardly or inwardly, depending on your location. Their teachings can be found under ***Biblio-Therapy*** for this chapter.

Another form of meditation is *Shinrin-yoku* (sometimes called Forest Bathing). You might be in a walking meditation similar to those beautifully taught by Thich Nhat Hanh if you try *Shinrin-yoku* in the forest. For a detailed description, see ***Self Therapy Tools, Rituals, and Practices for Stillness: Shinrin-yoku (Forest Bathing)*** later in this chapter. Finally, at the end of your yoga practice you might participate in *savasana*, a form of meditation that allows for integration of your yoga postures.

Please remember: meditation is called a practice for good reason. You practise! There may simply be one way of meditating that you have not been taught or that you have not tried. Try any of those explained above or another that calls to you.

Spiritual Journal Stems and Prompts

Choose your image for this month's work on Stillness. What resonates? Waves on the seashore never-ending? The waterfall continually falling? A snow-white landscape where even a footstep is muffled? Return to this image when you need to regroup and reconnect with yourself. Write about your image (or metaphor, or analogy) in your Spiritual Journal.

Use the following prompts to explore your thoughts and feelings in your Spiritual Journal, or contemplate these ideas at your altar:

- *"When I think that being absolutely still and present might actually help me eventually feel more calmly efficient, I think about why I resist this gift. Some of my resistance comes from..."*
- *"The cause of most suffering is resistance to accepting what actually is. Consider the possibility of a small opening or a crack in your own resistance by practising presence. Acceptance is letting go of resistance. This moment. Not a story about this moment. One moment at a time. One moment. One foot in Ego. One foot in consciousness."*

Spiritual Inspiration

Consider my personal practices, which I share to inspire you as you work through this chapter. Note your reflections in your journal.

I try keeping a quiet background relationship with my inner being, even as I am in conversation with others or attending to daily tasks.

I have quiet days where I intentionally communicate with no one except Source, my inner being, or natural elements like trees or water.

I refute our culture's preference for extroversion by allowing myself to indulge in solitude. This practice feeds my soul.

Dismantling Social Constructions and Unlearning Familial Patterns

Twelve minutes of stillness and silence might not feel very long to you if you have been socialized in our culture to default to "all or nothing" thinking. This limiting belief posits that if you just do more, you will succeed more, including spiritual evolution!

Your curiosity, openness, and humility are more important than the number of practices you do. Your comfort with mystery, consistency, intention, deliberation, and inner narration might be new. Deliberation is mindfulness. It coincides with silently narrating what you are doing. "I am now practising presence. I am now walking across the room in a mindful way. I am here now in this moment." Narrating can be likened to your

Deep Self training your mind to settle down and pay attention. Further practice with narrating will be explained later under ***Self Therapy Tools, Rituals, and Practices for Stillness: Mindfulness***.

When Carl Jung developed his theory of extroversion and introversion, he likely never expected his idea to be so bastardized in our culture by well-meaning extroverts. He taught that individually we land somewhere on a continuum of how we thrive or fail to thrive on energetic connections to others, and to ourselves. So, another pattern or cultural expectation that you may find yourself thwarting as you practise stillness or silence is the common societal habit of filling space with noise, talk, performance, or distraction. Our culture celebrates extroverts, rewarding them for participating in groups, giving presentations, playing well with others, and hosting or being invited to social events. Unfortunately, our culture also punishes introverts labelling them "shy" or "insular" or "standoffish" or otherwise pathologizing them.

While I empathize with the extrovert's bona fide need for energy from interactions with other people, I have had to help repair too many introverts' lack of self-acceptance, and even shame, for what they perceive in themselves as a deficiency. They have a genuine need for stillness and silence. Some of my beloved introverts put their extrovert masks on in the morning as they head off to work (or *performance*) and find the mask more exhausting than the work itself. They happily remove the mask at the end of the day. Susan Cain, author of *Quiet*, speaks about this in her now famous Ted Talk, *The Power of Introverts*[2].

Would you consider attempting to *not* fill the silence in conversation with another? What might it be like to simply sit together in silence? What I call "noise pollution" by individuals who are uncomfortable with silence is likely their anxiety around stillness, and the cultural expectation to be 'on' all the time. Introverts thrived during the pandemic while extroverts were seriously challenged during the lockdowns. "Either/or" thinking never served anyone, and this maxim is also true in this discussion. While we tend to gravitate toward one end of the introversion/extroversion continuum, we can respect each others' energetic needs with a little compassionate practice.

Self Therapy Tools, Rituals, and Practices for Stillness

Shinrin-yoku (Forest Bathing)

Shinrin-yoku, or Forest Bathing, offers a structured pathway to stillness. The idea is to walk mindfully and silently, stopping frequently for communion with the trees, plants, fungi, birds, and other creatures. Whether I am practising alone or leading a group, I release self-consciousness and greet familiar trees as friends. Try naming a favourite tree. You don't own it by naming it. You are inviting relationship. The tree becomes more obviously sentient, although it already is. Talk to each other. Nurture each other. Heal each other.

Try *shinrin-yoku* for yourself. Go into the forest, sit for at least twelve minutes, and imagine (then feel) a relationship with the birds, trees, plants, insects, and air around you. Bring your experiences to your safe space or your forest meditations into your body. Note your reflections in your spiritual journal.

To take this practice deeper, I invite you to try Starhawk's Plant Allies meditation in her beautiful book, *The Earth Path*. With this meditation, you make friends with plants and trees by spending time with them and then actually entering the plant's system (after you ask its permission, of course). Ask for an image or word (anchor) that you can use to return to the plant energies, or inquire if an offering or act of reciprocity to the plant is desirable. Can you begin to imagine the health of a planet that receives such reverence?

Together, we can discover a beautiful freedom if we can stop thinking about the past or the future, even for just a moment, by simply being with the forest and its inhabitants.

Mindfulness

When doing outreach counselling for school children, I used the Hawn Foundation's fabulous MindUP curriculum. Goldie Hawn and her colleagues researched neuroscience, social-emotional learning principles, and positive psychology to assist children's learning. The strategies helped kids understand how parts of the brain are involved in calming anxiety and stress. They learned to self calm to get on with their learning. I soon discovered MindUP principles were also effective for adults and often use the Core Practice to open therapy sessions or in the midst of a session if therapeutic content is triggering and we need to reset.

If children from four to seventeen can train their brain and body to calm down enough to learn, so can you. Sitting with the spine straight, you can tap a gong, then inhale through the nose, and exhale through the mouth, bringing the breath as deeply into your lungs as you can as though you are trying to fill your abdomen. Note its effects in your Spiritual Journal.

Here is another mindfulness experiment: When you feel overwhelmed at home, at work, or any time you feel like you're running on autopilot, stop and breathe for a moment. Then move from one part of your environment to another with absolute and total awareness. Make moving from point A to point B a slow, meditative experience. Once again, try narrating movements to anchor your intention. Remember that I call narrating the Dual Process, a psycho-spiritual strategy I use to strengthen my mindfulness muscle. Try it for yourself. You will be surprised. You are telling yourself what you are doing as you are doing it. For example, "I am now moving from the bedroom to the kitchen in a mindful way," or "I am now turning off the water in a conscious way." I call these mindfulness moments "pressing the reset button." Try moving mindfully with narration.

Note how it affects your focus and concentration, your body, and your mind.

Service to the Planet and Connecting with Others

Take no pride in multi-tasking. Approach each step in any process as mindfully as you can. Notice the alchemy of more loving, complete results when you do this. Consider encouraging our politicians and millionaires to take a Sacred Pause before making decisions or responding to provocation. A Sacred Pause before responding can alter the trajectory of a troubled relationship. A Sacred Pause allows time to consider the ethics of developing a scientific idea before it gathers momentum. A Sacred Pause before that next impulse purchase allows you to consider the many lives—both human and more-than-human—that went into its creation, helping you to be less impulsive and more thankful.

Forest bathing and forest meditation can deepen your love for and sense of responsibility for helping to save our living Earth. If this interests you, jump ahead to ***Chapter Seven*** and begin the work suggested under ***Service to the Planet and Connecting with Others***. Bringing mindfulness and intention to our everyday actions can change the world.

When you perform even one small action to protect our home planet, know that having a personal, spiritual relationship with this home can change you. Stillness and mindfulness will be your trustworthy companions on the journey.

Follow Up with Vera

Fellow traveller, were you able to explore stillness like Vera? She reported that she could no longer imagine *not* sacred pausing throughout her day. Sometimes she gave herself a "time out" and noticed that interactions following her stillness-in-solitude moment were calmer, more centred. Vera had learned what I call "the alchemy of stillness"—that we are more focused (and more productive, if that is important to you) when we interrupt our hectic 'what's next' trajectory with a moment of stillness-in-solitude. She catalogued her memories of natural stillness and stored them to access when she needed a Sacred Pause. I invite you to do the same.

Biblio-Therapy for Chapter Two

Books and Resources to Support Your Work with Stillness

- *The Power of Now: A Guide to Spiritual Enlightenment*, Eckhart Tolle
- *A New Earth: Awakening to Your Life's Purpose*, Eckhart Tolle
- *Braiding Sweetgrass: Indigenous Wisdom, Scientific Knowledge, and the Teachings of Plants*, Robin Wall Kimmerer
- *The Earth Path: Grounding Your Spirit in the Rhythms of Nature*, Starhawk
- *The Wise Heart: A Guide to the Universal Teachings of Buddhist Psychology*, Jack Kornfield
- *MindUP Curriculum*, The Hawn Foundation
- *Wherever You Go, There You Are: Mindfulness Meditation in Everyday Life*, Jon Kabat-Zinn
- *Mindfulness for Beginners: Reclaiming the Present Moment – and Your Life*, Jon Kabat-Zinn
- *Shinrin Yoku: The Japanese Art of Forest Bathing*, Yoshifumi Miyazaki
- *Walking Meditation: Easy Steps to Mindfulness*, Thich Nhat Hanh
- *Quiet*, Susan Cain
- *The Heart of the Buddha's Teaching: Transforming Suffering into Peace, Joy, and Liberation*, Thich Nhat Hanh

Chapter Three

spirituality

Dear Ms. Terry,

I wasn't raised in a particular religion but took myself to Sunday School at my friends' churches because I was curious and didn't want to miss out. My parents taught me that you couldn't know anything for sure if you didn't experience it directly, and this included the idea of God. They described themselves as agnostic, not atheist, so I did have some exposure to discussions of belief. However, I have had the sense that there is something mysterious and bigger than we are out there. Plus, I can't account for what I call the "supernatural" experiences I've had (and others I know have had) without thinking that there has to be something more than what we can perceive with our five senses. I'm ready to explore. Can you help me get started?

- Something More? Tracy

Tracy, like many people, wishes to explore spirituality in her personal life and relationships and wonders how spirituality might influence global events. We begin with an image that speaks to her of innocence: the first step on a staircase. I suggest a spiral staircase as she is at the start of a spiral, taking the first innocent "not knowing" step on a great adventure. Comfort with mystery keeps a person open to messages from the universe, the natural world, and their own psyche. Does the image of first steps on a staircase resonate for you?

I begin our work together by stating my own spiritual stance. If it does not resonate for her, if she feels uneasy with it, my ethical imperative is to help her find a counsellor or spiritual director she is more comfortable with.

First and foremost, I am deeply spiritual, but no longer religious in the "go to a building where other people believe the same thing you do" kind of way. This distinction will become an important part of Tracy's journey. You can be spiritual without being religious in the traditional sense, and you can be religious without being spiritual. I have genuine respect for those who choose to believe in the faith doctrines of their churches, as long as those beliefs are not hate crimes in disguise. In fact, I was a lay minister in a progressive Christian church (United Church of Canada) before choosing my own spiritual path. In some Christian churches, members model the attributes of Christ Mind—unconditional love, inclusiveness, nonjudgment, acceptance, compassion, and openness to change and new ideas. In other churches, members do not. Unfortunately, many adherents of contemporary dominant religions have forgotten the original spiritual principles underlying their traditions. Their rituals have become rote. Egos, literal interpretations, zealots, fanaticism, and extremists have undermined the best intentions in these traditions. I am transparent with Tracy about my biases, reiterating my belief that human rights and the health of Mother Earth take precedence over religious privilege.

Having a background in a religious tradition can both help and hinder forward momentum in spiritual exploration, but at the end of the day it is up to each of us to work out our own salvation, our spirituality. We each become our own *thealogian* designing our own cosmology. I use the term 'thealogian' instead of the more familiar 'theologian' to designate each person's uniquely feminine creation of their cosmology.

Many of my teachers have emphasized how it is our responsibility to work out our own spirituality. Ask, "Who decides?" As you may recall from your work in Chapter One, it takes great courage to examine the doctrine of your own religion for teachings based on fear. Disguised as love and protection, some religious doctrines instill fear for even questioning the teachings. Homophobia, sexism, racism, exploitation of our planet, and other hate crimes are rationalized or justified using the reward-and-punishment mindset.

I am my own thealogian, comfortable with mystery and with having many more questions than answers. As a syncretist, I believe there are many paths to an evolving personal consciousness, or self-realization, and that blending these paths is acceptable as long as I am humble, respectful, and cautious not to participate in disrespectful cultural appropriation. The elements, rituals, mantras, and spiritual strategies that I participate in and teach come from teachers, leaders, and gurus of various spiritual traditions, with the clear expectation that I honour my sources and do not misuse or misrepresent their original intention.

Finally, I am a non-dualist, believing each of us is an inseparable part of a universal consciousness or unified spiritual intelligence. Our Egos try to keep us separate from each other, cling to being "special". We can unconsciously accept Ego's determination or seek and support the soul connection beyond the surface of things. I have found many overlaps among spiritual traditions around the world, in shared stories, parables, and myths (there's a flood story in almost every tradition, as well as a death/rebirth narrative), or in commonalities of ritual or ceremony, or similar attitudes toward service to the planet. I visualize a Venn diagram and seek the overlap where love and non-duality live. I land there.

Having been immersed in various faith traditions and taught by amazing sages, gurus, and spiritual leaders, I have developed a strong spiritual practice that involves meditation, contemplation, reverence, ritual, ceremony, and service to the planet. I live and breathe my beliefs. I consider myself (and everyone else) as one ray of consciousness, one emanation of Source, and my personality (body and brain) as a conduit for consciousness. Finally, and most importantly, I believe with all of my being that as each of us evolves in consciousness, the entire world will evolve in consciousness. We can save the planet this way. I know this.

Fellow sojourner, if you and Tracy are okay with this rich and varied background of experience and knowledge, shall we explore together?

Nuts and Bolts

Maintaining a Spiritual Diary/Journal

If you started this book at ***Chapter One***, you already have a Spiritual Journal. If not, find one now. Some people like a binder with lined pages, while others prefer notebooks or scribblers. While there are several routes to creating your own belief system, thealogy, or cosmology, the most fruitful path for my clients is often writing their own spiritual autobiography.

The Spiritual Autobiography

Write your spiritual autobiography. Here is a simple way to start. Leaving spaces around each item, do a quick chronological overview, tracing both your earliest personal experiences of the mystical or spiritual and the more formal organized teachings of your family faith. Work through your adolescent years, your adult years, up to now. This begins as a record of significant events with the date or your approximate age. Some examples are: Baptism; an early encounter with the mystical; Sunday School;

a private sense of kinship with nature; church camp; formal catechism or confirmation; a psychedelic experience; a spiritual group event; an organized wilderness experience; discovering your zone in running, mountain biking, swimming, or gardening; entering into covenants, vows, or commitments like engagement, marriage, or giving birth; a career calling; or a formal spiritual vocation stage or call to religious vocation.

Next, write in the spaces how your understanding of the Divine evolved through each event. For example, many people recount feeling like God was a parent-like entity (usually male) in their early years. Others pictured a bearded man in the sky. Some people had a Zeus-like, all-powerful god figure (again usually male) who was capricious and not particularly personal. Some theologians suggest the "bearded guy in the sky," that many think of as God, is actually a Zeus lookalike that developed out of the historical transition from matriarchy to patriarchy.

During my Goddess Pilgrimage on Crete, in Heraklion, before and after the official site visits, I studied Minoan culture and learned how pre-patriarchal Goddesses were demoted or destroyed in newer myths, their original feminine power and reverence stripped away or re-storied in often derogatory ways. Male gods usurped Goddesses. Goddess the Mother was replaced by God the Father.

My spirituality evolved from simply accepting patriarchal religious teachings designed to keep me in my place with a male god-father, to wondering if there was a Source who might share my femaleness.

Whether you remember choosing a mother figure or a father-like character in your childhood, continue to note your evolving understanding over time and through your list of personal experiences with the Divine. One way to start is to look at each event and ask, "How did this life experience change my understanding of myself, of the Divine, of my responsibility to children, to women, to the marginalized, to the exploited or disenfranchised, to the planet, and to the human community?" I call this way of exploring your spirituality a phenomenological approach. This means that you look at your own personal experiences with the Divine in real time, in your own life, in your own body, and in your own way. These experiences are your own, not borrowed from someone else or written for you to accept as doctrine. Return to your spiritual autobiography as you continue the work in this book. You may be delightfully surprised by how your idea of the Divine changes over time.

Some Spiritual Questions

Each of the following exploratory questions could have its own separate page, (or its own journal!) as explorations, investigations, and experiences evolve over time. Recall that spiral staircase? Spiritual exploration is like travelling on a spiral. As you evolve and change, you go deeper on the journey, but you encounter some of the same ideas, issues, and questions on ever deepening levels. You are becoming your own thealogian.

- *What are the differences between spirituality and religion?*
- *If there is an afterlife, what does it look and feel like?*
- *What part of you is eternal?*
- *What is your Soul, Higher Self, Divine Inner Intelligence asking of you?*
- *What connections have you experienced with your ancestors? How do you explain these experiences?*
- *If there is a Source, Divine Intelligence, or Divine Mind, a unified field, or an overarching Consciousness, is this entity male or female or neither?*
- *How comfortable are you with mystery, with not knowing, but not giving up the search? Are you a seeker?*
- *Can you recall those moments when you comfortably move in non-duality, soft acceptance of what is, or when you find yourself easily*

holding two ideas or points of view at the same time? Who are you with? What is the context?

- *Now, write about those moments when you get caught in black and white thinking, right and wrong, this or that (but not both). Again, who are you spending time with when this happens?*

Spiritual Practice – Ego Forward or Spirit First?

We live in a culture that is Ego Forward. Yes, of course, we need our Egos in order to stop at red lights and show up at the grocery store with clothes on. Ego helps us conform to societal expectations and that is not necessarily a bad thing. However, unthinking, Ego-driven conforming does not move us forward on our spiritual journey. When Ego determines every action, including all of our motives for behaving in a particular way, we are definitely in trouble. As a self-check spiritual practice, make two columns, headed *Spirit* and *Ego*. Under each heading, make a list of attributes you associate with that concept. I will start you off with "Love" under *Spirit* and "Fear" under *Ego*.

Consider how Ego consumes. Ego tries to shore itself up, feels like it is never enough, wants to be in control and special, constantly compares itself to others, gravitates toward the past or the future, abhors the present, competes, strives endlessly, and constantly feels lacking in some way. Spirit is open, creative, generous, quiet. Spirit wants to contribute through your body (your instrument). Spirit is deeply present and abides in a reality of abundance. When I am in the Spirit First position, my gaze is diffused, taking in a broader perspective rather than intensely focusing on minutiae.

Here are some associations that repeatedly appear in my practice.

Can you add more?

Ego	Spirit
fear	love
scarcity	abundance
dismissive	reverence
defensive	expansive
closed	open
doing	being
competitive	creative
critical voice	the friend (galb)
shaming	accepting
controlling	allowing
exclusive	inclusive
blame	understand
past and future	the now/presence
false self; small self; persona	true self; deep self; essence
facade/mask	authentic
reactive	responsive
rigid	flexible
definitive	curious
static	evolving
linear	circular
pain; heaviness	lightness; flow
____________________	____________________
____________________	____________________
____________________	____________________
____________________	____________________
____________________	____________________
____________________	____________________
____________________	____________________
____________________	____________________
____________________	____________________

Now that you have your lists, experiment in your interactions with others: are you responding openly, creatively, expansively with this person, or defensively, critically, or competitively? Note any discoveries in your Spiritual Journal. Are you Ego Forward or Spirit First?

Yes, the Ego-created identity, role, or persona is necessary in our culture. But we are *not* our roles. When all identifiers are stripped away—gender, role, occupation, marital status, house, car, money, privilege, friends—what is left? Your beautiful Self, Essence, or Soul. When given an opportunity, choose love. Acknowledge the present moment and allow Spirit to be first instead of an afterthought. This is a radical act in a culture that serves Ego.

For this spiritual practice, you may need to set reminders in your phone, your calendar, or your computer: "Reminder—move from Spirit First." Or place a sticky note in plain view, at your workstation, on your fridge, or on a mirror with your columns of Ego words and Spirit words.

You may love this work and its effect on your daily interactions. If so, jump to ***Chapter Seven*** and the section titled ***Taming the Dragon***.

Taking This Practice Deeper – Somatic Work

Take some time to feel exactly where in your body Ego resides. Where does it experience fear, scarcity, defensiveness? What part feels closed, competitive, or critical? If you feel defensiveness in your gut, the next time you feel that sensation, you will know Ego wants to run the show. Where does your physical body feel love, abundance, expansiveness, openness, and creativity? It is a very different somatic response. You can trust your Big Brain (what I call your body in ***Chapter Four: Balance***). I ask people to mindfully shift between both sensations—where they feel Spirit and where they feel Ego—to gain some control over their responses. When you feel tempted to react from Ego, your body signals give you time to step back, take a moment, and respond mindfully. Note your findings from this investigation in your Spiritual Journal.

Soul Work (Homework or Heartwork)

Schedule specific days for deeper explorations of your Spirit. On those mornings, set your intention to notice when you feel *in the zone* (calm, grounded, peaceful, measured, centred, connected in a loving way with yourself and others). Find your innocent place of "not knowing," and be open to whatever comes. Discard old teachings that tell you spirituality is 'woo woo' or religious or for other, more special, people. Many people find that their sense of spirituality comes when gardening. Others find it when running or climbing. Others find it when they sing, paint, write, do yoga, or hang out with children. When do you feel happy, peaceful, calm, and connected? Note your findings in your Spiritual Journal.

Spiritual Journal Stems and Prompts

- *What image did you choose that speaks of innocence to you? Does this image still guide you to the first steps at the beginning of a spiral, the beginning of being in an innocent "not knowing" stance?*
- *Re-read Tracy's letter that opens this chapter. What is your own felt sense of her concerns now that you have done some of your own work?*
- *How does it feel to learn you can design your own cosmology, become your own thealogian? What if you're told this is your responsibility? Do you feel resistance? Would you rather be told what to do, when to do it, and how?*

Spiritual Inspiration

Many strategies for this chapter are from those I designed for participants in my year-long Sophia Women's Wisdom groups. Sophia is from the Hebrew word *hokhmah,* which means wisdom, and where wisdom has always been characterized or personified as a woman in scripture. I invite you to read the *Book of Wisdom* for the beautiful renditions of wisdom as a woman.

In many ways, your decision to work through this book month by month can be the gestation of your new Self. You may decide to be reborn every year as you revisit the book next year, and the year after, watching yourself evolve and grow. Your commitment to your spiritual work and play can be in the form of a daily morning practice in your private She Space.

Dismantling the Social Construction or Unlearning the Familial Pattern

There are those who want to convince you that spirituality is a special place or condition that you must strive for or be taught. This is a false teaching. You already are Spirit, in a physical body. You cannot... *not*... be spiritual. It is impossible. You are mind, body, and Spirit simultaneously.

You may find it audacious to design your own spirituality, your own cosmology, your own thealogy. It may be that you don't trust yourself. Possibly you yearn to abdicate responsibility or to hand it off to someone in authority. If you are loving in your design and congruent, with your actions matching your values, you are not trying to be superior or judgmental. Take care, though, that you are not participating in disguised hate crimes whether misogynistic, racist, homophobic, destructive of our Earth Mother, or any other form of exclusivity.

The social construction that Source is male and that all religions are led by males (with special permission given to women to lead in some spaces) is one you may wish to unpack now, or later, in ***Chapter Five: Freedom.*** To begin this unpacking now, you may wish to read the Gnostic Gospels.

You may have learned how the Cathars (or the Albigensians) were systematically killed in a Christian crusade in the Middle Ages. They lived in southern France and northern Spain, and while their seeds were Christian, they were considered heretical because they believed women could be clergy. The Cathars fought hard and long from their mountain castles, like Montsegur in the Pyrenees, but they were eventually all eliminated. Is it possible that you yourself fear being labelled and punished as a heretic if you explore on your own? Offer yourself a journal reflection on this possible fear.

Self Therapy Tools, Rituals, and Practices for Spirituality

Samyam Saptah

The spiritual teacher Anandamayi Ma taught and encouraged the practice of Samyam Saptah—deliberately choosing one day of private spiritual practices. They might include monitoring dietary intake, observing silence, undertaking meditation periods spaced throughout the day, contemplative prayer, listening to or reading spiritual teachers, or any spiritual practice or ritual that helps you remember you are Spirit in human form. Ma's devotees organized an entire week of Samyam Saptah during which mahatmas were invited to speak, and spiritual practices were supported. These weeks are still practised at Ma's ashrams in India.

Some spiritual traditions associate phases of the moon with the Divine Feminine, designating certain days for inward reflection, natural days for rest, ritual, and spiritual practice. Perhaps you yourself feel inspired to practise Samyam Saptah at home or by booking private personal retreats. Perhaps you would like to create your own "moon day" dedicated to stillness, reflection, and spiritual nourishment.

Manifestos

The statement of biases I shared with Tracy (and with you, dear reader) could be considered my current manifesto, my evolving thealogy. Create your own current manifesto or statements of belief. These are organic and will change as you evolve. There are many examples and models to choose from. The sunscreen manifesto I heard on the radio back in the day felt like advice or a commencement speech. It was a spoken word piece by Baz Lurhmann based on "Everybody's Free to Wear Sunscreen" written by *Chicago Tribune* columnist Mary Schmich. You might giggle at its sentiments nowadays, but the beauty of manifestos is they give you something to reach for, to stretch toward. Pamela Redmond Satran's beautiful manifesto, "Every Woman Should..." is one of my favourites. Another favourite is Oriahe Mountain Dreamer's "Invitation," which you might also find inspiring as you work out your own manifesto.

Writing your own manifesto or credo helps to codify your current beliefs and attitudes, both toward life in general and toward your spiritual goals. Congruence happens when you live them. Talk is cheap. People are found in what they do, not in their rote, auto-piloted doctrine, creed, or prayer. Your manifesto is your first tentative step in creating your personal thealogy.

Revisit your manifestos from time to time. Do they match your behaviour? Get honest about whether you still believe in each one. Are you attempting to act from these each day or simply wishing them true? It is fine, either way. Just be honest with yourself in your Spiritual Journal.

Goddess Spirituality

If you yearn to explore Goddess Spirituality, you can jump ahead to ***Chapter Five: Freedom.*** I encourage you to continue designing your own spirituality by noting what speaks to your heart when you dream, when you are drawn to particular art pieces, or when you hear a podcast on Minoan culture. Try lifting your arms to the Divine Feminine, then kneeling down to ground yourself as you put your hands in the soil of Mother Earth. Give thanks for the food you are about to consume. Notice what happens in your body when you do these practices. You may feel shy at first, and maybe even a little daring. Don't allow internal critical voices created by our culture to hold you back from discovering your own spiritual freedom. You may also wish to integrate the results of your inner search into your daily altar experiences with reverence.

Service to the Planet and Connecting with Others

Challenging, a little scary, but ultimately fulfilling, we can choose to commit to the task of connecting deeply with our own divine nature. By doing so, we can have a personal effect on the evolving consciousness of the planet. You will find like-minded people on this journey if you remain aware and alert. Together, we can change the world. Human consciousness is evolving, and the current backlash is simply a testament to the fear of change this may mean for those who remain unconscious.

Talk is cheap. Model your own commitment to exploring and designing your own spirituality, based in love, openness, non-judgment, and respect for Mother Earth, through action. Can you volunteer for projects in your community that promote peace and wholeness? Can you find your place in your town's efforts toward watershed cleanup, soil restoration, and endangered species protection? If you do, you will find your people, and you will feel like you belong.

A Cautionary Note on Spiritual Bypass

Spiritual bypass is when you avoid the dirty work of difficult conversations, conflict resolution, and hands-on, planet-changing work by claiming to be "above all that". Spiritual addiction, piety, or spiritual superiority is a common pitfall of those who desire to evolve spiritually. It has been a very real part of my own journey and those of many clients. Leaning into our negative emotions and life challenges *is* our spiritual journey. Relationships are where we take our recovery show on the road. Eventually we must test our newfound fortitude and spiritual realizations in the crucible of real life, real relationships... the nitty-gritty of the day to day. In his beautiful book *The Clear Light: Spiritual Reflections and Meditations,* Steve Taylor wrote a poem called "Coming Down from the Mountain"[1] in which he captures this idea beautifully. I invite you to check it out as part of your spiritual inspiration for remaining cautious of spiritual bypass.

For further enrichment, explore *The Gaia Hypothesis* by James Lovelock (1972). You may discover that you are moving toward a spirituality of deep love for our Earth. You may discover this *and* still retain allegiance to the religion of your upbringing. Profound grief may arise as you realize all we have done to Mother Earth. It may express itself as worry and anxiety about our future survival on this planet, the future lives of our children and grandchildren. You might despair over historical choices made by past authorities.

Of course you will grieve. This is a natural reaction to what you see has been done to our planet.

Grieve, yes. Pray, yes. Meditate, yes. However, part of your grief work can be to make your gifts of restoration to Mother Earth as joyful as possible. Get your hands dirty. Do something, yes. What else can you do to help save our Home? Do it.

Follow Up with Tracy

Dear reader, were you as fascinated by your own spiritual autobiography as Tracy was? She reported that it felt like the bare bones of a memoir. At the end of our work together, she was a little shy about sharing her working manifesto. Part of her felt it was provisional. I validated her great courage in the undertaking and encouraged her to return to the spiral staircase image, carrying her ever deeper into the same mysteries. Her more difficult challenge was congruency—that is, acting on her newly found spirituality. It compelled her to join in efforts to save the planet and restore women's rightful sacred place as "life givers".

Biblio-Therapy for Chapter Three

Books and Resources to Support Your Work with Spirituality

- *The Chalice and the Blade*, Riane Eisler
- *Womanspirit Rising,* Carol Christ and Judith Plaskow
- *Tao Te Ching*, Laozi
- *The Veda*
- *The Tripitaka*
- *Tibetan Book of the Dead*
- *The Spiral Dance*, Starhawk
- *Original Blessing*, Matthew Fox
- *Finding Meaning in the Second Half of Life: How to Finally, Really Grow Up*, James Hollis
- *The Gnostic Gospels*, Elaine Pagels
- *The Power of Myth*, Joseph Campbell (with Bill Moyers)
- *Universal Human*, Gary Zukav
- *Living in the Light: Follow Your Inner Guidance to Create a New Life and a New World,* Shakti Gawain
- *The Goddess Companion: Daily Meditations on the Feminine Spirit*, Patricia Monaghan
- *Roar Like a Goddess*, Acharya Shunya
- *A Goddess Among Us: The Divine Life of Anandmayi Ma*, Swami Kedarnath
- *Life's Companion: Journal Writing as a Spiritual Quest*, Christina Baldwin
- Rumi

- *A New Earth*, Eckhart Tolle
- *The Power of Now*, Eckhart Tolle
- *The Clear Light*, Steve Taylor
- *A Course in Miracles*
- *The Torah*
- *The Qu'arn*

Risking Vulnerability, Walking the Talk, and Keeping it Real

This Therapist Shares Her Experience. Congruence Moment: Reverence

Terry'ism: "What you ritualize, you sanctify or make sacred—but always remember the underlying intention of your ceremony."

Acknowledging my Deep Self daily with reverence is a reminder that I am Spirit living in human form. My daily ritual tunes me in, sets the overall tone for the day, gives shape and form to my intention, and invites me to be open to assistance from the non-physical realm. I also have prayer beads (similar to a rosary but within the Buddhist tradition), a gong to anchor the end of my ritual, framed photos of myself as a child, ancestor rocks (more on these in ***Chapter Ten***), a Green Tara, Rumi quotations, and a mirror above my altar at eye level. I approach my altar formally in morning and evening, and I practise informally throughout the day, whenever I speak *from* my Higher Self and *to* the Higher Self of each client. An attitude of reverence keeps me humble and stands against Ego's fight for sovereignty. You may find a particular element (earth, air, fire, or water) or direction (north, east, south, or west) resonates more for you at different times in your life. I gravitate (no pun intended) toward north and Earth more often than not.

Congruence Moment: Stillness (from Chapter Two)

Terry'ism: "If it's urgent, it can wait."

Working with Stillness has changed my life. I ponder the damage to our psyches resulting from what I call "noise pollution". It may sound ironic that as a hearing-impaired person, I find extraneous unnecessary noise deeply offensive to me. I find auditory dissonance disturbing. I support municipal attempts to curb excess noise pollution, such as fining those with obnoxiously loud cars. Befriending my deepest Stillness has led me to moments of pure bliss.

There is a kind, friendly, loving aspect to this level of consciousness that I never want to be apart from. During particularly traumatic moments, my greatest solace comes from connecting to Source in Silence. I call Her the Friend. To calm my mind at bedtime, I often use a stillness practice: travelling to a beautiful waterfall in my mind's eye, experiencing the wonder of its perpetual flow in the darkness and solitude.

During the day, I might see a hummingbird using its small, narrow, tweezer-beak to pull fluff from the dried cattail I put by the feeder. The fluff trail as she flits away to build her tiny nest is bigger than she is! This is love; this is a portal to presence. Sometimes, when I need to get centred between clients, I pull out a gem, a rock, or a piece of labradorite. I think about all that had to happen to create this mineral. I am grateful to be holding it now and for its ability to bring me into the Now.

Congruence Moment: Spirituality (from Chapter Three)

Terry'ism: "All that is good about me, that emanates from me, is the Divine in me seeking expression." Terry'ism: "Every day my Soul gets to look out through my eyes, use my hands, speak through my voice."

My *sadhana* (Hindu for spiritual practices that prepare oneself for self-realization) began just after I turned ten. One could argue it began in an earlier lifetime, in the womb, or during my early childhood but age ten was my first personal consciousness of Source, Divine Intelligence, Unified Field, or whatever name you want to give Her. In adulthood I am aware when I have been guided supernaturally by the profound sense of peace and gratitude that washes over me.

My understanding of the Friend continues to evolve through the works of Jalal al-Din Rumi, a Sufi mystic from the 13th century. Coleman Barks' translations of Rumi's poetry are captivating and astonishing. Some believe Rumi's references to the Friend were elaborations on his relationship to his soul friend Shams, a wandering dervish monk. Others consider the Friend a field between formlessness and form where we meet each other at our deepest spiritual levels, what Sufis call *qalb*. I consult my Friend when I most need help turning off my inner critical voice or Ego, when I'm hungry for unconditional love, compassion, and peace from my Inner Parent or Beloved Other.

I truly believe that when each one of us evolves consciously, we evolve global consciousness. Evolved global consciousness will save the planet. This is my life's purpose.

Practising What I Preach: Winter Moments
Earth-based Spiritual Practices, Winter Solstice (Yule)

Imbolc (Candlemas)

In Celtic and Pagan Earth-based Spiritual traditions, there are eight major annual Earth celebrations called Sabbats. These are usually observed at sunset and continue for forty-eight hours.

Samhain (Halloween – October 31/November 1) is often considered the first Sabbat or New Year in Celtic and Pagan Earth-based traditions.

However, I will not start with Samhain. For this particular book, it is more appropriate to end with it during our Autumn work together in the concluding ***Chapter Twelve***.

The day after Samhain is considered the start of winter, so I will begin with the psycho-spiritual offerings of Winter Solstice. Set aside your old, fear-based overwhelmed life and start fresh as this Sabbat offers a new focus of growth and change ahead as you begin your work through this book.

- ***Winter Solstice (Yule)*** December 21
- ***Imbolc (Candlemas)*** February 1
- ***Ostara (Spring Equinox)*** March 19 - 21 (approx.)
- ***Beltane (May Day)*** May 1
- ***Summer Solstice (Litha)*** June 20 - 21 (approx.)
- ***Lughnasadh (Lammas)*** August 1
- ***Mabon (Autumnal Equinox)*** September 23 (approx.)
- ***Samhain (Hallowe'en)*** October 31/November 1

Winter Solstice or Yule – December 21

Winter Solstice is a very special time in our Earth-based Spiritual tradition. From my early Christian experiences of celebrating the quiet candlelight of Advent, I often think of Winter Solstice as a 'gathering in' period, a time of quiet reflection on the year past. Halcyon Days before and after December 21 are days of quiet, calm, and peace. They can feel foreign if you are caught up in materialism, consumerism, and stressful preparations. I wish you the courage and curiosity to choose a different, quieter, calmer, and more peaceful approach to late December: the spiritual still point of our Archetypal Human Year. May it be so. Blessed be.

Appropriately, Winter Solstice is also that point of the year where the night is longest and the day is shortest. I liken this day to the death and rebirth of the sun, so I celebrate the most sacred time of our calendar year: *The Return of the Light*. The carefully considered architecture of some megalithic monuments around the world acknowledges this most sacred time by revealing the sunrise light only once a year through a small opening in roofs at Newgrange, Ireland, or sunrise at Stonehenge, England. Other megaliths are in Scotland, Germany, and Mexico. You may wish to research these humbling testaments to our ancestors' honouring of our sun's movements. If you are lucky, you may even visit these sacred sites. Give thanks.

At my house, for days prior to Solstice, I prepare to let go of that which no longer serves me in healthy ways. I strip the altar of all that was collected throughout the year and compost it, as it is all organic. Then I move into Stillness, honouring the still point with reflection, quietude, and lovely sanctity. After that I celebrate the return of the light with a fire or a symbolic gathering of family and friends. In the Celtic tradition, I bring in fallen evergreens like holly, wintergreen, or ivy to form wreaths or garland. If you choose to do this ritual, be conscious and gather from windfall if you can, rather than cutting from our living sisters.

Imbolc or Candlemas (February 1 and 2)

This is the halfway point between Winter Solstice (Yule) and Spring Equinox (Ostara). I celebrate the Celtic tradition of looking for signs of emerging green life in our natural world. I include the whimsy of Groundhog Day. In our part of the world, early spring crocuses poke their little noses out of the soil (or snow!). This is also a time of cleansing so I may do some spring cleaning, which in my home also represents spiritual cleansing to make room for new life, new possibilities, new embodiment that puts my winter planning into action. I often honour the Celtic Goddess Brigid at this time as she was known as the Goddess of fire, fertility, water wells, and other water sources. I might have my first beach or outdoor fire or meditate beside a river or stream.

Feel free to design ceremonies that feel personal and meaningful to you. You may wish to review my suggestions for setting up a ritual from ***Chapter One: Deepening Your Understanding of the Four Directions***. This involves preparing yourself, calling in the four directions and the five elements (including Spirit) to create a sacred space, then setting your intention. You can follow this with invoking your guide(s) for supernatural assistance, proceeding with an activity that feels like the best way to meet your intention, reflecting, then thanking your helpers. You may choose to feast afterwards. Always give thanks for divine assistance, whether it is from deities you invoke, or for the generosity of the four directions.

Spring

Balance, Freedom, Overly Responsive to Others (Codependence)

Chapter Four

balance

Dear Ms. Terry,

I'm exhausted and cranky. I'm becoming forgetful and jumpy. I don't know why I feel this way when I have the most amazing life and I know I am privileged. I feel guilty for whining but sometimes I just feel so overwhelmed. Can you help me understand what's wrong with me?

- Missing something, Sherry

During intake, Sherry confided that, as a professional mom, she took pride in doing it all. She homeschooled her three children, sat on committees, managed a large, busy home, and handled everyone's health appointments. Unfortunately, fatigue affected her overall health, her moods, and her ability to juggle it all. Predictably, she was burning out. My intuitive sense was that she had lost or forgotten allegiance to herself. She did not know her own worth. Perhaps you see parts of yourself in her frustration?

We began our relationship by celebrating her decision to ask for help. Then I offered her an image to work with that would inspire balance: the familiar Yin Yang symbol. Its origins are in the Taoist spiritual tradition, which I honour, respect, and attempt to emulate. Balance is vital to sound mental, physical, and spiritual health. Yin Yang is tattooed on my body, and it is my therapy practice logo. Fellow traveller, I invite you to hold Yin Yang in your psyche as you journey through this chapter with Sherry.

Nuts and Bolts

The Wellness Wheel has four quadrants: spiritual, emotional, physical, and intellectual. As integrated beings, of course we are not split into four parts, so think of the wheel as a convenient tool. Download my template from my website or draw a large circle on a page. Mark the four quadrants: spiritual, emotional, physical, and intellectual.

Wellness Wheel - Self Awareness - Balance - Self Compassion

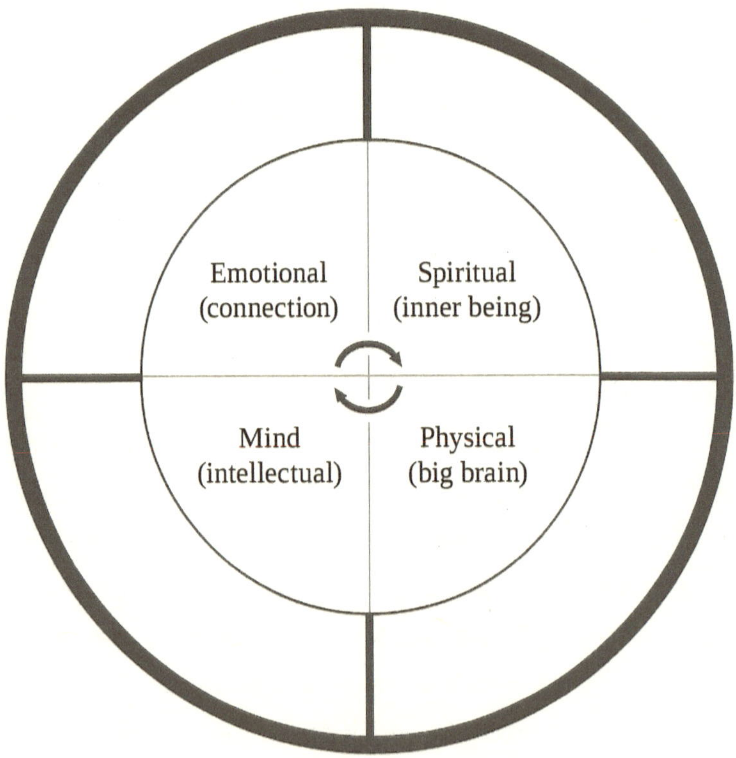

Shade in the quadrants with colours that reflect the attention you are currently giving to your physical, emotional, intellectual, and spiritual needs. If writing feels more natural to you than colouring or shading, jot notes in each quadrant instead.

The Physical Domain – Your Big Brain

Your *Big Brain* constitutes the neck down. She speaks to you, without words, continuously because... and this might sound corny... because She loves you unconditionally. She wants you to be well and continuously re-calibrates herself for your wellness and healing. She is nonverbal, speaking to you via symptoms. However, if She cannot get your attention with one message, She ups her ante, intensifying the symptoms or adding new ones.

What is your Big Brain trying to tell you? Under the physical realm, consider not only symptoms but sleep hygiene, fresh air, happy movement, clean food, hydration, personal rhythms, addictions, and sexual fulfillment.

The Emotional Domain – Relationship to Self

Under the emotional quadrant, consider your relationship with yourself. How well you are attending to your emotional life? What is your self talk like? How emotionally flexible are you? Can you be aware of both thoughts and feelings at the same time? How do you practise emotional self-regulation? Do you make space to notice emotions in your body before you respond to an emotionally charged event? Is your emotional vocabulary wide and specific? How safe do you feel being your authentic self in your relationships? Would you like some help with emotional management?

The Intellectual Domain – Your Escape Route?

In Western culture, we spend a lot of time in our heads—at work, reading, studying, thinking, analyzing, problem solving. Some say we escape the emotional disappointments and challenges in our life by retreating to our intellect. In what way is this true for you? Do you escape your body, heart, and Spirit sometimes by intellectualizing your experiences? Do you read about spirituality but sometimes forget to live it? Does your wheel feel wobbly in this area?

The Spiritual Domain – Your Connection to the Divine Within and Without

Consider your openness to connecting to the non-physical realm. When and where to you feel the deepest connection to your Source, Soul, Spirit, Essence, Higher Self, True Self, or the Witness? Joggers find Spirit in their run, gardeners with their plants, hikers among the forests, mountains, and rivers, mountain bikers on the trails, artists in their creative zone, professional moms in the minutia of home and family management. Each of these examples has connections to Spirit both within and without... imminent and transcendent... at the same time.

Where in your world do you feel your deepest connection? What do you believe about the afterlife? How do you explain mediums? What part of you is eternal? How comfortable are you with mystery? Are you a seeker?

On your wheel you noted in each quadrant the activities you participate in daily for yourself. *For yourself.* Whichever method you used—shading/colouring or writing—study your wheel now and consider the priorities that emerge. Is your wheel wobbly? Fairly balanced? Are some quadrants filled with activities and attention while others are mostly blank? In which areas would you add more energy or take some away through scheduling new activities or removing existing ones? Use your reflections to shift from simple awareness to goal setting and re-prioritizing.

Spiritual Practice – Wellness Wheel Daily Check In

A blank Wellness Wheel can be posted on the refrigerator for a quick wholeness/balance check each day. You could start a breakfast habit of looking at the wheel and re-calibrating the day ahead. Expand into a monthly, biannual, or annual spiritual deeper look to guide your personal assessment, accountability, and goal setting.

Including the spiritual realm as an essential part of the well-balanced life can surprise women who are busy meeting the emotional, physical, and even intellectual needs of others before their own. Yet when the spiritual life is given attention and commitment, a certain alchemy manifests. Everything feels easier. Acknowledging *what is* is the first step for change, which is why I started with the ***Nuts and Bolts*** of getting honest about what is actually happening.

Reading about the integrated life or the four realms is not the same as practising balance. Noticing incongruousness between your stated core values and actual daily activities can be destabilizing at first. There may be grief or self-punishment around how you have neglected yourself and your core beliefs. We can work through grief, but more challenging is resentment. It is harder to admit to and escape from. But resentment is your responsibility to deal with. By doing so, you are saving important relationships, including with yourself, and letting the Big Brain know you have heard its message.

If this chapter intrigues you, the dis-ease of codependence (or what I call the "overly responsive to others at your own expense" malady) is addressed further in ***Chapter Six***.

Soul Work (Homework or Heartwork)

This seemingly simple tool, the Wellness Wheel, can be the catalyst for incredible growth. Considering what constitutes a "spiritual activity" helps us examine differences between organized religion and personal spirituality. Contemplating how activities in the emotional quadrant are different from those in the intellectual domain help can help distinguish our taught obligations from our authentically chosen ones. Some activities fit in all four realms in an integrated way. My yoga practice connects me to my intellect, my emotional self, my Spirit, and of course, my physical self.

Deepen your Wellness Wheel practice by honestly assessing what value you place on each domain and then comparing this with how you actually live your daily life. A strategy that will help you is to start with another blank Wellness Wheel but divide each quadrant in half again. In one half-quadrant shade (or write, or scale from 1-10) your professed value. In the other half-quadrant, shade in the *actual* daily attention you give it. This shows you how congruent your life is. You may be startled to realize how your work role and your identity have become tightly woven. Saying the emotional dimension is an important value is very different from actually paying attention to your emotional life. As Sherry filled each quadrant with daily activities, her tears flowed. Under her hand the reality emerged—not only was her wheel wobbly, but many activities in each domain were for others, not for herself. The wheel can keep us honest.

Sherry admitted that she would never miss a medical, dental, or program appointment for one of her children or her partner. However, she had neglected to put her own self-care on the family calendar. It is a radical and necessary act to perceive your own self-care as equal to or even, occasionally, more important than the care-taking of others. For your final piece of Soul Work for this chapter, schedule your self-care time on the family calendar. You would never miss someone else's appointment. Why miss your own?

Spiritual Journal Stems and Prompts

Sherry used the Taoist symbol Yin Yang for balance, and you might like to continue using it. Possibly the quadrant wheel works better for you. Whichever you choose, write about how it helps you with restoring balance and self-care. Use the following prompts to expand on your thoughts and feelings:

- *"When I study my wheel, I realize that I..."*
- *"The thought of actually putting myself first makes me feel..."*
- *"Ms. Terry tells me that resentment can have a negative effect on my body and my overall health. This idea has me wondering if..."*
- *"To me, balance means..."*

Dismantling Social Constructions and Unlearning Familial Patterns

Until we move away from our current gender-centric culture, the roles imposed upon those born female are those of caregivers, nurturers, help-mates, givers... *to others.* As women we are inundated with cultural and familial approval for selflessness. Has anyone told us our first responsibility is to ourselves? What was modelled for you? Do you judge women who attend to their own needs first?

Answer the above questions in your journal in a loving, self-compassionate way. You can unlearn the social constructions of the dominant culture or the teachings of your family of origin. You can remember who you are underneath labels, roles, job assignments, and titles. Your BEINGness is what will sustain you when the job or family giving role is stripped away, irrelevant, or when you choose to retire.

Self Therapy Tools, Rituals, and Practices for Balance

Body Forgiveness and Body Acceptance

Our bodies love us. They want to have a relationship with us. They are always trying to communicate that love to us. In my decades of service, I have yet to meet a woman who can say she returns that love toward her body in its totality. Can you imagine forgiving your body for its imperfections? Can you imagine quitting negative self talk around the body? Can you consider giving up believing your body is somehow betraying you?

As an experiment, forgive your body for responding to your thoughts. After all, that is exactly what your body is doing when you complain about it—responding to your thoughts. Would you not be sad if someone constantly told you that you were not good enough? Would you not be discouraged if someone insisted on complaining about a specific part of you, personally? This ever-flowing conversation goes both ways: your Big Brain (your body) speaks to you, and you speak to it. How loving are your words?

In your journal, imagine telling your body you love it even though it might not be perfect. Imagine developing a loving relationship with your body, flaws and all. Imagine sending these different thoughts to your Big Brain. Try this regularly, as a conversation with your body in your journal, for a hundred days. Notice your overall improvement in general health and flexibility. I challenge you. You can receive assistance with my challenge by reading Steve Taylor's beautiful poem, *Your Body.*[1]

Qigong

Balance is vital for sound mental, physical, and spiritual health. Some integrated spiritual body practices related to balance include Qigong and Tai Chi. Grandmaster Mantak Chia, a gentle Qigong teacher in the Taoist tradition, teaches inner alchemy with an emphasis on how to maintain the PH balance required in our bodies through various sounding techniques. Among other practices, he teaches the various sounds you can make with your mouth that connect with your vital organs, as you smile inwardly at each of these organs. The idea is not only to create balance, but to compost then transmute negative energy and the negative emotions associated with each organ into positive energy. The experience is delicately freeing and refreshing. The common sounds and their relevant organs are as follows:

'shhh'	-	liver
'haww'	-	heart
'huu'	-	spleen; pancreas
'sssss'	-	lungs
'whoo'	-	kidney
'heee'	-	full body (known as the triple warmer)[2]

My Qigong teacher, Robynn Honeychurch, incorporates these healing sounds in each of our current weekly sessions. Her healing sounds are *Ho (heart); Hu (spleen); Tzu (liver); Shuh (lungs); Shee (three heaters); and Chuwee (kidneys).* Robynn comments, "I know that as time goes by things like the healing sounds end up evolving and changing, so I'm not saying the way I learned is the right way, by any means." (personal communication, 2023). Can you investigate Qigong or Tai Chi classes available in your community?

Reiki, Healing Touch, and Bio-Energetics

You may wish to deepen your balance and healing spiritual somatic practices by receiving treatments from a Reiki Master or a Certified Healing Touch Practitioner, or by learning how to do these treatments on others and on yourself.

Be sure that the person serving or teaching you has received ethical training and is not Ego Forward. What this means is that the ethical practitioner will acknowledge that they are simply a conduit or reed for universal healing energy that is available to *anyone* and *everyone.* They will not claim special status or claim to be *healing you.* They simply said "Yes" to becoming an instrument for the energy that already exists for *everyone.* They chose to be trained by a dedicated teacher or master in how to shape, contour, and direct that energy with agape loving intention.

A second cautionary note if you choose to participate in bio-energetics.

Be sure the practitioner does not claim to be an expert on your healing process and is not wearing a Super Heroine cape. Any genuine servant of healing energy will humbly acknowledge your own inner healing resources, not theirs. We have a saying in our practice: "The healer is on the table."

Finally, the practitioner will ask for and receive your informed consent before proceeding. They will only treat within their scope of practice and will abide by the ethical standards of bio-energy work. Most importantly, they will *not* try to provide therapy or counselling. If they sense you could benefit from a mental health referral, the ethical bio-energetic practitioner will refer you to a licensed, competent, skilled, trained, and certified psychotherapist for particular mental health issues that come up during your session.

My primary references for both forms of bio-energetic treatments (Reiki and Healing Touch) are Anodea Judith's *Eastern Body, Western Mind*[3], Barbara Brennan's *Hands of Light*[4], and Sister Eileen Curteis's *Reiki: Universal Gift of God's Healing Love*[5]. There are other resources you may wish to consider in the Biblio-Therapy section of this chapter.

Chakras

Balancing the chakras is for healing in Reiki, Healing Touch, and other bio-energetic practices. Chakras were mentioned in ***Chapter One: Reverence***. Here we go deeper. There are many energy centres in the body, called chakras, from the Hindu Ayuerveda. They are often envisioned as spinning wheels or disks of energy that correspond to body parts. Balancing your chakras also positively enhances your emotions. Concentrating on the seven major chakras, deepen your spiritual somatic practice by exploring balance with the following:

- Chakra 1 – Root – Located at the base of your spine. Your sense of home, foundation, Earth, feeling grounded, pragmatics, stability, 'rootedness'.

- Chakra 2 – Sacral – Located at your pelvis area, below your belly button. Your sense of yourself as a sexual, sensual, creative, emotional being.
- Chakra 3 – Solar Plexus – Located above your belly button, your stomach area. Your sense of personal power, volition, will, confidence in moving forward in an active way.
- Chakra 4 – Heart – Located at the centre of your chest (not biologically where your physical heart actually is). Your sense of loving and receiving love, feeling compassion, and receiving compassion.
- Chakra 5 – Throat – Located at your throat area. Your sense of being able to listen to yourself, communicating your needs, listening to others, and feeling understood.
- Chakra 6 – Third Eye – Located just above your eyes in the middle of your forehead. Your gut sense, intuition, knowing through the sixth sense, and your imagination.
- Chakra 7 – Crown – Located at the top of your head and just above it. Your connection to the universe, transcendence, your life's purpose, and the divine.

Other Balance Practices You May Wish to Explore

The highly respected Ayurveda from the Indian healing sciences will help you explore, among many other beautiful practices and teachings, the balance required by your body type: Vata, Pitta, and Kapha.

You may wish to receive treatments from a qualified acupuncturist who is knowledgeable in balancing your system using Chinese medicine.

You may decide to explore balancing your Big Brain's many systems through dedicated yoga practice.

I use Stanley Rosenberg's work with the vagus nerve in the balance practices I teach for trauma, depression, and anxiety. Rosenberg widely shares self-help exercises online if you wish to experiment with the vagus nerve[6].

Service to the Planet and Connecting with Others

Our planet is in serious need of balance. We reflect and impact our world. As we re-balance ourselves, we contribute to the restoration of the planet. I sometimes imagine eavesdropping on a conversation between Robin Wall Kimmerer and Starhawk about Earth-based Spirituality. As they discuss how to save our Earth, I sense their mutual excitement and admiration for each others' ideas on natural observation, conservation, sustainability, permaculture, reciprocity, gratitude, activism, and carbon footprint reduction. They *do* as well as teach.

You, too, can walk the talk. My best experiences of having an actual impact on the planet have been when I joined forces with others. These projects went from identifying needs, conceptualizing a path of least resistance, and designing a plan together. Each of us in these groups had our own tasks, while other bigger jobs were completed together in coordination. Whether it is removing invasive ivy from my local forest or directing Eve Ensler's *The Vagina Monologues* and raising thousands of dollars for my local shelter, these community projects have a lasting impact on the world. My experience of belonging to a community of like-minded people with a mission keeps me returning to these voluntary groups. All of my group projects are deeply satisfying because in some way, I am involved in restoring balance in our world. *Shall we join this community together?*

Follow Up with Sherry

Dear reader, did you experience pushback as you worked through this chapter? When Sherry found the courage to schedule self-care into the family calendar, she noticed flack from family members who preferred she stay in the role they were comfortable with. This flack ranged from guilt inducement, passive-aggressive behaviours (sabotage, silent treatment, dramatic crises that would force her to focus on them, and even outright anger). We prepared for these reactions, rehearsing how she could find compassion for loved ones who feared if she loved herself more, she would love them less. I offered hope that when they realized how much healthier, happier, and more fulfilled she was, they would decide they loved her enough to wish her to be the best person she could be. However, the pressure to return to that more familiar role became overwhelming for Sherry.

This is when we decided to delve much deeper into that age-old disease: codependence, or what I prefer to call ***Overly Responsive to Others' Needs (Chapter Six)***. The Yin Yang image evolved into a symbol for her deeper balance work of addressing codependence.

Biblio-Therapy for Chapter Four

Books and Resources to Support Your Work with Balance

- *Accessing the Healing Power of the Vagus Nerve: Self-Help Exercises for Anxiety, Depression, Trauma, and Autism*, Stanley Rosenberg
- *Hands of Light: A Guide to Healing Through the Human Energy Field*, Barbara Ann Brennan
- *Reiki: Universal Gift of God's Healing Love,* Eileen Curteis
- *Eastern Body, Western Mind*, Anodea Judith
- *You Can Heal Your Life*, Louise Hay
- *Anatomy of the Spirit: The Seven Stages of Power and Healing,* Carolyn Myss

Chapter Five

freedom

Dear Ms. Terry,

I have this constant underlying feeling that I'm just not enough. I feel like I'm always trying to prove my worth. Sometimes I wish I'd been born male so I could coast through life knowing I was born "enough" because I'm a guy. These are weird thoughts, I know. Guys have it hard too, I'm sure. I keep myself very, very busy. Whenever I yearn to relax, soak in my tub, journal, nap, read my book, paint or craft, putter in my garden, or simply stare out the window, I come up with a million reasons why I should be doing something more productive. I feel guilty if I'm resting or doing something enjoyable. I worry about other people judging me, or that I may have forgotten a chore or task I promised I would do for someone. I long for some "me" time, but the only thing I do for myself is indulge in a glass of wine while cooking dinner.

- Thinking wine is not enough, Marcie

A woman born into our patriarchal (androcratic) culture may never feel like she is enough, never free to do what she wishes. The rigid roles in androcracy maintain the patriarchal status quo. Like many women, Marcie was plagued by 'shoulds' linked to the roles she was taught belong to females. Whenever she started to relax into an enjoyable activity, like art, yoga, or gardening, Marcie immediately doubted her right. Surely, she should tackle something on her extensive to-do list. She had no image of herself existing in freedom from these duties. Complicating matters, her Ego liked the approval gained from doing favours and going the extra mile. It felt good in the moment, but afterwards she expected thanks or a return favour that did not come or did not satisfy. She had once again left her own desires for last and was out of time for herself. Her evening glass of wine felt justified as the only thing she did for herself. My initial intuitive image of Marcie was as a bird soaring over the ocean, playing on air currents, allowing life to simply happen. Fellow sojourner, what is your image of freedom?

Nuts and Bolts

Shoe Box Ritual – Part One: The Rules

Many women mistake approval for love. I have found in my work with psychologist Carol Gilligan's ideas that this merging of approval and love happens around the age of nine for young girls but typically anywhere between seven and twelve years of age.[1] I have a directive in my therapy practice: No 'should-ing' on yourself allowed within these four walls. This need for approval is explored in more depth later. For now, allow the idea of approval mimicking love to rest in your psyche, or journal about it before proceeding with your shoe box ritual.

For this ritual you will need a shoe box and slips of paper, on which you'll print any rules you learned in childhood from parents, other family members, teachers, community, organized religion, or television and other media. Did rules restrict your being, relaxing, reading, creating, playing, treating yourself, or daydreaming? What rules appear as limiting beliefs or an internal, critical voice that is still telling you how you should behave?

Your rules might include:

1. I *should* always put others' needs before my own.

2. What people think of my giving *should* be more important than anything.

3. I *should* avoid saying "No" to requests from spouses, parents, children, bosses, or friends.

4. If I think about my own needs and preferences, I *should* label myself as selfish.

5. If I do not like someone's behaviour, I *should* justify it by referring to their childhood trauma, upbringing, or current crisis, or take pride that they are misunderstood by everyone else but me.

6. I *should* avoid feeling my own feelings and distract myself by feeling for others.

7. I *should* not relax until all of my chores or errands are complete.

8. I *should* earn any self indulgence by how much I do for others.

9. I *should* not think that I have the right to change your mind.

10. My obligations to others *should* be more important than obligations to myself.

11. Everyone *should* think I am a nice person.

12. Approval equals love, and I *should* know this.

13. I *should* feel lucky that, as a woman, I am no longer considered property (or chattel) in North America and that I am now legally a human citizen with the right to vote.

One by one, reflect on whether you created these rules for yourself or if they were learned through reinforcement. Reinforcement simply means that someone gave a positive response to a behaviour. The positive response made you feel good about yourself. Approval is an important positive reinforcer because it feeds the Ego's need to belong. Historically, belonging meant we would be fed; we would survive. Now look at each rule slip and ask yourself how it improved your life or how it gave you what you wanted.

Be aware that these rules may have served you well for a while. They were coping mechanisms, core beliefs, or historical commitments or vows you made, perhaps unconsciously. Now you are conscious of them and no longer blindly living according to rules you've never previously questioned.

When you read a rule that is no longer serving you or your happiness, put it into the shoe box. When the box is filled and no slips remain, visualize handing it back to the people, communities, and institutions who instilled the rules. Then dispose of the whole box. Bury it, recycle it, even burn it, being aware of the environmental impact of your choice. For example, you might decide that the rules are represented by carrot peelings or other composted vegetable matter. You can bury that and be doing good for the Earth as you clear out your unhelpful rules.

Over time you may recognize other buried rules emerging. Determine whether each rule is working for or against you. Ask yourself "Who decides?" Symbolically give back to its messenger any rule that does not serve you in the present. You may feel like you are waking from a spell when you do the important work of this book. Lift the blinders. You are strong enough to see clearly.

Shoe Box Ritual – Part Two: Your Birth Rites

Many of the women I serve are shocked when I share their birthright to basic human rights. It has simply never occurred to them that they have unconsciously given up some very important rights over time. You may have been socially conditioned to reject or forfeit your rights in order to keep the peace, or your family of origin may have taught you that you are not entitled to particular human rights for fear that you would stir the family pot.

In your journal, please reflect on some of the following rights I teach. Decide which ones you would like to practice.

You have the right to be direct in asking for what you want, and the right to say no to requests. You have the right to be imperfect, and the right to create your own belief system. You have the right to change your core values as you mature, and to change your behaviour to honor those values. You have the right to represent only yourself, and to decline representing someone else. You have the right to radical self-acceptance, and to refute judgments about your behaviour. You have the right to be angry (as long as you express it in a safe way and not internalize it), the right to be afraid, and the right to say no. You have the right to privacy, autonomy, quiet time, "you-time", and a private space to reflect uninterrupted. You are allowed to be happy, to play, and to relax. You are actually allowed to evolve beyond those around you, perhaps modelling self-care without being accused of being selfish. You are actually allowed to change your mind. Did you know that?

After your first round of reflections on these rights in your journal, replace the word 'right' with the word 'responsibility'. Note how this feels for each statement. For example, "I have the responsibility to be direct when asking for what I want." Note that the word 'responsibility' does not always fit perfectly for each right, but for those where it does work, the results can be astonishing!

Finally, to take this strategy to the next level, choose one right that you find problematic and work on developing some comfort with it over the next month. Then move on to another right to work on the following month, and so on. If you carefully read through your list every day, eventually you will learn to accept that YOU are entitled to each of these rights.

There are two rights that many women stumble over. One is the right to change your mind. The patriarchal stereotype is that 'women always change their minds' so women often go out of their way to disprove this, and to show the world that they are loyal and committed. Unfortunately, this often backfires. Some women stay in bad situations because they fear being perceived as 'flaky' at best, or traitorous at worst. There is no winning when you are attempting to disprove a stereotype—hence the double bind. Remember, this works for certain individuals who wish to keep you loyal to an oppressive system. When men change their minds, they are considered discerning and strong of character. The double standard is a basic tool of the oppressor. Practice changing your mind about little choices before working your way up to more momentous decisions.

The other problematic right is your right to be healthier than those around you, or to evolve in consciousness. The social conditioning women receive around the glory of martyrdom and self-sacrifice can compel them to rank their own mental and physical health last on their to-do lists. We explored this in ***Chapter Four: Balance***, but this might be a good time to refresh the concepts you learned and practised there. What did you write in your journal then? Do you see it differently now? Are you indeed evolving by doing this work?

Spiritual Practice – Assertiveness/Directness

Not everyone would consider attempting to speak directly or be assertive as a spiritual practice. Yet I see it as a spiritual practice because it is honest. It takes great courage to let go of manipulation, passive aggression, martyrdom, or indirectness and to replace it with firm clarity. You can still be kind. You may still have to accept "No" as the answer if you are direct and kind. At the very least, you will have expressed yourself truthfully.

Carol Gilligan's research found that women and girls are so conditioned to depend on approval that they may unconsciously change their voice to increase their chances of getting what they need.[2] I have noticed over decades of serving women and girls that if they are seeking approval, their voices are higher. It's almost as if they are attempting to soften requests for what they truly want by infantilizing their voices.

Does this resonate with you? Reflect in your journal about girls and women you know who change the pitch or tone of their voices around men or people in authority. Can you observe this propensity in your own communications, or in the voices of your daughters? I invite you to bring this tendency to consciousness and to try to speak from your lower register when you are tempted otherwise. Do you dare to be direct not only in your requests, but in the tone of those requests?

According to anthropologist and author Marija Gimbutas, women have been in exile from our own power for at least 5000 years.[3] In your journal, consider exploring her important work or that of Riane Eisler[4] or Carol Christ and Judith Plaskow[5]. Fair warning! Accurate historical details of *her-story* were not included when you studied his-tory in our culture's school system.

If we accept Marija Gimbutas' extensive archaeological findings and research that women have indeed been in exile for millennia, is it any wonder that we adapted our behaviour to survive as *outlanders*? Women are often accused of being manipulative, but this form of artfulness may be an adaptive strategy learned, honed, and developed over thousands of years in order to survive. However, women's behaviour is too often stereotyped by *both* women and men to keep women "in their place". Internalized misogyny is very real. Women turn on women to stop them rocking the boat. Women may appeal to male authority to get their wants and needs met, even if it means throwing a sister under the bus.

Knowing the origins of these behaviours is not an excuse or rationalization for continuing it. It is your responsibility to be aware of and reject stereotypes, to build yourself and your sisters up, teach when you can, and to learn to speak clearly and directly. The ideas presented here may be new to you and you may have a strong reaction. Write about your feelings in your journal. Work it out in your own mind. Continue to think for yourself, to investigate, and to be honest with yourself.

For your spiritual practice this month, remember that it takes fortitude to be direct in your requests, and even more bravery to call out 'mansplaining' when you are the target of such condescension. I invite you to change the way you ask for what you want in your home and workplace. Be direct, clear, and firm, and accept the response if it is fair.

Vulnerability Scripts

Try writing a vulnerability script wherein you express your needs in a heartfelt, honest, and vulnerable way. I assist many women with this practice. While I use vulnerability scripts for many issues, the following example using self-care will give you a general idea of what a script looks like. "I am working on practising self-care without feeling guilty or like I am neglecting you. I am struggling with giving myself permission. This is awkward for me, but I'd really like your support in my attempts. I love you and my guilt and worry about your needs is my problem, I know, but I just wanted to let you know what I'm trying to do." If you look closely at this script, how can you possibly find fault with the person's attempt to bring another on side of her work?

I always recommend script writing because it can be uncomfortable or downright scary to be direct and honest expressing your needs to your loved one, colleague, or employer. You may have been colonized, socialized, parented, or otherwise convinced that you are responsible for other people's responses to your decisions. This is a difficult lie to unlearn. I congratulate you for even trying! Sometimes the women I serve read their scripts out loud to their loved ones or employers, then leave the script with the person to consider privately. Sometimes my clients use the script as a guide or memorize parts of it, so their delivery feels more natural.

Soul Work (Homework or Heartwork)

All Women Matter

In my work with many postpartum women, I see that much of their depression and anxiety rises from the lack of reverence, awe, gratitude, congratulations, respect, and veneration they should be receiving for performing the miracle of carrying life in their bodies for almost ten months (40 weeks) then delivering that life out into the world. This unbelievable miracle must be acknowledged for the truly amazing feat that it is.

I am indebted to the feminists of the past for bringing us this far out of exile. Yet only on the day our cultures fully honour women, equally fund research of the uterus, acknowledge women's right to choose what they do with their bodies, honour childbirth, compensate women spiritually and economically for their incredible birthing and parenting tasks, and prioritize childcare—on that day, you and I (and everyone else) can truly celebrate our freedom.

You might find yourself grieving the reality we must live with as women. It is distressing to face the truth that we have less freedom of movement and lower compensation simply because we are women. We are more than half of the human race, and there would be no humans without us. Journal about how you feel when you realize that we were only recognized as citizens, only given the right to vote, about a hundred years ago.

Work at Home Wages

As another piece of Soul Work, consider investigating another women's reality: little if any compensation for the most important job on the planet. I started reading *Ms. Magazine* when I was 13 years old. At the time, the idea that women could even consider claiming a daily wage for their work managing a home was revolutionary. Several years later, in 2019, according to data from *salary.com*, a stay-at-home parent would earn an annual salary of $178,201.00 USD for managing a home 24 hours a day, 7 days a week, 365 days a year (8,760 hours). The hourly wage would be a paltry $20.31 per hour, without benefits or a pension plan! Factor in benefits, pension plan, and employment insurance (and danger pay!), and it's closer to $40.00 per hour. For the incredible pressure that society puts on women to raise loving, responsible, healthy, integrated beings, that hourly wage is insulting. What is more offensive is that women who choose this profession, house and family management, are not even paid for it in our culture, never mind receiving benefits and a pension plan.

Please remember this *Terry'ism: "Every human is born of Woman. Revere Her."*

When we legally, economically, spiritually, and practically support women, we are supporting children, too.

Freedom is often earned or discovered in levels or degrees, rarely all at once. Addiction is one of our worst prisons, but the mindless following of cultural expectations is a less recognized but serious form of self-entrapment. Who or what is master here? A social construction? A cultural imperative? An ideology? An addiction to approval? Who is the slave? Who decides?

All Women Matter.

Does it shock you to know that women were only "given" the right to vote or stand for election just over a hundred years ago? Does it mean anything to you that girls and women were not allowed to receive an education prior to 1800, and that in many countries today women are denied the right to access education or to be literate? Did you know that a woman in Canada was not allowed to open a bank account without her husband's approval before 1964, let alone obtain a mortgage on her own? Are you familiar with which countries deny a woman the right to decide what she can do with her own body?

Who decides?

We have many women and conscious men from history to thank for the improvements we've seen in women's rights. Yes, we have come a long way. However, you may be noticing what looks like a regression in our world today when it comes to women's rights. The good news is that some scholars of history believe this current backlash from frightened men (and some women) is simply evidence of the strength of our current transformation toward equality.

Spiritual Journal Stems and Prompts

The image I offered Marcie was of a bird soaring on the thermals. Choose your image for this month's work. What does freedom mean to you? Is there an image of peace, calm, and lightness of being that speaks to you of freedom? Keep this image in your mind. Draw or paint it in your journal, cut it out of a magazine, or take a photograph. Consider the following thoughts in your journaling:

- *"I was ______ years old when I first began to believe that my obligation to others was more important than my obligation to myself. A few life examples that led me to believe this are..."*
- *"I was ______ years old when I first began to believe that approval is the same as love. A life example that led me to believe this was when..."*
- *"Who decides what rules I follow? If I'm honest, I have to say..."*

Spiritual Inspiration: Goddesses in Every Woman

For this next spiritually inspired strategy, review *Dance of the Dissident Daughter* by Sue Monk Kidd; play with *Goddesses in Everywoman: A New Psychology of Women* by Jean Shinoda Bolen; have fun with the *Goddess Oracle Deck and Book Set* by Amy Marashinsky; dive into *The Goddess Path* by Patricia Monaghan, and immerse yourself in Achurya

Shunya's *Roar Like a Goddess: Every Woman's Guide to Becoming Unapologetically Powerful, Prosperous, and Peaceful.*

Dance of the Dissident Daughter will change you. Reading it became the catalyst for my own participation in the Ariadne Institute's fall Goddess Pilgrimage on Crete, Greece, in September of 2023.[6] Perhaps you will be inspired, too. In her insightful book, *Goddesses in Everywoman: A New Psychology of Women*, Jungian analyst Jean Shinoda Bolen introduces you to seven major Goddesses and helps you discern whether these archetypes (inner patterns) are active in your current phase of life. She also describes the psychological challenges of each Goddess, how to cultivate particular Goddess qualities you might need now, and how to grow beyond some of the limitations of particular Goddesses.[7] I invite you to enjoy this process.

Amy Sophia Marashinsky's gorgeous *Goddess Oracle Deck and Book Set* introduces fifty-two Goddesses, each beginning with a poetic statement the Goddess might utter and followed by her mythological history. Each card discusses its possible meaning and describes a ritual that is specific to the energy of your chosen Goddess. Enjoy![8]

I know you will be inspired by the Goddess archetypes you encounter in Patricia Monaghan's *The Goddess Path*, as well as in Acharya Shunya's astonishing book, *Roar Like a Goddess*, in which she offers modern interpretations of India's beloved major Goddess archetypes and invites you to consider how they might be activated in your life. The myths of Durga, Lakshmi, and Saraswati, in their various manifestations, become inspiration for you to fully embrace your power.

Dismantling Social Constructions and Unlearning Familial Patterns

Who decides? Keep asking this question. The "rules" or "shoulds" we are taught can become limiting beliefs. Question everything. The need to belong was a matter of life and death in our primeval past. If we were shunned or excluded, we would not eat. Is this still true? Women are often pitted against each other to distract us from the real work of saving the planet and raising loving, woman- and Earth-honouring children. How can we realize our power and inner divinity if we are fighting each other? Internalized androcracy, even internalized misogyny (hatred of women), is very real. The need for approval makes us desperate to belong, and aligning ourselves with power insures we live. When you find yourself "going along to belong", ask yourself, "Is this something that I really believe in?" Ask yourself, "Who decided that this was so?"

A strategy to move out of this fear of not belonging, or not fitting in, or not being approved of, is to explore the discomfort of practising going against the norm. Your tolerance for this anxiety decreases as your personal and authentic freedom increases. Keep practising expressing yourself and asserting, and you will gradually find your need to approve of yourself supersedes your need for outside approval. This is a core value shift. Please consider carefully before you tell other women that you are already free and that you do not understand what all this feminist fuss is about.

Explore your own internalized androcracy. Reflect on how you have literally turned yourself into a pretzel just to get along, to avoid rocking the boat, to get by without conflict of any kind.

When you do your personal work for freedom as a female, you are challenging powerful social structures that have been in place for thousands of years. We have been in exile a long, long time. As a result, you are also fighting internalized misogyny. What does this actually mean?

In order to fit in, get approval, and in some cases simply to survive, women have found themselves agreeing with their captors. In a twisted form of Stockholm Syndrome, women have even been known to attack their sisters in order to win the approval of male dominators. Women, having given birth, often do not condone war or sending their children into violence, but will find themselves agreeing to war as a result of internalized androcracy.

When women join their captors, no cage is needed.

Stop here and write your reflections on your own personal experience of "going along to get along." Pay specific attention to how you feel when you support your sisters, rather than compete with them.

I hold hope that once you see the dynamics of patriarchy, you will find ways to change them. You may indeed feel free in the privacy of your own home or in the private internal dynamics of your relationships with the men and boys in your life. Can you carry this equality and freedom publicly, in all instances, in front of everyone?

Feminists are not saying women should be superior to men. Feminists do not condone misandry (hatred of men). We do not burn our bras (although at the end of some long days I am tempted). Many male feminists work valiantly along side women to right egregious wrongs. If you enjoy the privilege of freedom in your world, lucky you. Please help make that possible for other women and girls. Be courageous enough to check yourself for internalized misogyny. Then, once you have worked hard to make that course correction, please help your sisters, even the ones you disagree with. Especially them.

The Divine Feminine

Humans are realizing that the old toxic masculine paradigms are no longer serving us. Power over women and children, exploitation of our Earth's resources, and Ego dominance have led to genocide, prejudice, global warming, the subjugation of women, and misplaced resource use. People are realizing that accessing the Divine Feminine within each of us can save our planet and, therefore, save us as a species. Reverence for our Earth Mother, for all women who can carry life and give birth, for the feminine capacity in all humans—this can save us. Cooperation, creativity, equality, compassion, responsible Earth stewardship, and accepting that our Soul's journey is connected to everyone else's journey—these are what will save us in the end.

In the midst of their first, second, or third awakening, women often turn to the Old Religion to find a reflection of their own image in the Divine. Women's longing for partners instead of subjugators leads them to seek like-minded women and men who have the courage to look beyond the victor-written history someone else decided we should read and learn about. Many factual events were systematically cut out of the historical record to reinforce androcracy or to retain particular patriarchal advantages. By participating in androcracy, you are either complicit or in ignorance. Perhaps you did not recognize that you are imprisoned. But no more. Now you know.

The vocabulary of feminism is the language of "both/and", which frees us from choosing sides or creating unnecessary dualism. "Either/or" thinking or "black and white" thinking seems easier; no effort goes toward understanding complexity or differing points of view. Living with ambiguity is uncomfortable; the Ego wants everything wrapped up in a neat tidy package. Yet our multifaceted lives are much more complicated than that. Experiment with this spiritual practice: next time you are asked your position on an issue, stop. Ask yourself if you can tolerate the temporary discomfort of seeing two points of view at the same time. Become suspicious of black and white thinking, either-or language, or "us versus them" ideas. *Who decides?*

Self Therapy Tools, Rituals, and Practices for Freedom

Exploring Your Matrilineal Line

In the Sophia Women's Wisdom Spirituality Group I facilitate, participants are invited to trace their kinship through their female line. This quickly becomes a challenge since we live in a patriarchy. I traced my own female kinship line with several personal and historical challenges, one of which is that my mom's mother died when my mom was an infant, and my mom was adopted by another family. The moment a woman in the group stands up to recite her matrilineal line is deeply moving. Here is one woman's example:

"My name is Margaret Anne Humphrey, and I go by Maggie Callan. I was born seventh of eight children by Catherine Elizabeth Humphrey, who goes by Cathy Callan. I draw strength from Catherine Elizabeth Humphrey's stories of courage and from her cautionary tales. My mother was born of Georgina Anne Callan. She drew strength from Georgina's stories of courage and from her cautionary tales. Georgina Anne Callan was born of Morag Lynn Bartson. She drew strength from Morag's stories..." and so on.

Some people add the following to help round out this practice:

"I also draw strength from my father's sisters (my aunties) and his mother and the mothers in her line, and from her sisters (my great aunties). I draw much strength from my current female friends, female ancestors (both friends and family) and from all aspects of the Divine Feminine who show up as guides, goddess oracles, and other transcendent feminine beings. I am deeply grateful for my matrilineal line, the women and girls in my life, my female ancestors, and the Divine Feminine in all her guises. And so, it is."

The foregoing does not contain real names of real people. I wanted to give you a sense of what it feels like to recite your matrilineal line. It will feel foreign for good reason! It can also be profoundly poignant. I invite you to feel the reverence and awe of honouring your matrilineal line by reciting out loud in front of your altar or a close, safe friend.

Sexual Freedom - Role Reversal

A fantastic awakening activity you might like to try with another woman or a group of women is a guided visualization called *Woman –*

Which Includes Man, of Course by feminist educator Theodora Wells.[9] In this visualization, you imagine yourself in a role reversal situation guided by another person's voice. You experience what it would feel like to be a man who enjoys all of the advantages of being male, and you get a sense of what a man might feel if these privileges were stripped from him and he had to live with the sanctioned inequalities women face now. The visualization walks you through what it might feel like as a disenfranchised male to have clitoris envy and womb envy. You can then debrief by asking questions such as, who is at greater risk for mental illness, more apt to feel body shame, or be more susceptible to abuse? Sigmund Freud may have contributed much to our understanding of human psychology, but he single-handedly destroyed many women's sexual freedoms when he taught that women have penis envy, that the clitoral orgasm was "less mature"[10] than orgasm by vaginal penetration, and that women are totally preoccupied with reproduction. You will note that in the role reversal guided fantasy, it is far easier to see the absurdity of these ideas when they are applied to men. Ask: Why is that?

In Riane Eisler's dominator model, those with less power need to know more about the powerful, as a matter of survival, than the powerful know about those they dominate. The falsehood that those with more power protect those with less power has no basis in reality. Dominators often abuse women and children, rather than using their power to support, protect, and rectify imbalances.[11] Once you understand the dynamics of power, you can determine what power you wish to claim back for yourself and your sisters. Like all dominated, we will need to develop a plan together.

Feminism and Spiritual Freedom – Carol Christ

I felt great sadness with the death of one of my mentors and the quintessential Goddess Pilgrimage guide, Carol Christ, in July of 2021. I had been saving my pennies, reading everything she wrote, and preparing for a

Goddess Pilgrimage to Crete, Greece, for several years so I could immerse myself in Minoan culture. Carol's notes on thealogy and her thoughts and reflections on feminine cosmology opened new ways of thinking for me.[12]

Carol Christ helped me understand that when you are expected to worship an idea of Source or Divine Intelligence as male or 'fatherly', it changes the way you view religious authority and your place in the world as a female from girlhood to womanhood. When all the symbols are male symbols, where do you, as a woman, fit in? When all priests or religious leaders are male, you wonder what your place is in the grand scheme of things. Males are leaders because the male god ordained it so. Did this same god allow rape of women and rape of the Earth as divine rights? Dominion over nature—a standard interpretation of man's right expressed in the book of Genesis—is destroying this planet, our Mother. Surely it is time to rethink these antiquated, inhuman interpretations if we want to save our home. Disguised misogyny, hate crimes against more than half of the human race, and religious permission to have dominion over nature, to exploit our planet's resources, must be exposed for exactly what they are. Our collective trauma as women over many centuries is individualized by each of us: it shows up in our lives.

Write in your journal your feelings about these ideas. Grieve. Lean into the feelings. Then determine to act.

Emotional and Intellectual Freedom – Carol Gilligan

Most people who take an introductory psychology course in college or university are taught Kohlberg's theory of moral development. Kohlberg's ideas were based on research on the morality and ethics in the behaviour of young white males. Feminist psychologist Carol Gilligan (Kohlberg's research assistant) found that women and girls approach morality and ethics differently, yet traditional teachings still use Kohlberg's male-oriented research. How can half of the human race be dismissed this way?

Kohlberg states that males move through various stages of moral development from pre-conventional rule-following (only where it benefits the self), to conventional morality (being a good citizen), to the post conventional stage where principles of justice are considered. He characterized these principles of justice as abstract and universal, not context or situation driven. He also found most of his subjects did not reach the final stage of morality.

Carol Gilligan, on the other hand, found that women develop morality alongside their evolving sense of selfhood. Following an ethic of care, women consider interpersonal relationships and the context or situation of ethical or moral decision making.[13] As a woman matures into her sense of herself, she learns that her initial focus on her own needs is deemed selfish, and at the same time she is aware of both her desire for connection and her responsibility to others. Can she fulfill those without relinquishing care for herself? If she cannot, her journey is fraught with confusion and self recrimination. The culture we live in does not encourage women to put themselves first, or even anywhere in the equation.

In my Sophia Women's Wisdom Spirituality Groups, we often discuss how, if women were in charge of the world, we would never send our children off to war. We would not even have war. Yes, there would be conflict, but we feel we could find ways to resolve issues without killing one another. The very idea of ending someone's life because you disagree with them, feel threatened, or want what they have, feels ludicrous when you stop and think about it. Reflect on Carol Gilligan's ideas in your journal.

Service to the Planet and Connecting with Others

We change the world one person at a time by persistently modelling our worth and self-respect, and by refusing to cooperate with injustice and violence. This approach is one example of *satyagraha* or "truth force" that Riane Eisler describes as Gandhi's "positive transformative energy."[14] Another way to build power is by first giving it to ourselves and then sharing with other women in community. I believe that women can claim our own autonomous spaces and in them build the world we envision. I offer such a space with my Sophia Women's Wisdom Spirituality Groups, and there are many other communities of this kind.

If you are reading this chapter as a male, I challenge you to check your own privilege. Learn the history of how you gained it and then make a clear decision to join other women-honouring men in righting the wrongs.

I have undergone a great deal of personal work overcoming the effects of colonization on my assumptions and behavior. I have found myself humbled and committed to truth and reconciliation when I acknowledge my own and my ancestors' participation in horrible prejudice. I dream of a world where courageous men unpack their privilege and work to right egregious wrongs against women and Mother Earth.

Personal freedom is precious but often taken for granted or misused in the First World. Boredom, personal or global grief, the need to belong, the need to control something because you feel otherwise powerless, or all four may lead you to justify irresponsible behaviour. There is no excuse for boredom. With so many humans in poverty, so many homeless, so many children needing someone to read to them, so many marginalized individuals, so many vulnerable women, so many animals in need of protection, so many trees to plant, so much need out there—it all calls us to act. Choose a need and help fill it. Respect your freedom by being responsible for it. Respect your freedom by acknowledging that it is a precious privilege. Use it to free others.

During the worldwide pandemic, the anxiety felt by clients and the sometimes-outrageous global behaviour seemed a grief response. The virus affected the respiratory system; in my somatic world grief is felt in the lungs. Resistance to change is the germ of grief. How fortunate are we to have the luxury of acknowledging our grief and seeking healing for it.

That is freedom.

The need to control something, anything, during a powerless season coincides with the need to belong, forming a perfect storm of illogical behaviour that can impinge on the freedom of others. It was often excruciating to watch this phenomenon during the COVID crisis. Freedom means giving yourself permission to question everything, including your own motivation. Are you helping? Or are you complaining? What exactly are you doing with the privilege of your freedom? Who decides?

A Special Note: Female Genital Mutilation

This next section was a very difficult piece to write. It may be even more difficult to read. For this next piece, be sure to have your support system in place before proceeding.

Breathe.

My life's passion and work have been empowering women and girls. Yet over 200 million young girls and women in thirty countries are forced into genital mutilation. Knowing this makes me nauseous and causes a convulsive somatic response. I understand if you want to avoid looking at this truth. However, I am also challenging you to go there with me. Together we can work to stop this atrocity, but first we must face the reality that it is happening.

According to the World Health Organization, there are four main forms of female genital mutilation practised today. The first involves the removal, or partial removal, of the visible part of the clitoris and/or the clitoral hood. The second includes the removal, or partial removal, of the clitoris along with the inner folds of the vulva (the labia minora), and sometimes the outer folds (the labia majora). The third form, known as infibulation, involves narrowing the vaginal opening by creating a covering seal formed through cutting and repositioning the labia, sometimes with stitching, and with or without removal of clitoral tissue. The fourth category includes all other non-medical procedures performed on female genitalia, such as piercing, scraping, or cauterizing.[15]

The short- and long-term damage is horrific, but all too real, verified by the World Health Organization. Hyper-sexualization of women, which underlies so much of the discrimination against us, is rooted in men being afraid they cannot control their own sexual impulses. For example, women's hair is considered too intimate to be publicly shown in some cultures because it might tempt men. The same holds for doctrines that require women to hide their mouths and ankles. The Madonna/Whore syndrome (women characterized as either paragons of virtue or prostitutes) leaves very little leeway for women to represent themselves authentically.

If you find yourself feeling deep anger, nausea, and unbelievable sadness as you read about the genital mutilation of our young sisters, know that your rage and outrage is righteous.

In your journal, reflect on how you express your anger when it surfaces in your life. Do you squelch it, stuff it, repress it, ignore it, or talk yourself out of it?

In my service to women, I am concerned about the negative effects on women's bodies when they internalize their anger. Elevated cortisol levels can wreak havoc on women's health. I teach that anger is the great clarifier. Anger helps us see and understand the edges of our boundaries that have been violated. Some anger is indeed justified. It calls for a response. However, I teach that in the interests of physical health, anger also needs to be expressed, not repressed. Together, we brainstorm ways to safely express this important emotion so we can get it out of our bodies and dissipate the energy. Some women hurl stones in the ocean, lake, or river. Some drive down country roads alone in their cars, yelling at the top of their lungs. Singing is easier on the throat. Some work out, run, or mountain bike. Dancing is a favorite. My only caveat is that they do my Dual Process strategy as they are expressing their anger in a safe way. You may recall this psycho-spiritual practice asks you to narrate what you are doing as you are doing it.

What is your anger and outrage calling you to do? Do it.

Follow Up with Marcie

Perhaps you, dear reader, have found yourself considering freedom and moving through stages of grief over how and when it is denied you. In our work together, Marcie discovered freedoms she did not previously know existed. It had never occurred to her to question what was handed to her from well-meaning parents, cultural constructions, and the unspoken rules of the patriarchy. Her addiction to alcohol was one prison, but it was also a symptom of her attempt to cope with a much harsher reality. As a woman, she was considered "less than" in her faith community, her political group, her culture and community, and in her own home. She worked very hard to move through to ever deeper levels of freedom and to take responsibility by helping to free other women.

The image of a bird soaring wild and free became very important to her. Your images of freedom are important for you too. Keep photos or artifacts around you to inspire you daily.

Biblio-Therapy for Chapter Five

Books and Resources to Support Your Work with Freedom

- *Dance of the Dissident Daughter*, Sue Monk Kidd
- *The Living Goddesses*, Marija Gimutas
- *The Gnostic Gospels*, Elaine Pagels
- *The Chalice and the Blade*, Riane Eisler
- *WomenSpirit Rising,* edited by Carol Christ and Judith Plaskow
- *Woman –Which Includes Man, of Course*, Theodora Wells
- *In a Different Voice*, Carol Gilligan
- *Revolution from Within,* Gloria Steinem

- *The Spiral Dance,* Starhawk
- *The Earth Path,* Starhawk
- *The Goddess Path,* Patricia Monaghan
- *Roar Like a Goddess,* Acharya Shunya
- *Goddesses in Everywoman: A New Psychology of Women*, Jean Shinoda Bolen
- *Goddess Oracle Deck and Book Set*, Amy Marashinsky
- *Girl God Books*, Trista Hendren
- *Minoan Impressions Paintings,* Barbara Daling

Chapter Six

overly responsive to others (codependence)

Dear Ms. Terry,

Now I'm tired. I think my partner might have mental health issues, uses substances to self-medicate for chronic pain, and is very sensitive (defensive) to any of my encouragements to get professional help. I have been the main breadwinner for most of our time together and have been taking responsibility for everything including our children, pets, finances, household, and other aspects of our lives. I am the one who cleans up the messes, phones my partner's employer if they can't make it to work. I keep track of how often my partner uses substances and how much they spend. I'm tired. I am also feeling resentful a lot of the time. I feel like I have no life. I don't want to be intimate, and I don't think my partner wants to be either. I'm really struggling. So is my partner, but I want to change something to make my situation better so I'm reaching out to you.

- Something's Got to Give, Leslie

There is a common misconception that needs to be corrected before we go any further: *codependence* is not a word people like use to describe their life challenge. They think it means they must be in a relationship with someone addicted to drugs, alcohol, sex, shopping, gambling, or other problematic behaviours. This is simply not true. You can be codependent with anyone you worry about, fixate over, or wish would change. Some people characterize codependence as an addiction to another person's business.

My codependence groups (sometimes called *Living with Difficult People* or *Boundaries for Your Freedom* or *Self-care in Challenging Relationships* or *Letting Go of Trying to Control Others*, or my favourite, *Overly Responsive to Others' Needs)* serve many clients who are simply other-focused. Potential participants cannot quite put their finger on why they feel so resentful in their primary relationships, whether with a parent, young adult or adult child, sibling, or partner. These beautiful souls have big hearts and only want the best for their loved ones, but they struggle to understand that their attempts to control the behaviour of others are doomed to failure.

I invited Leslie to recall taking a flight somewhere. Did she remember the flight attendant advising her, in the event of an emergency, to don her oxygen mask before assisting another passenger? The metaphor for our work together was putting an airplane mask on her own face before trying to assist others. Fellow traveller, would this image work for you?

Nuts and Bolts

If Leslie's letter resonates with you, if you are struggling to help someone in healthy ways, or if you are wishing you could attend one of my groups, then think of *three* people you are trying to help. Write each of their names at the top of three different blank pages in your therapy journal. Answer each of the following questions *before* helping *any* one of your three people, or before continuing to help them if you already are.

The Essential Questions

1. *Am I comfortable taking the time to answer these questions before I decide to help or continue to help this person?*

2. *Who decides the urgency of any situation? Can I practice saying "I need time to think about that. Let me get back to you?"*

3. *Does this person have a right to their own journey? Do I have a right to my own journey? Can we feel bonded even if we are on separate journeys?*

4. *Am I struggling with what this person is struggling with, and if I am, what do I need to do for myself right now that would help me? If I am not struggling with what this person is struggling with, what is my personal primary growth concern and what do I need to do in this moment to help myself?*

5. *Do I know this person better than I know myself? Do I think I know this person better than they know themselves?*

6. *Has this person that I feel compelled to help* <u>*actually asked*</u> *for my help?*

7. *Do I feel superior to this person? Do I feel I know better? Do I feel this person is weak?*

8. *Can this person reasonably be expected to be able to do this for themselves?*

9. *Would helping this person to accomplish this task make me feel better or make them feel better?*

10. *How would this person feel if this person were able to accomplish this task on their own?*

11. *Do people generally learn from their own experiences and mis-*

takes? What is one example from my own life where I learned from my own experience and mistakes?

12. *Can I actually change someone? Can I make someone love me more by changing them?*

13. *If I actually help this person, do I believe they will love me more?*

14. *Am I avoiding my own journey, my own challenges, my own addictions by distracting myself through helping this person? Am I using this person to avoid facing my own life?*

15. *Do I feel a need to be thanked and acknowledged by this person for all that I have done for the, or for all that I have put up with in my life with them?*

16. *Do I somehow feel that I own this person? Do I somehow feel that this person owes me for some reason?*

17. *Would I survive if this person failed at their life task at this time?*

18. *Do I enjoy the drama of other peoples' crises? Where can I find a healthier outlet for my desire, need for, or addiction to drama?*

19. *Do I stand for myself, my choices, and my behaviour? Do this person's choices and behaviour somehow reflect me?*

20. *If I stop helping this person, what flack can I expect from them? Would they be surprised and disappointed? Would they try to make me feel guilty, get angry, withdraw, threaten self harm, or victimize themselves further in an attempt to pull me back in? Can I withstand this flack? Would I survive if they followed through on their threats? Seriously?*

21. *Is it possible that I give myself more flack because I am breaking a family rule that says, "Love equals Rescuing"?*

22. *How could I explain to this person my struggles with helping (or not) in terms of my need for approval from them? How could I explain myself in a way that is loving but firm?*

23. *Can I live with the anxiety of not helping? Can I live with any real or imagined disappointment from others?*
24. *Can I find other ways to improve my own self-esteem besides helping this person? Are there others who would benefit from my help who I have no desire to control? Could I volunteer somewhere and get a similar measure of satisfaction?*
25. *How does my body tell me that I have tipped over into over involvement? Where do I feel resentment in my body?*

Spiritual Practice – Motivation and Intention

Johari Window (Reflective Practice)

Psychologists Joseph Luft and Harrington Ingham introduced what became known as the Johari Window[1] as a way of exploring self-awareness in relationship. I draw inspiration from this work, not as a personality model to master, but as a reflective practice to help you examine your motivation and intention when you feel compelled to help others. Discernment is an ancient spiritual practice. It is not easy, but it is always necessary.

Rather than thinking in terms of fixed categories or diagrams, consider different aspects of yourself that move in and out of awareness—some you know well, some you keep private, some you are still discovering, and some that are revealed primarily through relationship. In your journal, or in dialogue with a safe friend or trusted therapist, explore the reflections below.

First, reflect on the aspects of yourself that feel visible and familiar—both to you and to others. This is often the self you present publicly: the version of you that feels acceptable, competent, or safe to share. Some people call this the persona or façade. It may reflect who you truly are, or it may be a mask you learned to wear in order to belong. As you journal, ask yourself whether you would like to be more authentic, and what safety you would need to do so. By authenticity, I mean being honest with yourself about what you are really thinking and feeling, even if you never say it out loud to another. This is integrity. This is congruency. Since authenticity requires safety, begin by telling yourself the truth.

Next, turn your attention to the parts of yourself you know well but tend to keep private. What do you choose not to share, and why? Privacy, autonomy, and solitude are not signs of selfishness; they are signs of self-respect. Some of the women I serve have never considered it permissible to keep parts of themselves private, including their own thoughts. One of the first permissions I teach is this: you are allowed to enjoy the privacy of your own mind. Historic boundary violations can deeply disrupt this inner safety. Believe me—your abuser could not, and cannot, read your mind. For some women, the mind becomes the safest place of resistance until more external safety is possible. In your journal, reflect on what you keep private and whether that privacy feels chosen or enforced.

Now, gently explore the parts of yourself that remain outside your conscious awareness. These unconscious aspects often make themselves known through the body, dreams, creative expression, or emotional reactions that surprise you. Jungian psychology teaches that what we are unaware of, we may act out or project onto others.

Messages from your psyche often surface through your Big Brain—your body—as well as through dreams, images, music, stream-of-consciousness writing, art, or imagination. You might try giving your deeper self a name and inviting it into conversation through journaling or visualization. Ask it to communicate with you in ways you can understand. Your deeper self wants you to be well. It will respond when invited.

Finally, consider the possibility that others may sometimes see things about you that you have not yet recognized. These blind spots are not failures; they are simply areas of growth. In safe groups, drama therapy exercises can highlight how our behaviour affects others without our awareness.

In your journal, list the qualities you hope others experience when they are with you. Then reflect honestly on whether your behaviour aligns with how you wish to be perceived. Awareness is not about blame; it is about responsibility. It is very difficult—if not impossible—to change what we are not aware of.

If you feel especially courageous and wish to deepen this work, consider Byron Katie's[2] compassionate inquiry into the stories we tell ourselves. Her Judge-Your-Neighbor worksheet can be a powerful way to clarify your motivations when you believe someone else should change. The insights are often surprising and freeing.

What does this reflective work have to do with codependence recovery? Each of these inquiries helps you become more conscious of *why* you help—whether your actions arise from love, fear, guilt, control, or a need for approval. People who struggle with codependence are often deeply kind and generous. The work here is not to become less kind, but to become more conscious.

Soul Work (Homework or Heartwork)

Karpman Drama Triangle

This seminal strategy—seminal means that it is historically older but very effective—is astonishingly insightful and effective for codependence recovery. My Spiritually Integrated strategy builds on Dr. Stephen Karpman's work.[3] Draw a triangle. At one point put "Rescuer". At another point put "Victim". At the final point put "Persecutor".[4] Now draw arrows moving around the outside of the triangle from one role to the other in a never-ending cycle.

You have likely played all three roles at various times in your life but there is usually one that you lean toward in a conflict or potential conflict situation in your family, in your workplace, or in your own mind. If you are feeling powerless over your life, or feel incapable of making decisions, or find yourself saying, "Poor me..." or wonder "Why does this always happen to me?" then you are likely in the *Victim* role. Remember, there is usually a story that is created in this role that may only be true in the role player's imagination.

If you are feeling powerless over *another* person's life, incapable of changing *them*, or find yourself saying "After all I've done for you!" or "How can I help you?" then you are likely in the *Rescuer* role. Again, there is a story created in your mind that justifies this role.

Finally, if you are feeling self-righteous, defensive, critical, demanding, blaming, angry, or find yourself thinking that you know better how a person should live their life than they do, you are likely in the *Persecutor* role.

The *drama* part of the Karpman Drama Triangle lies in watching yourself move around the triangle in your relationship with another person. This can happen in a matter of minutes or over several days. It can begin to feel like a cycle. This is good news! It means that you are becoming more aware of your own role in the cycle or drama pattern. Become familiar with your default role and when it is usually played out in the cycle. Think carefully about how you move from rescuer, to victim, to persecutor. It might follow a trajectory from 'woman on a mission' to 'why won't you change?' to 'I give up so you're on your own... for now" then back to 'woman on a mission'.

How do you step out of a role in the Karpman Drama Triangle? All change begins with awareness. If you know you revert to the victim role, explore your fear of taking responsibility for yourself and how often you look to others to take care of you. Your work will be finding the courage to explore who you really are, discover what your strengths are, and look in a mirror when you are tempted to relinquish your responsibility for yourself. Your recovery will require that you ask for help from people who can guide you, not do it *for* you.

If you would like to step out of the rescuer role, rescue yourself. Tend your own garden. Choose to stop avoiding yourself. One quick way to get back in your own garden is to go back to the Wellness Wheel in ***Chapter Four: Balance***. You may also want to review ***The Essential Questions*** at the beginning of this chapter.

If you would like to move out of the persecutor role, it is time to get humble. Look in the mirror. Consider what areas of your life you would like to improve. Again, tend your own garden. You might also like to complete a *Judge-Your-Neighbor* worksheet mentioned earlier in the ***Johari Window Strategy***.

A surefire way to get off the triangle that I personally use, and one that I teach others, is this: instead of considering your role in relation to others (victim, rescuer, persecutor), visualize yourself literally stepping off the triangle and self-differentiating (individuating). Envision yourself outside the triangle, outside of any dramatic relationship with anyone else, and picture yourself instead as a complete, whole person on your own terms. Build that woman. Consider her spiritual, emotional, intellectual, and physical needs, unrelated to anyone else's agenda.

Spiritual Journal Stems and Prompts

Choose your image for this month's work and write about it in your journal. Leslie's was putting her own airplane mask on before trying to assist others. You may find that a different archetype, symbol, landscape, journey, or image better captures your personal work in this area. Some people quite like looking in the mirror above their altar for this work (see ***Mirror Work*** in ***Chapter One***). Among other positive effects, looking in the mirror helps them remember who they are actually responsible for.

Remember to journal around these ideas. Challenge yourself to get clear on your motivation as you build self-knowledge.

Boundary Work and Values: What is the Connection?

Much has been written about boundaries, but it always comes back to getting to know yourself. Examine your own beliefs and values. This knowledge helps you set boundaries and maintain them. If boundary work is of interest to you, go to ***Chapter Eleven***, the section titled ***Self Therapy Tools, Rituals, and Practices for Partnerships, Trust, and Anxiety.*** For now, consider the two key values worth cultivating in codependence recovery which are compassionate detachment (or detached compassion) and respectful non-interference.

You may believe you value each person's right to live out their lives, learn from their mistakes, and enjoy the rewards of new growth no matter how painful. In other words, you may profess to holding the boundary and the value of *respectful non-interference*. You might also say that you believe in *compassionate detachment*, that this is a value you live by. It means you trust that the person is going through what they need to be going through to learn, and that while you may not be willing or able to stop their pain, you can feel compassion for their struggle. Compassionate detachment is both the value and the boundary of *trusting the process*.

How do you now move from professed values to actual behaviours? In other words, how do you avoid hypocrisy and move toward congruency/integrity?

If you are a rescuer, you may need to find healthier ways to get your Ego stroked than compulsively helping others. You may also need to detach from the outcomes of your efforts. You may need to take off the superhero cape and let go of your need to be acknowledged or given credit for another person's success. Do you feel like you somehow *own* the person you are rescuing or that they owe you for helping them? This level of self-honesty takes incredible courage. Boundaries are rarely about the other person. You are giving yourself the boundary of respecting another's right to their own journey. You are giving yourself both the value and the boundary of non-interference. The values you hold and the boundaries you give yourself are inextricably connected.

Spiritual Inspiration

Terry'ism: "I have a centre that vibrates even when I am alone"

This simple affirmation has a deep and profound effect on individuals recovering from being overly responsive to others' needs (codependent). There are several psycho-spiritual reasons for this. The affirmation relaxes the anxiously attached person by providing a small opening to an inner life that she can now become responsive to. She may realize after much reflection and meditating on these words that she can maintain the bond she has with others at the same time as she relinquishes an old role. The mantra also interrupts her default pattern or auto-pilot compulsion to be other-focused, especially if she thinks she will be paradoxically abandoned if she stops care-taking or rescuing. Finally, the wording invites her to consider who she might be underneath the role she has been trained to take on just because she is female or because codependence was role modelled for her by the women in her matrilineal line.

As you work with the affirmation above in your journal, consider listening to the Meditation Moment I prepared on my website. This is a gift I offer to all of my site guests. The meditation captures many of the psycho-spiritual strategies offered in this book, and in this chapter particularly: *spiritfirstcounselling.ca/meditation-moment*

In his stunning book of poetry, *The Clear Light: Spiritual Reflections and Meditations,* Steve Taylor wrote a poem called *The Role,*[5] which captures your entrapment in a role you may be ready to throw off as you continue your codependence recovery. I invite you to sit with this poem, then record your reflections in your journal.

Dismantling the Social Construction and Unlearning Familial Patterns

In North American and other patriarchal cultures, from the moment their gender is assigned, and well before they have a say, most females are trained to be selfless, nurturing, tirelessly giving, and unthinkingly working for other people's needs. It takes great courage to unlearn this training but doing so may save your life. It will not be easy. Unlearning your social or familial conditioning requires you to face your own shadows.

Remember that shadows disappear under the intense noonday sun. Shadow work can be very freeing, and if it intrigues you, go to the ***Spiritual Practice: Parts and Positions Strategy*** in ***Chapter Seven: Feeling and Emotional Self-regulation.*** One of my personal metaphysical counsellors taught me that Karma is complete when we forgive ourselves, and I find this is so with shadow work. Forgive yourself for being human! You are Spirit in human form, and being human comes with the drama-seeking Ego and the limitations of this body. Your spiritual practice becomes a process of discernment, facing your shadow, forgiving yourself. I am here to remind you that your simply being is enough. You do not have to prove yourself by rescuing others.

Terry'ism: *"I am enough simply by my being, by my very existence."*

In your journal, explore your personal feelings around the truth of this affirmation in your daily life and relationships.

Enmeshment – Estrangement Continuum

In your journal, draw a line with the word *enmeshment* at one end and *Estrangement* at the other end. Enmeshment is a family or relationship dynamic in which you are not always clear where you end and another person begins. You may even take pride in thinking you can read each other's minds or finish each other's sentences. This seems cute and harmless, but it can be unbelievably unhealthy when it is extreme. Why? There are no or very few boundaries in the enmeshed family. If you crave privacy or a stronger sense of self, if you dream of some autonomy, or rebel by taking an extremely independent path (a pendulum reaction to frustration within a system), these are all messages about weak or missing boundaries. Attachment styles in the enmeshed family are usually quite anxious. When you choose to go against the norm (as perceived by members of the system) other members may find your boundaries almost intolerable. They may throw flack to try to force you back to what lessens their anxiety. Be compassionate but be resolute.

Estrangement is the polar opposite: individuals in relationship or families are isolated from each other, completely cut off, even though they might be living in the same house. Many individuals in estranged family systems are quite lonely. Again, this is a not a healthy dynamic for a system that requires interpersonal agreements, social contracts, and loving interactions.

When you look at the line you drew in your journal, at what point between enmeshment and estrangement do you sit in your family system or relationship? Can you see where on the line might be a healthier position? Question yourself about the family dynamic you grew up in. Decide what rules from there you would like to unlearn to shift to a healthier position in your family system or current relationship.

Anxious Attachment and Codependence

People who are other-focused tend to have anxious attachment patterns. There are many websites you can go to explore your attachment pattern and its ramifications. I like the *Attachment Project*[6] because the approach is positive, highlighting the gifts of particular attachment patterns. However, our work focuses on helping people attach to *themselves* instead of to another person. Your attachment to yourself is one of the primary goals of the work in ***Chapter One*** and it will be reinforced again in ***Chapter Eleven: Partnerships, Trust, and Anxiety***.

Self Therapy Tools, Rituals, and Practices for Codependence Recovery, *Flack in Codependence Recovery*

Where can you feel the truth of the following affirmation in your body?

Terry'ism: "I am not responsible for your response to my self-care decisions."

If your answer is, "I don't feel the truth of those words anywhere in my body. The affirmation does not resonate for me" then I have a gentle challenge for you: Can you imagine yourself caring less about others' responses to your self-care decisions? Can you test your tolerance for the anxiety you experience when other people disapprove of your choices for yourself?

Often in codependence recovery, we experience flack from those who profess to love us and who say they want the best for us. These individuals say they want us to live our best lives and offer to support us in any way necessary. At the same time, however, these same people will do everything they can to make us continue to maintain *their* homeostasis, the emotional regulation that they themselves should be responsible for. When you grow or change, those around you may feel pressured to change themselves. Maintaining status quo is critical to them. You may experience flack or pressure to return to status quo so they feel less pressure to look at themselves. You can have compassion for their fear of change, as much as for your fear of it, but you may have to be firm in your self-care resolve.

In ***Chapter Five: Freedom***, I taught the Vulnerability Script strategy. Return to this strategy now if you feel compassionate but determined to practise affirming your resolve to practise healthier boundaries. You can write your own vulnerability script in your own unique way, using your own language. It might look something like this:

"I love you and I understand that you may feel threatened by my decision to commit to my own self-care. It is awkward for me to continue because I am only guessing how you feel. I am also experiencing self doubt because I have been taught that to practise self-care makes me a selfish person. I would appreciate your support as I face my own internal critical voice, the voices of society, my faith community, my parents, and many others who teach that it is my responsibility to care for everyone else but myself. If you decide you want to join me, we can support each other. However, I will also continue on my own and there will be some activities that I will want to do alone. I love you. I want you to know how difficult this is for me, but I also want you to know that I am determined to do it, no matter how awkward I am at it at first."

When I completed my practicum with clinical supervision at a government run mental health and addiction outpatient clinic, I learned a great deal about flack in the Women's Codependence groups. My clients continue to teach me about flack. I have experienced flack myself when I have attempted to improve my life, and I discuss this in my ***Congruence Moment*** at the bridge between ***Spring*** and ***Summer***.

Flack can come in many forms. Some ways people may challenge your right to care for yourself are: guilt, outright anger, passive aggression, the silent treatment, withdrawal of affection, outright departure, threats, temper tantrums, crying, worsening problem behaviour, rallying support from family members and others, covert and overt insults, sabotaging your self-care regimen, somatic illness, and references to past unspoken verbal agreements or social contracts within the relationship.

Besides these forms of flack, your own critical inner voice can become flack if you are not aware enough of its whispers to challenge it. It takes great courage to unlearn societal, parental, religious, or historical conditioning, and to autonomously choose your own value system with integrity.

Here is another strategy to strengthen your self-care muscle. Try treating *yourself* the way you wish others would treat you for just one month. One month. Note in your therapy journal what you notice throughout this experiment.

Codependence in the Workplace

If you find yourself in a codependent cycle at work, recognize that you are on a trajectory to burn out, vicarious trauma, or compassion fatigue. All three of these symptoms of codependence appear in my clients who are physicians, therapists, teachers, nurses, social workers, and professional moms. One teacher who I encourage you to explore if you fall into this category is Vikki Reynolds and her *Zone of Fabulousness*.[7] Vicki and I shared the same supervisor, Dr. Allan Wade. Both Vikki and Allan helped me to find a balance between supporting another and taking on too much or taking work worries home. My self-care must remain an ethical imperative if I am to do exceptional work.

Radical Self-Care is the best short cut I know of to nip these codependence symptoms in the bud. Immediately return to your Wellness Wheel from **Chapter Four**. Look at each of the four realms: emotional, physical, intellectual, and spiritual. Ask yourself two questions: "What am I avoiding in my own life by attending to someone else's garden?" and "What can I do to take care of myself in each of the four areas of my Wellness Wheel?" Then do one activity from each of the quadrants immediately.

Service to the Planet and Connecting with Others

Terry'ism: "Worry is prayer without action."

Our planet is in desperate need of your service. If your identity is caught up in service, then serve! However, serve from a 'clean' place, not to avoid your own personal work, or to feel superior to others, or to change anyone. Giving is a beautiful quality when there are no expectations for change in another as a result of your service and no assumption of gratitude from the receiver.

Volunteering is one option. Detachment is much easier when it is not someone you know or have an intimate connection with, or when it is part of your job. When you are vulnerable to being other-focused, you can look in the mirror, perform a charade of putting on your oxygen mask, and check the four domains of your Wellness Wheel for self-care activities first. You can then provide service from an honest place. You might consider volunteering at a shelter or a non-profit thrift store. You may decide to work with others by serving on committees with Naranon, Alanon, or other groups like SMART Recovery for Family and Friends.

Terry'ism: "Trade drama for dharma."

If you discover an addiction to drama in your codependence recovery work, consider how you might be of service to evolving consciousness, yours and the collective, rather than participating in activities or social media exchanges that contribute nothing to our planet.

Follow Up with Leslie

Fellow traveller, were you able to open yourself to the challenges of discernment as you worked alongside Leslie in this chapter? She thought codependence was a relationship dynamic only between a person who did not suffer from an addiction and one who did. This is a common misconception. The term "other-focused" helped clarify the reality of codependence. She learned that she had based her entire identity and her good feelings about herself on giving to others, rescuing, and being seen as indispensable. Strokes to her Ego began to wear thin when she stared at herself in the mirror on a day when no one needed her.

During our work together, Leslie began to feel lost and restless. She did not know how to be responsible to herself, to her own personal growth. Nor did she know how to fill her time with activities she enjoyed. She confessed she did not even know what she wanted to do or what made her genuinely happy. She was also confused by her resentment toward those she was helping. This instability at the beginning of treatment for codependence (or being overly focused on others) is common. As we continued the strategies, activities, and spiritual practices in this chapter, Leslie eventually began to see her service to others as one part of her whole person. She began the journey of self discovery even though at the beginning it felt selfish. As she became more and more attached to herself, she became less anxious about her attachment to others. It was a beautiful journey to be part of.

Biblio-Therapy for Chapter Six

Books and Resources to Support Your Work with Codependence Recovery

- *The Language of Letting Go: Daily Meditations on Codependency*, Melody Beattie
- *More Language of Letting Go: 366 New Daily Meditations*, Melody Beattie
- *Codependent No More*, Melody Beattie
- *Beyond Codependency*, Melody Beattie
- *Loving What Is*, Byron Katie
- *Boundary Boss: The Essential Guide to Talk True, Be Seen, and (Finally) Live Free*, Terri Cole
- *Addiction and Grace: Love and Spirituality in the Healing of Addictions*, Gerald May
- *SMART Recovery Family & Friends Handbook: For People Affected by the Addictive Behaviour of a Loved One* edited by Roxanne Allen
- *Get Your Loved One Sober: Alternatives to Nagging, Pleading, and Threatening*, Robert Meyers and Brenda Wolfe
- Naranon and Alanon Literature (if your loved one is affected by addiction)

Risking Vulnerability, Walking the Talk, and Keeping it Real

This Therapist Shares Her Experience. Congruence Moment: Balance

When I present at women's health symposiums and conferences or deliver workshops or facilitate groups, the Wellness Wheel is often a focus of my presentation. I teach what I most need to continue learning. My intellect has always been my safe place. Working with and teaching the Wellness Wheel woke me up to how disembodied I was. I practised compassion for myself as I began the process of coming home to my body, heart, and Spirit. My daily yoga practice, my weekly dance and qi gong practices, my strength training, and hiking commitments bring me back home to my body each and every day.

Congruence Moment: Freedom (from Chapter Five)

Terry'ism: "She is every man; he is every woman."

I knew I was Spirit in human form by the time I was ten, and I knew I was a feminist by the time I was thirteen, but I did not know I was allowed to honour my love for women, so I married my high school boyfriend.

I chose to do what was expected, not what I truly wanted. I have no regrets as my beautiful daughter was born from my union and marriage to her father. Slowly and deliberately over time, I let go of behaviours and interactions that were dictated by social conditioning, colonization, and the familial training of the 'good girl'. At first, questioning everything was exhausting. I was deeply angry that I lived in a culture that taught me to put myself and the environment last. Then I grieved. I knew that under the anger was deep sadness. My freedom actually came from questioning everything. I asked myself, "Who decides?"

Claiming one specific level of my personal freedom meant owning my truth: that I felt most authentically me when I allowed myself to love a woman spiritually, emotionally, intellectually, and physically.

And yet... freedom can still feel elusive if you are female on this planet. I was on an extended pilgrimage to the southwest states. I was hot and tired after a long day of driving, so I felt grateful that my hotel had an outdoor patio pool with a place for me to sit and read my book after a dip. A man was cooking his dinner outside on one of the guest barbeques. There was no one else around. I got comfortable on my lounger but covered parts of myself because he was there. Call it a habit. He came over to my lounger and offered me a beer. I declined graciously and went back to my book. He left his meal cooking and disappeared. I knew exactly what he was about to do. With a sigh, I gathered my things and prepared to go to my hotel room. Sure enough, we crossed paths on my way in. He had two beer and held one up for me. I looked at him and said "No, thank you," (again!) and walked around him to the exit.

You may have opinions about this encounter. I am sure you do. You may decide that I should lighten up, go along, accept the drink, get over myself, make a new 'friend' or 'chill'. I was tired. I wanted a swim and a reading break. I had already said no. Freedom is the ability to make choices. Freedom is the opportunity to live our preferences.

Congruence Moment: Codependence (from Chapter Six)

Terry'ism: "People tend to treat you the way you treat yourself."

When I was first introduced to the Karpman Drama Triangle, I was still studying for my master's degree in counselling psychology and still unconscious of the way this important triangle was playing out in my personal life. I experienced various forms of flack firsthand as I saved my own life and sanity while living with those with addictions, people in chronic pain, and rage-aholics. I am no longer in these situations, and it was my self-care regimen that got me out. In my personal journey, I learned about flack from the amazing Melody Beattie and from both Naranon and SMART Recovery for Family and Friends. Fleshing out and naming the various positive and negative parts of myself was an important method for stripping away Ego definitions of myself. If all the roles, definitions, and parts of me are stripped away, what is left? Timeless, formless presence. The Eternal Self or the Self that Never Dies. Consciousness. The Observer or Witness or the One Who Knows. Yes, I am a woman. I am a feminist. I am a mother. I am a daughter. I am a psychotherapist. Despite all these descriptors, I identify most strongly with the Self beneath, above, and beyond them all.

Practising What I Preach: Spring Moments
Earth-based Spiritual Practices
Spring Equinox (Vernal Equinox) or Ostara
Beltane (May Day)

In my home, I celebrate the following late winter and early spring seasonal rituals. They connect me to the Archetypal Human Year, The Great Turning of the Wheel, and my own body responses to the seasonal energetic shifts. Once again, I draw from my ritual box—books with ideas, sacred objects, candles, and smudging materials. I create my own rituals from resources in the Pagan, Earth-based Spirituality, and Reclaiming Traditions. You may find the following ideas inspirational. Keep what you like, discard the rest.

Spring Equinox (Vernal Equinox) or Ostara (March 19, 20, or 21) – This marks the time when day and night are of equal length (this happens again at Autumnal Equinox) so I focus on balance and potentiality. I add some traditional Celtic/Pagan symbols of birth, fertility, new beginnings, balance, pregnancy, and hope to my outdoor altar: buds, seed pods, eggs, Spring flowers like crocuses, violas, and primulas, and images of baby animals like lambs, bunnies, and chicks.

I create an Ofrenda at my house altar, even though this beautiful display of flower petals and seeds is usually reserved for early November (Dia de los Muertos, after Samhain). In our part of the world, the herring are running. I plant some early seeds, do another cleanse of my home to make room for new ideas and growth, and donate many good quality pieces to local charities. I think about what has lied dormant in my personal growth and what might be ready to 'sprout' into action.

Beltane or May Day (May 1) – Beltane is halfway between Spring (Vernal) Equinox and Summer Solstice. Beltane can be loosely translated as "bright fire" and is commonly referred to as May Day in the Gaelic tradition. You may be more familiar with the tradition of dancing around a May pole. I am thrilled to lie on the grass and stare at the sky, gather flowers, and have my first outdoor fire. Sometimes I save burning rituals for Beltane, symbolically letting go of what no longer serves me by writing notes and committing them to fire.

Summer

Feelings, Emotional Self-regulation, Addiction and Compulsion, Abundance and Gratitude (Reciprocity)

Chapter Seven

feelings and emotional self-regulation

Dear Ms. Terry,

I have a love/hate relationship with my feelings. Everyone tells me to pay attention to my feelings, that they are important. But I also get told I'm too sensitive. It's very confusing. I worry that I am a "moody" person or that other people see me that way. I sometimes find myself drawn into gossip and drama despite my attempts not to be. It almost feels addictive. I also find it hard to get out of particular negative feelings or moods once I'm in them. They colour my days, and sometimes even my nights when I can't seem to snap out of a mood so I can sleep. I sometimes squash down my feelings by numbing myself with snacks or alcohol and I know this is affecting my health. How do I befriend my feelings?

- Almost Afraid to Feel, Stephanie

Many women struggle with this paradox: accused of being too emotional and simultaneously encouraged by movies and other media to romanticize feelings, to wallow in them, and also to maintain self-control as they are responsible for the emotional labour in any relationship. Women are often berated in our culture for being too "emotional" (particularly at certain times of the month), or, like Stephanie, for being too sensitive. When we began working together, I suggested Stephanie add a daily affirmation: "I can think and feel at the same time." As we explored her problematic relationship with her own feelings, she shared what I've heard often from other clients: they're afraid of feeling a negative emotion because they might be consumed by it, that they won't be able to stop crying if they start, or the mess in their life from this feeling will be too big to ever clean up.

I often offer a metaphor or archetypal image as a guide to assist their psyche's work, or we arrive at an image together. For Stephanie's work, I offered her two images to work with. One was a picture of a *matryoshka*—a Russian nesting doll. This, we hoped, would be a reminder to see herself as multi-layered: her infant self, enveloped by herself at five years of age, enclosed inside her nine-year-old self, who in turn was encapsulated by herself at fifteen, and so on up to the present day. The other image I offered her was a visualization of herself walking a path between two forests. The forest to her left would represent her feeling/emotional self, while the forest on her right would be her rational/logical thinking self. Fellow traveller, what do you think? Can you see yourself being open to working with either one (or both) of these images in this chapter?

As long as women are encouraged and expected to do the emotional work on behalf of men, children, parents, and coworkers, even in our spiritual or religious communities, with no acceptable outlet for inevitable negative emotions, they are easy targets. They can be scapegoated or accused of being too emotional any time the feelings they bring to conversations are uncomfortable to others' emotions or challenging to the status quo. This double bind is unfair and untenable, causing confusion and a sense of betrayal among women who recognize that feeling is healing.

As a therapist I can provide a safe container for all feelings, and I believe you can learn to do the same for yourself. I believe we can develop our emotional intelligence, our emotional vocabulary, our own emotional self-regulation, and that we can become proficient in gleaning the gifts of feeling without them drowning us. Remember that your brain still works *while* you are feeling. It will not let your feelings run away from your control permanently. By practising self-compassion as you explore your messy feelings, you learn that messes almost always ease up naturally as they are released from containment. There is more detrimental effect on the body from not expressing feelings than from crying or otherwise airing them out in a safe way. Crying is the best detoxification I know of, so go for it. Can you go to oceans, rivers, or lakes to throw rocks? Take up kick boxing or another activity that dissipates excess energy? I send some clients out with instructions to yell in their car, while driving safely, of course.

Remember that it is not enough just to release these feelings, though. To heal from them you will also focus your intent through narrating—bringing intention to consciousness—what you are doing. For example, "I am releasing energy by doing this activity so it doesn't build to crescendo until I feel like I am losing control" or "I am doing this while I think about my stressful situation so I can get some perspective."

Nuts and Bolts

Creating a Personalized Feelings Inventory

When someone uses the common expression, "I became emotional" when telling a story, what does that mean, exactly? Is your feeling positive or negative? Can you find more specific words to describe it? Where do you first notice the feeling in your body? Our ***Nuts and Bolts*** work for this month is building our emotional vocabulary and learning how to observe our feelings from outside ourselves. Let's start a feelings list to help you narrate, witness, or observe more specifically when talking about your emotions.

I often encourage people to expand their emotional vocabulary so they can name their inner experience more clearly. One helpful feelings framework comes from the work of Marshall Rosenberg[1], which supports people in moving beyond general emotional states into more specific nuances. You may use the list that follows as a starting point, and I invite you to adapt it, adding to it and personalizing it so it reflects your own lived emotional experience.

For example, under the general heading *Anxious*, you might list the following words: jittery, antsy, fearful, panicked, nervous, shaky, unsure,

Anxious	**Happy**	**Angry**	**Loving**	**Confident**	**Ashamed**	**Lonely**
jittery	*joyful*	*tense*	*connected*	*sure*		
antsy	*elated*	*vibrating*	*joyful*	*able*		
fearful	*cheerful*	*explosive*	*welcoming*	*motivated*		
panicked	*hopeful*	*overwhelmed*	*harmonious*	*excited*		
nervous	*content*	*fuming*	*grateful*			
unsure	*exuberant*					
hesitant						

hesitant, or any other nuance of the feeling of being anxious. Likewise, under the general category of *Happy* you might write joyful, elated, cheerful, hopeful, content, or other subtle shades of what it means to feel happy.

Create your personalized feelings list for happy and anxious, and include each of the major categories of feelings including anger, ashamed, sad, confused, disconnected, vulnerable, overwhelmed, and restless. Then add feeling words to the list for positive feelings like loving, connected, hopeful, excited, confident, grateful, motivated, peaceful, and exuberant. Challenge yourself to come up with various shades and nuances in each category. You will be using this list regularly, so keep it within reach.

Putting Feelings in Perspective

Feelings, at their most basic, are transient energy charges in the brain. The Ego sometimes latches onto them to generate stories, or to keep Spirit, Self, or Psyche buried. Generally speaking, feelings change quite quickly once we notice and name them. We pay attention. Many people think paying attention means glomming on to a feeling, running with it, allowing it to colour their entire day, or wallowing in it. Yet a hallmark of sound mental health is emotional flexibility, the ability to move in and out of emotional states smoothly, fairly quickly, and without prolonged attachment. Easier said than done!

One spiritual strategy for strengthening your emotional self-regulation is conscious detachment from your feelings rather than identifying with them. Start by noticing the feeling. Find it on your feelings list. Naming the feeling specifically and precisely helps you move out of its whirlpool. Take another step, asking yourself, "Who is studying the feeling? Who is naming the feeling? Who is choosing the feeling from a list?" Putting the feeling 'over there' and studying it like a specimen takes the power out of it. It helps you stop identifying with it and prevents Ego from running a drama with it. You, the observer, the witness, or the knower, are in control.

Interestingly, more than one of my teachers has suggested that you imagine yourself sitting on top of the washing machine, watching the feelings agitate in the soapy sudsy water. You are not *inside* the agitating machine yourself. It is very freeing.

I often teach that feelings can be understood as messages—signals pointing toward something that needs our attention. While it is true that your deeper self can communicate through feeling, that does not mean you can or should act on every feeling you have. Instead, inquire: what is this feeling telling me about my life or my current situation? And remember, while we need Ego to get us up and moving in the morning, Ego can also lead us down a drama drain, using feelings like a bull's nose ring.

Terry'ism: "Feelings point—they mustn't pull."

In other words—yes, pay attention to your feelings as they may be pointing you in a necessary direction. But do not let them yank, lead, or pull you there. You can feel and think at the same time. Yes, you can.

Try this: dialogue with a feeling in your journal. Notice the feeling. Name it as specifically as you can. Add to your list if you don't already have exactly the right word for it. Note where you feel that emotion in your body. Ask yourself if the feeling is coming from fear (Ego) or love (Spirit). Narrate the feeling. "I am feeling frustrated. Not angry. Not confused. Frustrated." Ask what it might want you to pay attention to. "Frustration, what is it that you want me to see?" "What are you pointing to that I need to explore?"

Combine this dialogue with a genuine application of your feelings list any time to develop your emotional intelligence and emotional vocabulary. You may want to teach it to family members who need help with emotional expression. Your feelings list can be posted on the refrigerator for your next family discussion, couples' conversation, or to help your child put words to their feelings.

We can teach our daughters, nieces, and granddaughters that they are capable of thinking and feeling at the *same time*. Remember the path between the *feelings* forest and the *thinking* forest? We can teach them how to notice when Ego attaches itself to a feeling and creates a dramatic narrative to obsess over. We can also teach them how to recognize when they are projecting their feelings onto another person, something all of us slip into occasionally, whether to justify our emotional position or shore up our pride. Sometimes we project to protect our little selves—remember the matryoshka doll—from feeling alone and abandoned. That feeling is better addressed by acknowledging it and re-attaching to our younger self first, not by tricking our self into believing someone else is getting attached to us and will protect us.

Feelings point but they do not lead. Teach yourself and your loved ones that they can lean into a feeling and feel it all the way through and still survive. Show them by example that they do not have to let any feeling lead them around like a bully. Feelings point, not pull. Feelings show, not lead.

Spiritual Practice

Parts and Position Strategy

Here is an exercise with the potential for a deep and lasting impact on your healing journey. It combines Narrative Therapy[2], Transactional Analysis[3], Depth Psychology[4] and Richard Schwartz's Internal Family Systems[5] to result in my own Spiritually Integrated approach. The premise of my hybrid strategy is that when we externalize parts of ourselves (to be integrated back into our whole selves later), we are setting up conditions where we do not identify so much with these parts. Giving consciousness, our Deep Self (or pure awareness) this chance to shine naturally is very freeing. I observe profound healing in my practice with this strategy, so much so that it has become a requested tool.

For this activity, consider various parts of your personality, both positive (light) and negative (shadow). Give each part a name. You will *temporarily* consider them as separate characters and later integrate them back into you. You may wish to create a Parts Poster. Alternately, you may decide to devote one page per part in your journal.

Create Five Shadow Parts

As a general rule, shadow parts are those parts that prevent you from being your best self. They are often felt in the body as fear of some kind. For example, the part of you that gets anxious before a meeting, social engagement, or for no apparent reason can be called "Ms. Anxy".

Visualize Ms. Anxy. Name her. Draw her or find a magazine image that represents her. What is Ms. Anxy's agenda? To keep you feeling fearful, vigilant, guarded. Would Ms. Anxy carry a clutch purse or a briefcase? Would she carry a large handbag or shoulder pack, in which there is everything but the kitchen sink? Next, does she have favourite music? A colour? A catchphrase? For example, Ms. Anxy's phrase might be, "This is not going to go well and you know it." When Ms. Anxy is activated in your body, where do you feel her? Some people feel Ms. Anxy across their shoulders or as neck tension. Others feel her in the stomach or as a tightening in their throat.

Once you have an image and a name (it might not be Ms. Anxy), write words all around this anxious character that reference her *personality*—her agenda, her colour, her handbag, her music, her catchphrase, and where you feel her in your body when she is trying to run the show.

Move on to another shadow part of yourself and flesh her (or him) out. Is she Ms. CoDEE, or Ms. Other-Focused, or Judge Judy? Other shadow parts that often emerge are Ms. Seeking Approval, Ms. Critical, Ms. Self Doubt, Ms. Hopeless, or Ms. Obsessive.

Aim to create five shadow parts, each complete with an image (magazine photograph or your own drawing), her (or his) own name, an agenda, a handbag, tool or object, an associated music genre, a colour, a catchphrase, and the body part that is most affected when this shadow part is activated and trying to run your life.

Create Five Light Parts

Now move on to your light parts. More often than not, your light parts are the parts that move you forward in your life or help you feel comfortably present in the moment. One might be Ms. Capable. Sketch her or find a photo that represents her. Think about her motivation, her agenda. Is she meant to help you keep believing in yourself? What handbag or item would she carry? Would she carry a clipboard or a toolbox? What is her favourite colour? Her favourite music? Perhaps her catchphrase is "You've got this!" What part of your body feels activated when you are in touch with Ms. Capable? Some people feel self-confidence in their chest or heart area, while others feel it in their thighs. Again, write words all around her that reference her personality. Repeat the process with four more parts. Some light parts that have come to life in my practice are Ms. Focused, Ms. Self-Care, Ms. Directly Assertive, and Ms. Graciously Let's Go. Create and flesh out five light parts.

Understand that you are not *any one* of these parts. These are all parts of you, not all of you. Who you are is greater than all of them together. For now, just observe your parts and notice when they are taking control in your life and in your body.

You may also decide to explore when your so-called shadow parts have actually helped you and when your light parts worked against you (usually when they are taken to the extreme). Did your anxiety alert you to a person who seemed great but turned out to be unsafe? Did your confidence lead you into a dangerous situation?

Write a script wherein two parts converse. Learn how each sounds, the words they choose. You can self-regulate more easily if you're aware of which part is activated before you speak, act, or make an assumption.

Taming the Dragon: Ego as an Externalized Part

In ***Chapter Three: Spirituality*** you made a list of your personal associations with Spirit and Ego for greater self-awareness in life situations and conversations with others. When were you Spirit First or Ego Forward?

Today, let's externalize, flesh out, and name your Ego. To be clear, Ego is neither all shadow nor all light. We need Ego active in order to show up in the world, to shower, go about daily tasks, and not show up at the grocery store without clothes on! The trouble begins when Ego assumes it is in charge of your life choices or at least has special power over them. You learned in ***Chapter Three*** how to recognize when Ego is taking possession of you. Now you will learn to take control back when you want to. In my practice we joke about taming the dragon (Ego) as we begin to identify more and more with our true selves, and less and less with Ego. We become more able to see through the elaborate mechanism of the Ego structure so we can undermine it more quickly. Remember, Ego moves from fear, loves drama, is competitive and defensive, abhors the present moment, reacts, and thinks there is never enough.

Begin by naming this part. Some people call their Ego comical names like Fret, Gremlin, Squawker, or Whiner. Some people use the name of an egotistical individual they have encountered. Whatever works. In this exercise, Ego is a creation of your own imagination, neither shadow nor light although admittedly it often feels like shadow because it is fear-based.

It might be helpful for you to know that we often move into the Ego Forward position when we feel most powerless. How can you recognize when you are in the Ego Forward position? You might feel quite caught up in the drama or story of the moment. You might be acting defensive, combative, competitive, or resistant to hearing another's point of view.

Ego loves triangles, too. Why? Triangles are so dramatic, and Ego loves drama! Within a triangulated relationship, someone is always left out. Two people bond only by leaving the third person out. Are you one of those 'in' together or the lone one 'out'? Note where you feel this in your body. Some people have noticed that when they are in an Ego Forward position, their breath changes or their hearing changes.

Once you name your Ego, it is easier to direct it. While we love our dogs, they also have to be disciplined when they are going beyond what is reasonable to get our attention. Ego needs training too. How lovely would it be to tell Fret, Squawker, or Gremlin to "Go lay down" or "Go to your crate" whenever it tries to override your Spirit First positioning in an intimate conversation.

Notice where in your body you most often feel Ego's activation. Then give your named Ego an agenda, image, anchor item, colour, music, and catchphrase. You will discover your Spirit First position later in this strategy. For now, simply monitor yourself over the next few weeks and notice when you are in Ego Forward position. Make notes in your journal.

Inner Child Part and Inner Parent/Adult Part

For this strategy, deep inside the matryoshka doll, you will be drawing out your younger self, your inner child, as a separate entity, neither shadow nor light. Certainly not Ego! Find a photograph of yourself younger than the age of eight, preferably one that tugs at your heart or makes you feel pleasantly warm when you look at it. Give her your name, a childhood nickname you liked, or simply call her, Little Me. She is pure innocence, without fault, and dependent on the adults in her life for food, shelter, love, and safety. Remember as you get to know her that she does not have the skills that you have, as the adult you are now. She is dependent on you as her inner parent.

When you are in the *Child* position in any interaction, you may feel inexplicably responsible, vulnerable, confused, powerless, or desperate for this person's approval. A child is dependent on those in charge for basic life necessities. When the basics are threatened, approval-seeking behaviour is a vital survival skill. A *trigger,* by definition, is a memory of a time when you felt powerless. Children are often powerless, so if you are feeling powerless in your now-adult present time, a triggered memory may have reverted you back to the Child position.

Notice where you experience this childlike vulnerability in your body. Some people feel it as a loud rushing sound in their ears, others feel the urge to cry, with their throat tightening, and still others have a temper tantrum during which they temporarily lose the conscious connection to their own body.

In your therapy journal, write about a recent experience of being triggered into the Child position. Was it during a conversation with your partner, your supervisor, your parent, sibling, or another adult? How does your new understanding of your inner Child position help you make sense of that last conversation?

On the other hand, when you feel strong and confident, adult and self-assured, you are experiencing yourself in the *Adult* position. As an adult, you already have a name, and preferences, and tools. You can better judge what is truly a survival threat. You are not at the mercy of the trigger. As the parent of yourself, your job is to nurture your inner child in a way she may not have been in your actual childhood. You can remind her that you are the parent now, and "You've got this!" Her only job is to be her wonderful self, to play, to find out what makes her happy (her preferences), and to eventually (hopefully) learn to trust herself and her intuition.

After you have immersed yourself in this work for awhile, you may notice when some adults around you are in the Child position. They may have been triggered by an event in the present that sends them spinning back childhood powerlessness. You may see them having a temper tantrum or sense inappropriate guilt or worry over a situation that has nothing to do with them. They may suddenly seem defensive or resistant to adult conversation. If you can stay in your Adult position and *not join them in Child,* you have options: you may decide to end the conversation (for now), give yourself (and them) a time out, and continue the conversation another day. If *you* find yourself in the Child position, know that it is unfair to put (or leave) your own little one in an adult interaction—she lacks the skills to interact in an adult way with other adults. She will only end up feeling anxious and exposed. She may even have a temper tantrum if she feels cornered or that her back is against the wall. Step away. Reassure her. When you are back in the Adult position, return to the conversation.

We will deepen this work later but for now, please note that Ego is *not* Child. They are two separate entities. Little You is pure innocence, worthy of your unconditional love, and without fault. She just wants to be loved and delighted in. Ego, on the other hand, is fear-based—a socially conditioned persona that understands social rules, wants control, and loves drama. Know how each feels in your body and keep Child and Ego separate in your understanding.

The Ultimate Goal: Arriving at the Spirit First Position by Answering the Pivotal Questions

Once you have created or imagined at least five light parts, five or more shadow parts, Ego, inner child, and inner parent as separate entities. ask yourself the pivotal questions:

1. *Who created these parts? Who is the creator?*
2. *Who manages these parts now? Who is the manager?*

The answer to these questions should be the same.

Your inner manager, director, puppeteer, or lady boss is the Creatrix of all of your parts. This 'creator' is your Deep Self or True Self, the Beloved, the Psyche, or the Friend—your spiritual Essence, if you will. Some people think of their inner manager or creator as the observer, the witness, the knower. Others call this part their Soul, Inner Spirit, or Essence. It is the part of you that is eternal, the part of you that was here before you were born into form, and the part of you that will continue after you leave your body, or become unmanifest. I encourage people to name this Deep Self so they can call on the Friend whenever necessary.

Surprisingly, this True Self often has an androgynous name and becomes a dependable, stable, lifelong Guide or Friend. This internal, ultimate, eternal guide for your life, this Creator/Manager of all the parts, including your adult persona, is as close as your breath and unconditionally loving toward you. Notice where in your body you feel this presence. Become familiar with this sensation. This entity is your lifelong Inner Guide and is absolutely reliable, but you must develop your bond with this Guide. Strategies for accessing this True You are offered in ***Chapter Two: Stillness***, with particular attention to ***Portals to Presence***.

Soul Work (Homework or Heartwork)

Your Big Brain, remember, is your body. It loves you unconditionally, wants only your healing and, being nonverbal, speaks to you through physical sensations and symptoms. If you ignore those sensations, it will lovingly *up the ante* and try to get your attention in a more dramatic way. Your Big Brain is constantly scanning the environment. Noticing where you hold anxiety, sadness, anger, or fear is such a gift to give yourself. Sometimes you may feel the physical symptoms of panic, for example, before the actual event occurs. Rather than pushing the emotion or feeling down, try leaning into it. Acknowledge it. Shine the light of truth on it, see what it is trying to warn you about, and watch it dissolve.

Do not resist the feeling. This may feel like a radical act since we are often taught to resist our feelings, to run from them, to try to get rid of them, or to bury them under numbing agents like alcohol, drugs, shopping, gambling, or sex.

But *do* resist Ego's attempts to make up a story about the feeling, one that makes you feel worse or justifies self-sabotage or rationalizes words and actions that hurt other people or the planet. You can always trust your body's messages, but you *cannot* always trust the stories your Ego makes up about them.

Spiritual Journal Stems and Prompts

Journal around the following ideas:

Remember the two images I offered Stephanie for the work of this chapter? One was the Russian nesting doll. If you chose the matryoshka, journal about how the image informed your work for this chapter.

The other image I offered her was the visual of travelling a wide, walk-able centre path between two wooded areas representing her feeling self on the left, and her logical rational self on her right. If you chose to work with this image, journal about how capable you feel staying on the middle way, or what I like to call the Tao position.

A well-known psychological concept suggests that, over time, we can develop a protective "outer self" to shield what is most tender and true in us. I reinterpret this idea in the following way: if you get to know your True Self, it can become your protector, ally, and best friend. Record your own thoughts around this idea in your journal.

Now, journal around the following ideas:

1. *When I think about who is the "boss lady" or manager of all of these parts, I understand this to be...*

2. *If I consider my Deep Self, my Higher Self, my Realized Self, or in* *some spiritual traditions, my True Self, to be the maestro or the manager of all of these parts, I discover that...*

3. *As an experiment I am going to have different parts talk to each other. I will record this dialectic or dialogue by writing an imaginary scripted dialogue. For example...*

4. *Understanding that only a part of me is codependent (or a martyr or an approval-seeking doormat), helps me understand that this role is not my true nature. She usually emerges when I am feeling powerless. For example...*

5. *I am worried that if I do not acknowledge my feelings, I will forget about the original reason for them and the person who 'caused' them will get away with something.*

Spiritual Inspiration

Spend some time in conversation with your Inner Being (Deep Self, Higher Self, Realized Self, True Self). I recommend you write this conversation as a dialogue in your journal. Remember, your Inner Being is your lifetime best friend. This part of you loves you unconditionally. Ask Her directly how She uses feelings to get your attention.

Dismantling the Social Construction and Unlearning Familial Patterns

The expectation that women are always the emotional caregivers is unfair to men, as well. The nurturing expectation placed on women seems to be a natural offshoot of birth-giving. However, men are born of women and equally capable of psychological and physical nurturing toward themselves and others. Reality TV and soap operas aside, our culture seems as afraid of feeling as it is afraid of sexuality. In the old mind/body split paradigm, the body was seen as seductive, base, lower, or animalistic while the mind was seen as cerebral, higher, above it all, not caught up in emotion, and somehow purer. A male's lack of personal control or lack of shadow examination gives him permission to blame females for the mere existence of their bodies and their emotions. He may even absolve himself of responsibility for his own body. When it behaves badly, that, too, can be someone else's fault. Fear of menstruation, long hair, bare feet, or women's righteous anger lead to phrases like, "She asked for it" or "She must be menstruating" under the *'blame women for everything'* paradigm. As a result of the mind/body split, feelings also tend to get the same bad rap. A male's emotions can also be deemed a woman's fault. "She made me mad." What do you think about this mind/body split? About women's burden of nurturing? Do you reject it in thought but find yourself accepting it in deed? Journal around this mind/body split.

Unfortunately, this split has also shaped how many of us relate to the Earth—treating nature as something "separate" from us, and therefore easier to control, use, or ignore. In some belief systems, this separation has justified placing humans above the natural world rather than interdependent with it. From my perspective, healing asks for a different posture: connection instead of disconnection, reverence instead of domination, and relationship instead of extraction. When we remember that body and mind are one, it becomes easier to remember that we, too, belong to the Earth and are inseparable from her living systems.

Self Therapy Tools, Rituals, and Practices for Feelings and Emotional Self-regulation

Managing Guilt and Worry, and Other So-Called Negative Emotions

In your therapy journal, explore the idea of leaning into your emotions. Own what you feel and acknowledge that you have the rational capacity to choose how to act. We can think and feel at the same time. Some teachings invite us to see emotions not as obstacles, but as carriers of wisdom, with each one offering a different kind of guidance. From this perspective, fear may carry discernment, guilt may invite repair (if the guilt is truly yours to own), and pain may point to something in need of tenderness. For our purposes here, it is enough to begin welcoming emotions, sometimes leaning into them, and clearing them through our journals. Think of the buffalo: when they sense a storm coming across the grasslands, instead of huddling with their heads together to wait out a storm, they turn into the storm and move through it to the other side, so it is behind them more quickly.

The Origins of Guilt and Worry

Early in their development, children are egotistical, seeking autonomy, and to find their place in their small world of family. Everything revolves around the child, so everything that happens is somehow about them. If the child hears parents arguing, she may think it is because she left her trike on the driveway or made some other mistake. To us as adults, capable of abstract thinking, this is not an obvious connection, but it still feels like one to the child. Children are egotistical because they are supposed to be. It is developmentally appropriate for them. However, because everything is about them, then everything that happens is *because* of them. Some of children's magical thinking arises from this personalizing behaviour. Most children are powerless in their dependency for food, shelter, safety, and love. If the child wants to feel more in control, she may experience two forms of *false* power: worry and guilt. Worry feels like power because it emotionally mimics "doing something". It is false power because it accomplishes nothing.

Remember that a trigger is a memory of a time in childhood when you felt powerless. We can be taken back to the powerlessness moment by a conversation (as mentioned earlier), a scent, a song, an image, a current experience, which may include an anniversary, or a felt sensation. As an adult, you might be triggered by a conversation with a partner, parent, colleague, supervisor, or even an adult child. You slip into the Child position. Sometimes you feel responsible for something that is not truly your responsibility. With worry you feel like you are doing something because you are worrying. In reality, although you have an unusual feeling of power, these powerless emotions do not actually change anything externally.

If you are feeling guilt while in the Adult position, it could mean that you have not yet owned your decision. You may not feel ready to accept the consequences of your choice even if you know the choice is a good one for you. The consequence you may be avoiding by feeling guilty is disappointing someone else. Their approval matters. When you own your adult decision, you can build your capacity to sit with the discomfort of disappointing another.

So, let us turn this around. What if guilt and worry, are actually gifts that help you to see you have moved from the Adult position into the Child position?

Now you can step away, regroup, reassure your inner child that you are the adult now, and far from being powerless, you are in charge. You can choose to step away, to realize that this current event is not personal, is not about you. You are not responsible for everything, and worrying will not change anything. Freedom!

It is fascinating to identify a trigger and to become more aware of why we behave in certain ways when a particular stimulus is present. It can be helpful to revisit the original powerless moment and re-imagine a different response from here, in the safe, often more mature position you now inhabit. Sometimes it feels a little bit like the movie *Back to the Future*: we change how we feel today by changing one moment in the past, if only in our imagination.

Much has been written in this book and elsewhere about not confusing the Ego position with the Child position. By now you are learning to notice where in your body you feel each position. The Ego position is more defiant, competitive, rigid, defensive, dramatic, self-serving. The bodily sensations of the Child position feel more like confusion or anxiety. In your adult interactions, try to become conscious of these positions and to distinguish between them.

A note of caution is worth repeating here. There is a difference between child egocentricity and adult egoism. Your inner child is innocent, deserving of all of your inner spiritual parent's consistent love and patience. She is to be loved, delighted in, enjoyed, played with, and reassured. When you as an adult are triggered into the Child position by an adult event, you must step away. You cannot leave your little one there to face an adult situation. It is not fair. She does not have the tools that you as an adult have learned over the years. She will likely cry or get anxious, as she did then.

As an adult who is triggered, you may feel this anxiety and helplessness in your body. You may cry. Step away from the adult interaction and regroup. Quietly tell your little one you have got this. Do not make her handle an adult interaction she is not equipped to handle. Revisit your earlier journaling from this chapter to refresh what you have noticed about your body sensations and symptoms when you are in Child position and when you are in Ego.

Service to the Planet and Connecting with Others

If you decide to parallel your personal healing journey with the healing of our planet, seek the spiritual medicine of trees for emotional regulation.

My regular romps in forests here on Vancouver Island have convinced me of the healing qualities of spending time with trees. I teach *Shinrin-yoku* because my own healing journey toward wholeness convinced me of its efficacy. Botanist and medical biochemist Diana Beresford-Kroeger explains how the aerosols released by specific tree species have measurable, positive effects on both physical and emotional health.[6] Her work is fascinating. You may wish to seek out like-minded allies of Mother Earth and watch *Call of the Forest: The Forgotten Wisdom of Trees together*. After the film, consider planting trees as a shared act of healing and reciprocity.

This practice can be taken further by connecting with the deva of plants and trees for solace and com-fort. For more on *Shinrin-yoku* (Forest Bathing), return to ***Chapter Two: Stillness***.

Follow Up with Stephanie

Stephanie's biggest relief arose from giving herself permission to think and feel *at the same time*. Positioning herself outside of Ego's story-telling gave her the power to see more clearly its shenanigans and desire for drama. Fellow sojourner, did you experience similar "aha" moments in your work around emotional self-regulation? Externalizing, then integrating, her shadow parts and light parts helped Stephanie to see that she herself created these parts. She wrote letters of compassion and love to her younger selves, and the self forgiveness she experienced was incredibly moving. Does the image of the matryoshka help you have compassion for your younger selves?

Biblio-Therapy for Chapter Seven

Books and Resources to Support Your Work with Feelings and Emotional Self-regulation

- *Greater Than the Sum of the Parts,* Dr. Richard C. Schwartz (Six Session Audio Course)
- *Loving What Is,* Byron Katie
- *The Four-Fold Way*, Roy Henry Vickers
- *The Seven Emotions and Their Gifts*, Roy Henry Vickers
- *Pair-a-Dimes for Your Thoughts,* Interview between David Truss and Roy Henry Vickers
- *The Medicine of Trees, Ninth Haig-Brown Lecture,* Diana Beresford-Kroeger
- *Homecoming,* John Bradshaw
- *Braiding Sweetgrass: Indigenous Wisdom, Scientific Knowledge, and*

the Teachings of Plants, Robin Wall Kimmerer

- *The Earth Path: Grounding Your Spirit in the Rhythms of Nature*, Starhawk
- *Nonviolent Communication,* Marshall Rosenberg
- *The Seat of the Soul*, Gary Zukav
- *Narrative Means to Therapeutic Ends*, Michael White and David Epston

Chapter Eight

addiction and compulsion

Dear Ms. Terry,

I'm struggling with quitting smoking. I tell myself it calms me, but it doesn't really. I just get anxious between smokes. I've tried seriously quitting maybe five times, and the longest I've lasted is three days. I probably drink more than I should too, but again, I tell myself that I'm taking the edge off, relaxing after a long day. Besides, drinking and smoking kind of go together, don't you think? These are both habits I'd like to break, but smoking is probably my top priority. I know these changes will impact my life in big ways. Can you help me get started?

- Willing to Change, Erin

Erin is to be immediately applauded for several reasons, and she has not even started her Quit Journey . First and foremost is her decision to ask for help. Secondly, for her courage to continue trying to reclaim mastery over her life. Each previous attempt has brought her closer to success.

When we are all faced with so many changes beyond our control, choosing change is a radical act of defiantly claiming power. Choosing to stop obsessing about another person, or to stop shopping, gambling, smoking, drinking, using marijuana, or ingesting illicit drugs like heroin, fentanyl, cocaine, or crystal meth is a profound spiritual decision, the most courageous act I have ever had the honour of guiding.

The Stages of Change Model (sometimes called the Transtheoretical model) first posited by James Prochaska and Carlo DiClemente in the 70s, is a process model. It recognizes there can be an actual plan to quit. Yes, you can go 'cold turkey' and white knuckle it on your own, if you like. However, developing a plan and attempting to follow your own steps has shown itself successful and sustainable in my practice. I use the model to determine which stage of change is the person in:

1. Precontemplation (sees no cons with using and does not plan to quit)
2. Contemplation (sees some cons in continuing to use and might be thinking about quitting)
3. Preparation (sees more pros in quitting and more cons in using, starts taking little steps, and might develop a plan to quit)
4. Action (attempting to quit and learning new ways of coping)
5. Maintenance (sustaining the quit by working on preventing relapse)
6. Termination (has no intention to use ever again)[1]

Our letter writer Erin is in the preparation stage. The strategy I offered Erin (and you, dear sojourner, if you feel ready) is the archetypal Heroine's journey. This journey follows the Stages of Change model fairly closely. The classic text *The Hero With a Thousand Faces*[2] by Joseph Campbell teaches that the archetypal heroic journey is standard fare in various global mythologies, literature, and the movies, particularly *The Star Wars* series. This heroic myth is archetypal (sometimes called a *monomyth*), a narrative used in many, if not all, stories of heroes across cultures and geographic locations. Campbell uses the term "hero," implying a male prerogative, but the story can apply to all individuals whether female or male. I draw quite heavily on Campbell's work and his astonishing interviews with Bill Moyers in my approach to overcoming addiction of any kind. In *The Heroine's Journey,* Maureen Murdock adjusted Campbell's archetypal myth to more accurately reflect the feminine experience. I offer her journey overview in ***Deepening Your Practice*** near the end of this chapter. Overcoming an addiction is essentially a decision to embark on a journey through your own grief.

Nuts and Bolts

Start a Quit Journal for the stages and tasks below. Exercising power and control at each of the twelve stages of the Heroine's journey is part of the success of this approach.

Stage 1: Ordinary World – Limited Awareness of Problem

Using the tasks below, see yourself as the Heroine centred in your normal surroundings and your familiar world. Understand that what you now consider normal will not look the same at the end of this journey.

- Task 1: Look unflinchingly at the reality of *what is.* Honestly track how much you use or obsess for at least two weeks. Do not do anything else. Just write down when, how many, and the context. For example, "I smoked two cigarettes before breakfast" or "I had two six-ounce glasses of wine, one while cooking dinner and one while eating it."
- Task 2: Over these two (or more) tracking weeks, note in your Quit Journal any feelings, insights, and realizations that surface.
- Task 3: Write a Thank You letter to the substance or obsession. This

is not a Goodbye letter. This is a letter of genuine letter of gratitude for what the substance or fixation has actually done for you over the years and how it has helped you in specific situations. Writing this letter allows you to explore your relationship or preoccupation with the substance.

- Task 4: As you write your Thank You letter, note in your Quit Journal any feelings, insights, and realizations that surface.

Stage Two: Call to Adventure – Increased Awareness of the Need for Change

Using the tasks below, describe the challenge or problem you are setting up for yourself in realistic terms.

- Task 1: Get honest about the known long-term physical effects of continuing to use this substance or fixation. Research the many sites that provide this information. Take some quiet time to sit with these scientific or psychological facts. Allow them to sink in as much as possible. Remember that denial has been very useful in keeping you using, and facing reality is difficult when you're out of practice, so exercise exquisite compassion with yourself.
- Task 2: Describe your Big Brain's messages to you when you use this substance or obsess. What sensations do you experience in the moment of using? What have you noticed about the effects on your body over the years?
- Task 3: What does "freedom" mean to you? In what ways are you the master of your daily life? In other words, what daily decisions are within your control? Catalogue these decisions from the moment of awakening to lights out at night.
- Task 4: Which parts of your life have you lost mastery over?

Stage Three: Refusal of the Call – Resistance to Change

This is the beginning of grieving the end of your relationship with the substance you use or the object of your obsession.

- Task 1: What is one of your private fears about choosing to stop using this substance or acting out this behaviour? What is another one? Are there other private fears you have about what might happen if you stop using?
- Task 2: What do you fear will happen to your body or mind if you continue to use this substance participate in this activity? What is another one? Are there other fears you have about what might happen if you keep using?
- Task 3: How will your identity be affected by your decision to stop using? In other words, how do you think you will be different? What do you fear about those differences? How do you think others will perceive you if you are no longer using?
- Task 4: If you are afraid you will not know what to do with your time if you stop using or behaving this way, describe how much actual time it takes.
- Task 5: Make a list of activities you can do that might fill your time. These might include going to meetings, knitting, running, swimming, participating in extra counselling, singing, meditating, walking or hiking, cooking, writing, or wood working.
- Task 6: If you are afraid of withdrawal and what it could feel like, try cutting your use in half for seven days with the focused intention of exploring the edges of withdrawal. Allow yourself this investigation of edges. Take this step a little further and notice what happens when you push yourself to your limit. You are not quitting now. You are simply investigating the outer perimeter of withdrawal. How much discomfort can you tolerate?

- Task 7: What do you notice about a typical wave of withdrawal? Withdrawal waves shorten over time. They also become less intense. Withdrawal waves get further and further apart as time passes. How is this helpful for you to know?

Stage Four: Mentor – Overcoming Fear

The mentor is often a wise old woman (or wise old man) who assists you in your preparations for the journey. Sometimes your mentor will be gentle and if you are a 'good grasshopper', she may give you a gift to use now or later in your journey. Sometimes your mentor will be harsh and non-indulgent, without the gentle touch.

- Task 1: Most substance use or obsession over another person begins with an attempt to come to terms with trauma or traumatized attachment. Find a counsellor or therapist who can help you work through historical trauma. I have worked extensively with trauma victims-survivors-flourishers but that is the subject of another book.
- Task 2: A mentor has earned her wisdom through learning, sacrifice, and commitment. Describe your ideal mentor. Do you have a role model who has been successful in her (or his) recovery? Interview her and note what you might learn from this mentor.
- Task 3: Describe the person who would be most affected by your decision to quit fixating or using this substance (besides yourself). Describe another person who would be affected. Are there more than two?
- Task 4: What would be the best gift your mentor could possibly give you that would be the most helpful on your journey?
- Task 5: If there are quit aids out there for you, take advantage of them by ordering them, getting prescriptions, researching how to use them, and exploring how you might cope with the side effects of these quit

aids. Follow all recommended preparatory steps with these gifts.

- Task 6: If there is an online forum, or a sponsor, or a competent professional who will check in with you on your progress, take advantage of this gift.

All of these tasks are preparation for your journey ahead, Heroine.

Stage Five: Crossing the First Threshold – Committing to Change

This is where the Heroine steps out from her ordinary world to start her adventure.

- Task 1: Choose a word that captures the state of being that you hope to experience as a result of quitting this substance or ceasing this obsessive behaviour. One of my clients chose the word "Pure" while another chose the word "Clear". Another individual chose "Freedom" and still another "Mastery". Your word could be any of these or any other. It is *your word.*
- Task 2: Meditate on your word. Draw a circle on a blank journal page and write the word in it. Web out ideas, associations, connections, and feelings related to this word by writing each somewhere around the circle, near or far away, and drawing a line between them. Continue until the journal page is full of thought webbing. To keep your vision of this hoped-for future in sight, you may wish to write the word on sticky notes and post them around your home.
- Task 3: Choose a Quit Date.
- Task 4: Attempt to quit.
- Task 5: Acknowledge that you are actually choosing to enter into the grief process. You may want to preview ***Chapter Ten: Grief, Change, and Loss*** to review tools that may be helpful to you now.

Stage Six: Tests, Allies, and Enemies – Experimenting with New Conditions

This is where you are faced with new challenges and tests, and you begin to understand a little bit about the way your new, Special World operates.

- Task 1: Notice who is on your cheerleading team. How do they cheer you on? Are there any surprises?
- Task 2: Notice who is sabotaging your success. How are they attempting this? Again, are there any surprises? (For more help coping with flack, go to ***Chapter Six: Overly Responsive to Others' Needs (Codependence)***.
- Task 3: For help building your Circle of Support, preview the strategy entitled ***Soul Work (Homework or Heartwork)*** in ***Chapter Eleven: Partnerships, Trust, and Anxiety***.
- Task 4: Prepare for withdrawal symptoms, both physical and psychological. Are there special preparations you can make at specific times to thwart negative inner voices or move through a temporary wave of withdrawal discomfort? Repeat to yourself that withdrawal waves are not permanent. Withdrawal waves shorten over time. Withdrawal waves get further and further apart over time. How is this helpful for you to remember?

Stage Seven: Approach the Innermost Cave – Preparing for Major Change

The innermost cave is the most dangerous place in the Special World. The Heroine knows it is coming and must plan ahead how she'll outwit the villain and the villain's guards.

- Task 1: Design a go-to plan for your most difficult withdrawal waves.

Remember both physical comfort and psychological well being. Here are some activities my Heroines have planned for difficult moments: running, meditating, swimming, going to SMART Recovery, NA, or AA meetings, knitting, making kombucha, taking anti-anxiety medications, phoning a sponsor, asking for help on a forum, booking an extra counselling appointment, taking some personal time away.

- Task 2: Take a half hour to review your Quit Journal. What pieces resonate now? What can you add that you have learned about yourself?
- Task 3: Who are your "villains"? Get honest. These folks may be afraid you will leave them, grow beyond them, or move away. They are used to you being in a particular role in their lives, and remember, they have not chosen change for themselves. Write about your feelings around their actions and *inaction*. Try to have compassion for those who are threatened by your attempts to heal and recover. Write a script that will capture your loving understanding of their fear *and* your determined commitment to yourself. Reinforce your hope that they can get behind you. For help with this vulnerability script, go to ***Chapter Six: Overly Responsive to Others' Needs (Codependence)***.
- Task 4: Your worst "villain" may be the critical voice inside your own head that asks, "Who are *you* to heal and grow?" Prepare your answer. You may discover the hidden unexplored potential in your internal villain, much like you would in shadow work.
- Task 5: Use the ***Spiritual Practice: Parts and Positions*** strategy from ***Chapter Seven: Feelings and Emotional Self-regulation***. Name one of your parts "Addiction" so that you can externalize and personify it as a shadow part, dialogue with it, and realize anew that Addiction is *not* you. It *was* a *part* of you. It is easier to be your own Heroine by confronting and fighting a part of you that feels like it is talking to you from outside yourself.
- Task 6: One of my teachers, Tina Zion, encourages us to call upon

divine and sacred experts in particular areas of our lives. Is there an ancestor, a spiritual guide, archangel, Goddess, or other deity that you can call upon to assist you in your Quit Journey? I could not have quit using tobacco without supernatural assistance.

Stage Eight: Supreme Ordeal – Big Change that has a Feeling of Life or Death

This is the moment our Heroine faces her biggest fear, deep in the Inmost Cave. It is a very dark moment. But knowing it is ahead lets you prepare.

- Task 1: Design a Reward Plan for your first month of sobriety. By sobriety, I mean one month of freedom from using your substance or obsessing over a particular individual. The reward you design, plan, and execute should be quite significant, a celebration of your courage and determination.
- Task 2: Design a Self-Compassion/Begin Again Plan for a possible relapse. My own mentor used to say, "Every relapse brings you closer to sobriety" when I was attempting to quit using nicotine. I recommend the beautiful work of Dr. Kristin Neff[3] at *self-compassion.org* for these moments.
- Task 3: Research the definition of *resilience* and describe how it applies to you, your personal life journey, and your current Heroine's journey here.

Stage Nine: Reward (Seizing the Sword) – Accepting the Gifts and Losses of Your New Life

Our Heroine takes ownership of the treasure "sword" along with her new self understanding, knowledge, and confidence. This bittersweet feeling accompanies letting go of your old way of being in the world and grieving for its ending. Grief processing is a very real part of quitting a substance or releasing a compulsion.

- Task 1: Identify what you are grieving. Are there individuals, places, related habits, or activities that you need to say goodbye to?
- Task 2: As your confidence improves, what are you noticing about yourself? Is it still 'one day at a time'? Are you finding yourself thinking 'one week at a time'?
- Task 3: What gifts are you enjoying? What positive results are now beginning to shine through?

Stage Ten: The Road Back – New Challenge and Re-dedication

In Spiritually Integrated psychotherapy, I call this the spiritual *law of reversibility*. Just when you are starting to feel more confident and assured of your Quit success, it is almost as if the universe is poking you and asking, "Are you sure? Are you absolutely sure?"

- Task 1: How is the law of reversibility showing up now? How are you being tested?
- Task 2: In your journal, answer this question: Are you sure? The law of reversibility is often not a test but an opportunity to see how far you have come and what remains to be strengthened. How is this true for you?

Stage Eleven: Death and Resurrection – Final Attempts and Last-Minute Dangers

This is the last ordeal. Again, our Heroine experiences what feels like a life-or-death struggle. However, this time it feels more like the death of the old self, the old way of being in the world.

It is a grieving time. Remember, crying is detoxing your emotions. Let yourself cry if that's what you need. For more grief strategies, see ***Chapter Ten: Grief, Change, and Loss .***

- Task 1: Don't impose a timeline for grieving the end of your relationship with a substance, compulsion, or other problem behaviour. The grief softens eventually, but it may never fully go away. In your journal, write a description of how you hope to feel when your grief softens.

Stage Twelve: Return with the Elixir – Mastery

Our Heroine returns to the community with a talisman from the Special World to help her community. This might be a magic potion, but more likely it is new knowledge that she can share with others who are quitting or thinking about quitting.

- Task 1: What have you learned about yourself in this Quit process?
- Task 2: How can you teach others what you have learned?

Spiritual Practice – Rituals for Endings and New Beginnings

Elevate your Quit Journey to the spiritual realm by designing a ritual. This ritual may be performed at any stage of your Quit Journey and repeated as often as necessary. The ritual may turn into a Ritual of Celebration and Thanksgiving near the end of your journey.

I offer a reminder here to always ground yourself before and after any ritual you design and practise yourself or with others. Grounding simply means you deliberately visualize yourself connected to the Earth in some specific way. I usually ground by imagining roots growing out of the bottom of my feet, or I do two or three sun salutations with the intention of connecting with Mother Earth. Create a ritual that captures the profundity of what you are actually doing for yourself.

1. Create a sacred space. You may decide to use your altar and/or the space around your altar for this ritual (see ***Chapter One: Reverence***). Have the four elements represented: earth, air, fire, and water, aligned with the four directions. As you face north, think about the Earth and how it supports you in fundamental ways. Facing east, consider how the air you breathe is life. Give thanks for the sun and its healing properties as you face south. Believe in the life-giving healing properties of water when you face west.
2. State your intention. In this case, your intention is to claim freedom and mastery from a substance or problem behaviour that has made your life unmanageable.
3. Call in the help of Source, ancestors, spiritual guides, and other supernatural assistants.
4. Repeat your chosen word for the work you are doing: "I choose _________". This word may be "freedom" or "clarity" or "mastery" or the word of your choice that feels like it has the most emotionally sustaining impact.
5. Safely burn a symbolic representation of the substance or compulsion. Follow all necessary safety precautions and respect our Mother Earth as you do this.
6. Give thanks to your guides and each direction as you reverse your movement (counterclockwise) around the sacred space or altar.

Soul Work (Homework or Heartwork)

Over the years, it has always amazed me what people learn about themselves when they choose to stop using a substance, stop obsessing over a particular individual, or end a compulsive behaviour. For example, when I underwent the Heroine's journey to quit smoking, I learned that I smoked to carve out time away from others and to have a little quiet privacy on busy days. I had no idea I was as introverted as I actually am. Learning this helped me meet my need for silent time alone in other ways including meditation, walking alone, or sitting quietly. Think about a deep personal need that you intuitively know you were meeting by your use. Now consider ways to replace this need that will not jeopardize your physical and mental health.

Spiritual Journal Stems or Prompts

Choose an image for this chapter's work. It might be a landscape: crossing a desert, or hiking alongside a river, or a trek up a mountain. As you journal through your process, note how your location on the journey changes.

Reflect on the word you chose in ***Stage 5: Task One*** that best captures your recovery journey.

"The idea that my recovery process from using ____________ or obsessing over _______________ could be my greatest spiritual journey makes me feel..."

Spiritual Inspiration

Gary Zukav taught me that overcoming addiction can be your greatest spiritual journey in this lifetime. I encourage you to read his seminal *The Seat of the Soul*. I promise you will be inspired.

Dismantling the Social Construction or Unlearning the Familial Pattern

It is a radical act to break a family pattern of addiction. The choice to step away from familial coping strategies, those learned in your family of origin through modelling behaviour, is the greatest act of courage. Unlearning unhealthy or maladaptive coping behaviours, then re-learning other ways of managing life like meditating, hiking, exercising, writing, participating in counselling, and rethinking life perspectives you were taught can be a very challenging process. Add to this that your family members may not necessarily encourage your decision to do life differently from them. Please congratulate yourself on your bravery at every opportunity, as sometimes you will feel very much alone in your endeavours, especially if you are dependent on the approval of your family and triggered by the threat of its withdrawal. Always consider ways you can harness the support and guidance of those who have been on the addiction recovery journey themselves, and how you can call upon and accept supernatural support for your success. The days add up gradually, and eventually "one day at a time" switches to "one week at a time" or one month, or longer. Celebrate and give thanks for every day.

Deepening the Practice from a Feminine Perspective

Some Twelve Step Programs have been successful for some people I have guided. However, one of the biggest complaints I get from the women I serve who check out traditional Alcoholics Anonymous meetings on their Quit Journey is that the structure and language of the meetings is decidedly patriarchal. Some women automatically transcribe the language and structure (as many of us have trained ourselves to do as humans in exile are wont to do), but others are deeply offended and simply cannot get past the voice of male privilege when they are working so hard to claim personal freedom. I give them feminist addiction experts who offer a reinterpreted set of steps that better reflect women's lived experience.

Two of the best feminist revisits of the 12 Steps are *A Feminist Reinterpretation of the Twelve Steps for Women* by Stephanie Covington[4] and Charlotte Kasl's *Many Roads, One Journey: Moving Beyond the 12 Steps.*[5]

In your Quit Journal or Spiritual Journal, whichever feels appropriate for you, slowly and carefully reflect on each of the traditional 12 Steps and compare them to the empowered, woman-honouring steps offered by Covington and Kasl.

Deepening the Practice

Try using Maureen Murdock's *Heroine's Journey*[6] template and see how closely your experience in overcoming addiction or compulsion matches her offering. Using Murdock's guide, in order to survive, receive approval, and be "successful" in the patriarchy, our Heroine separates from her feminine nature and aligns with the masculine. Meeting ogres and dragons in various guises, working at least twice as hard to achieve the same measure of success as her male counterpart, she feels that something vital is missing from this attainment. Life offers her an opening to return to her feminine aspect through an occurrence that feels like a descent into the Goddess, and there, she discovers within herself a deep yearning for the Divine Feminine. After healing both the Mother/Daughter split, and the Wounded Masculine, our Heroine finally emerges fully integrated in both her feminine and masculine aspects. Does any part of your journey match any part of this model?

Service to the Planet and Connecting with Others

Many people who manage to overcome an addiction are so deeply grateful for their victorious return to health and hope that they want to share their joy-filled experience with others. Some lead recovery groups, participate in outreach programs, or become beacons of hope for those still in the prison of addiction. There is a deep sense of purpose in sharing your wisdom, patience, and guidance.

Your connections to others outside the addiction and recovery world are also very important. Spend some time volunteering, taking fun classes, or participating in workshops that broaden your sphere of influence. Your circle of friends will change as you learn who is cheering for your recovery and who is waiting to watch you fail. There will be some grief work to do here. Our Earth Mother constantly teaches us that something has to die before something is born; death and rebirth are constant. What this could mean for you is that you may have to let some people go, making space for other healthier connections, or keep some relationships but change how you relate and how often.

Follow Up with Erin

Erin was triumphant, a true Heroine. Her process was the most challenging yet rewarding chapter of her life. Quitting smoking led her to reconsider her relationship with alcohol. Freedom became addictive! She also discovered other parts of her life where she had unquestioningly continued ways of coping to meet the expectations of her family or her various communities. The freedom to design a life she loved was more intoxicating than any other temptations. Dear sojourner, I hope this is also your experience.

Biblio-Therapy for Chapter Eight

Books and Resources to Support Your Work with Addiction and Compulsion

- *The Heroine's Journey: Woman's Quest for Wholeness*, Maureen Murdock
- *Addiction and Grace*, Gerald May
- *The Hero With a Thousand Faces*, Joseph Campbell
- *The Seat of the Soul*, Gary Zukav
- *Alan Carr's Easy Way for Women to Quit Smoking*, Alan Carr.
- *QuitNow online forum*, Province of British Columbia
- *Many Roads, One Journey – Moving Beyond the 12 Steps,* Charlotte Kasl
- *A Woman's Way Through the Twelve Steps*, Stephanie Covington

- *In the Realm of Hungry Ghosts*, Gabor Mate

Check your area's government-sponsored treatment programs, which are well researched and well supported.

Chapter Nine

abundance and gratitude (reciprocity)

Dear Ms. Terry,

My partner and I have worked very hard, and we are trying to enjoy the fruits of our labours but we both feel dissatisfied with our lives, each of us in different ways. We are restless. People look at our home, our vehicles, and our vacation rental and think we must be so very happy to have so much. It's hard to put my finger on exactly what's wrong. Sometimes we worry that the money we have saved will disappear and the beautiful things we have will be taken away. We rented a container to store some of our treasures, and we try to rotate these items through our various homes so we can enjoy all of them. We should be happy. I feel like I have this constant low-grade depression, and my partner sometimes has panic attacks out of the blue. There must be something more. What's wrong with this picture?

- One of the Worried Wealthy, Candace

Candace and her partner are rich in monetary terms but are impoverished spiritually and emotionally. Our culture applauds profit and the accumulation of possessions. Many people say they believe that money cannot buy happiness, but inside they believe it actually can. They assume a financially rich person must be special, more worthy, or somehow entitled to all they have accumulated. This underlying belief is fed by our economic system, consumerism, and marketing to be sure, but it is also fed by the Ego. My dear reader, take a moment to check your reactions to Candace's problem. You may relate to her, you may be envious, or you may judge her. Be honest.

I interpret her restlessness as *divine discontent,* an opportunity for spiritual growth if she is willing to do the work. She does not seem to want *more,* and I do intuit a desire to honour what she already has. However, there is no willingness to give, to be generous, to balance what she has with what others do not have. The fear of losing some possessions suggests low level hoarding.

My felt sense was that Candace would benefit by immersion in images with a flowing quality: water in rivers and creeks, the wind, birds soaring on thermals. The metaphor of flow aids our acceptance of the spiritual practice of reciprocity: the mutual exchange of gifts and talents orients us with the Universal flow. I gently challenge Candace to move from a place of privilege and entitlement into a relationship of gratitude and reciprocity with the Earth and her fellow Earth travellers, including animals and plants. This movement can only be accomplished by mindfully giving back.

Finding Your Inner Creatrix is a beautifully empowering strategy in my practice. We work together to design the most beautiful life you can imagine for yourself. I steer you away from unrealistic notions of wiggling your nose or clicking your heels together to make your dreams come true. When you combine your dreams with deliberate awareness of opportunities appearing, and maintain your readiness to act when they do, you co-create the life you want.

Starhawk first introduced me to Dion Fortune's definition of magic: "The art of changing consciousness at will."[1] This explanation of magic works because it puts volition, or will, right at the forefront. It is up to you to create the shift in your outer world by shifting your internal world. As within, so without. As above, so below.

John Randolph Price's abundance principles, combined with a strategy from Narrative therapy called the Miracle Question, and other respected pieces from the realm of manifestation, can help women like Candace seek 'something more' beyond the financial and material wealth they thought would make them happy. These are the strategies and approaches we will explore and work together.

Nuts and Bolts

Vision Boards move in and out of popularity, sometimes trending, and often a part of "coaching" sessions. However, in my Spiritually Integrated world, they take on new meaning. There is no secret mantra or affirmation that can take the place of actually doing the leg work to make your vision a reality. In my practice, we generally start the Vision Board process in the late fall, preparing for the New Year or years ahead.

First, using a large file, envelope, or plastic tote, begin collecting images (no text yet) from magazines or from internet sources where you are not violating copyright. Choose images that you feel drawn to intuitively, resisting the temptation to analyze your decisions. Images may include colours, faces, activities, landscapes, animals, earth, air, fire, or water elements, abstract designs, patterns, photos, even sketches or paintings you do yourself.

Do not include text yet. Stay in your right brain for this initial step. Your right brain processes in a global way, has spatial and visual processing abilities, loves visual imagery, and is imaginative, largely nonverbal, highly intuitive, and sometimes psychic. Staying in your right brain helps you not overthink or judge your choices and helps you stay in the flow. It is more spontaneous. Dreaming, visioning, playing with paper and colours, collecting and arranging pieces with your fingers and hands—these are all activities that not only appeal to your right brain, but they also appeal to the little one inside you, your younger self. You may find yourself accessing long forgotten yearnings.

Collect enough visual images to cover a 24-inch by 36-inch poster board. Begin loosely placing your pieces in an unstructured collage on your poster until you feel satisfied with the arrangement. Then glue them down. Leftover images can be tucked away for future use.

Now you can begin to choose text: any words or phrases that appeal to you for whatever reason. Again, loosely place these between or within your images, wherever they feel right. When you are satisfied, glue them down to the Vision Board. I use an inexpensive commercial poster frame for my own boards and place new boards over old ones, the better to marvel at the way the older images and words have become manifest in my life over time. Over the next year (or over the next five years, if you are committed to a five-year vision) be conscious of what emerges in your life from your Vision Board. You may be surprised that some visions manifest differently from the image you first thought was ideal. You may also be fascinated by *how* your vision manifests, as it unfolds in the perfect way for you.

For Candace, and for you if you sometimes share her need for "something more", the Vision Board process allows her to get in touch with deeper spiritual needs that go beyond 'stuff'. There emerges an overall gestalt in the process, a revelation of a desire for a change in your global perspective, atmosphere, or emotional universe.

Spiritual Practice – Exploring Abundance

For your spiritual practice this month, create a new section for your journal titled "Abundance". Consider your core beliefs around money. Where did these beliefs originate? Explore them in your journal before moving on. Follow my guidance below for this journaling work.

Are you stuck in the Reward and Punishment mindset? This conditioning feels very personal—if I do life wrong, I lose; if I do it right, I gain—and is very challenging to unlearn. It is so ingrained that something or someone outside of you is punishing you or rewarding you for your thoughts, your behaviour, your very nature. Unfortunately, this belief causes people to think they are special when good things happen to them, and somehow bad or sinful or evil when bad things happen. This is a distortion of the spiritual law of Karma, which is impersonal, matter of fact, and follows the laws of physics.

After exploring the punishment/reward mindset in your journal, read and explore John Randolph Prices's *The Abundance Book*[2], which includes the 40-Day Prosperity Plan. While Price uses the word *God* to describe Source, Creator, or Infinite Consciousness, you can simply choose a word to better reflect your thealogy, whether female or androgynous, or use any word or title that reflects your current understanding of Source. Price is not promising financial prosperity, although that is often one of the outcomes.

He invites us to shift our understanding of cause and effect. For example, many people believe that money is the source (cause) and that happiness is the effect. It is extremely difficult to shift social constructions that have us believing that money causes happiness. I have been working and playing with Price's Abundance program for close to twenty years, and I am humbled by what I learn every day. It takes diligence and open-mindedness to reverse this teaching of our culture. As challenging as Price's unlearning is, I can honestly tell you that it is worth the effort. The resulting miracles cannot be denied.

Terry'ism: "Happiness is a state of being; money follows."

Price suggests instead that you already have enough, and you are simply allowing it to flow, putting your unique gifts out into the Universe in the sure knowledge that what you need continuously flows in to refill you. Flow has more to do with being conscious and aware, alert and present in each moment as you attend to the continuous flow of abundance that you are already a part of.

Make no mistake, Price's abundance program is not about "wishing and waiting". An old Arabic adage that is attributed to the prophet Mohammed is more fitting to my hybrid version of manifesting and abundance: "Pray to Allah but tie your camel." You have to do the work. You have to shift your own consciousness and make your own magic. Price's abundance program is a true spiritual practice in that he challenges you to turn your conventional thinking about money, flow, abundance, cause, and effect into a new form of consciousness.

Both Price and I challenge you to twist or bend your thinking around to see that abundance effects are here, now, always, lavish, and inclusive. You simply have to be aware of this constancy. Your awareness itself is the cause! Fascinating, is it not?

Spend some quiet reflection and journaling time on this quote as it integrates with your new thinking around abundance, manifesting, and visioning.

Soul Work (Homework or Heartwork): ***The Miracle Question***[3]

In the 1970s, two solution-focused therapists, Insoo Kim Berg and Steve de Shazer, introduced this strategy for clients unable to envision a better future for themselves. I set the stage by inviting the client to consider their primary concern or problem. Then she is asked to imagine falling into a delicious, deep sleep, during which a miracle occurs. Her problem or concern is resolved. Upon awakening, how does she know the miracle happened? What does she feel before even opening her eyes? Often the first sensation upon awakening from the miracle night is deep peace, a calmness, or a sense that all is right with the world. I ask, "And then what happens?" or "After that, what happens?" and encourage clients to flesh it out so it feels truly real. You will also notice that the Miracle Question feeds the earlier Vision Board by putting you in touch with your deepest longings.

The key question following this descriptive fantasy is: What is one step you can take today that would make the miracle happen? For your Soul Work, drop into the Miracle Question and record your reflections. Then deliberately and with intention, take one step each day toward making the miracle a reality.

This Miracle Question strategy will impact your ongoing Manifesto work. Recall that you worked on your evolving manifesto (or credo) in ***Chapter Three: Spirituality*** when you attempted to codify your current spiritual beliefs and core values. Recall that you revisited this manifesto in ***Chapter Six: Overly Responsive to Others' Needs (Codependence)*** where you learned that your allegiance to your core beliefs and values actual strengthens your boundaries. Return to that organic and evolving manifesto now. Make the changes you want to make. How do you want to design your life?

Spiritual Journal Stems or Prompts

You may remember that I encouraged Candace to use a flowing image as her guiding metaphor for her work with me. Some flowing images include rivers, thermals, lava, melodies, paint, liquids, swirling colours, or rain drops sliding down windowpanes. You may have a different image that works for you. Journal about your image and what it means to you in your work with abundance and gratitude.

Return to your journal or a special section of your ongoing journal where you began your work for this month. Contemplate your reactions to the following ideas:

1. *Money is a symbol of the energy exchange between the seller and the buyer.*
2. *Money is a human-made symbol for the energy exchanged between someone who provides a service and the person who is receiving the service.*
3. *Money is a symbol of the continuous perpetual grace of Source.*
4. *Another key concept in Price's* Abundance Book *is his acronym for money: My Own Natural Energy Yield.*[4] *What does this idea mean to you?*

Your felt sense of abundance and your gratitude as spiritual practices can be deepened in many ways. In her beautiful book *Braiding Sweetgrass,* Robin Wall Kimmerer writes about gratitude, reciprocity, and the 'gift economy'[5] as taught her by her Indigenous teachers. Kimmerer has a deep and abiding relationship with the Potawotami Nation in New York state, which has helped her cultivate a sacred relationship with Mother Earth. She invites us to give ourselves permission to animate and name the trees and plants in your world. How does this change your relationship with the natural world if you feel you have an emotional and personal relationship with the trees, rivers, lakes, oceans, mountains, and the animals and birds that inhabit them? Would you be able to conceive of an exchange of energy? Would you be able to express personal gratitude in a different way? Since the act of reciprocity is a kind of giving back, a way of expressing gratitude, how might you show your gratitude in service to the planet? Write about these ideas in the Abundance section of your journal.

Spiritual Inspiration

Abundance invites us to reconsider what we mean by "cost." Not as money spent, but as life energy exchanged. Everything we choose requires something of us. Time, attention, presence, or commitment. These choices quietly shape the quality of our lives. When we become conscious of what we are giving our life force to, we are better able to decide whether the exchange is nourishing or depleting. Let your journaling take you beneath surface assumptions and into a deeper awareness of how gratitude, reciprocity, and conscious choice are woven together.

Dismantling the Social Construction or Unlearning the Familial Pattern

You may have been indoctrinated with ideas about money that hinder your spiritual growth. Your family mythology may be one of lack and scarcity, which you may find challenging yet ultimately satisfying to unlearn. The social constructions of striving and competing feed Ego's need to see itself as separate and to compete, have more, fill any lack, or horde what it has. Illusions of separateness limit us in profound ways. Yet we are all connected, not only to each other, but to the natural world. Your journey toward sustained abundance will challenge you to unlearn ideas from your family of origin, and from your culture. The natural world teaches us the basics of abundance and reciprocity if we just allow Her to.

Self Therapy Tools, Rituals, and Practices for Abundance and Gratitude

Gratitude is always the answer to feelings of lack and scarcity. Consider starting each day with a gratitude ritual. Recall your initial Soul Work with gratitude in ***Chapter One: Reverence.*** Remember that a gratitude practice is *not* a list of material items. Think about people, pets, activities, experiences, ideas, places, or aspects of the natural world—whatever brings joy to your heart and a nostalgic or poignant tear to your eye. Flesh it out by considering smells, tastes, sounds, felt sensations, and visual details. Find three distinct or related things to be thus deeply grateful for. Say “thank you for giving me...” and finish the sentence. Then close with, “I receive with pleasure. Thank you. I can give back by enjoying the gift, passing it on, or caring for it in a real and practical way.”

Unpacking Your Backpack of Privilege

To take your practice deeper, you may wish to read *White Privilege: Unpacking the Invisible Knapsack* by Peggy MacIntosh.[6] It is available in many formats. Just before reading and reflecting on the article, record what is good about your life. Read the article. Then record your reflections in your journal. How hard is it to accept and really look honestly at her challenge to you?

Psychic Feng Shui

Return to your ***Spiritual Practice – Ego Forward or Spirit First?*** work from ***Chapter Three: Spirituality***. Recall that if you are Ego Forward, you may be tricked by Ego into thinking there is not enough of anything to go to everyone who needs it. This is a lie. Ego would have you hoarding because its position is one of scarcity or lack. Wealth for a conscious individual can mean you always have more than enough so you can cheerfully give away surplus. Commit to a ritual cleanse of your home in which you consciously and with intention gather your surplus (clothes, trinkets, food, linens, dishes, art, and other creature comforts) and cheerfully give it all away. This spiritual practice creates space to breathe, contributes to the overall health of the planet in its re-calibration of balance, and reminds you of what is important in a very real and physical way. Many cultures have some form of ritual redistribution in celebration of their gratitude for abundance.

The Pygmalion Effect – What You Attend To Grows

For this strategy, meditate quietly and consider what aspects of your life you would like to grow. Think about what you want, not what you do not want. Arrive at three parts of your life you would like to see grow in a positive way. Nurture these parts like you would a plant you love. Attend quietly and lovingly. This may sound simple, but trusting in the process and in the abundant love of the Universe is really that simple when Ego is not in the way trying to make it more complicated.

As context, a story: When I was sixteen, my astute English teacher Mr. Swan let me study independently. I was drawn to a concept formulated by researchers Lenore Jacobsen and Robert Rosenthal in 1968 called the *Pygmalion effect,*[7] based on research into the effects of expectations on behaviour. In a nutshell, you get the behaviour you expect to get. Some students in a study were told the rats they must train to run a maze were dull; other students were told their rodents were smart. Students who thought their rodents were dull tended to ignore their charges, touched them less, didn't reward them for successful maze runs. Students who thought they had smart rats petted their subjects, spoke kindly to them, and rewarded them for successful maze runs. You can probably guess what happened, and you would be correct. The so-called 'smart' rats ended up being far better maze runners than the 'dull' ones. In truth, there really was *no* difference in the rodents allotted to the student groups. They were randomly assigned.

Yes, you get the behaviour you expect to get. I encourage you to use the Pygmalion effect in your interactions every day. What you attend to grows. What you are grateful for expands. It is really that simple.

Service to the Planet and Connecting with Others

If you have surplus energy, time, and resources, consider committing to social justice projects and activism. Write on sticky notes fifty ways you can give thanks by sharing your energy or time—not only your money—

with the planet. I have noticed that when individuals like Candace volunteer their time and energy on a community project or to an organization that needs hands-on help, their mental health improves dramatically. For them, money is easy; commitment is harder yet more rewarding.

Follow Up with Candace

As you followed Candace through this chapter, dear reader, what did you learn about yourself? What commitments have you determined to make? Candace's life, and her partner's, have been forever altered. There is sincerity now to their gift-giving, and they both get their hands dirty in local forest recovery efforts.

Biblio-Therapy for Chapter Nine

Books and Resources to Support Your Work with Abundance and Gratitude

- *White Privilege: Unpacking the Invisible Knapsack,* Peggy MacIntosh
- *Living in the Light: Follow Your Inner Guidance to Create a New Life and a New World,* Shakti Gawain
- *The Goddess Companion: Daily Meditations on the Feminine Spirit,* Patricia Monaghan
- *Creative Visualization*, Shakti Gawain
- *The Abundance Book*, Randolph Price
- *Braiding Sweetgrass: Indigenous Wisdom, Scientific Knowledge, and the Teachings of Plants,* Robin Wall Kimmerer

Risking Vulnerability, Walking the Talk, and Keeping it Real

Congruence Moment: Feelings and Emotional Self-regulation

Terry'ism: "Feelings may point. Refuse to let them lead."

Terry'ism: "You only feel guilt when you don't own or fully embrace your decision."

My somatic training began during my own therapy with excellent counsellors. As we worked together on my healing journey, these women would consistently ask where in my body I felt a particular feeling, memory, or reflection. It was very difficult at first to discern the exact locations in my body where I could connect with specific feelings, memories, and thoughts. I felt like I was guessing half the time or making it up. Luckily, my therapists told me that it was perfectly fine to guess or to use my imagination. I was learning a new language. It helped enormously when I was taught the basic Chakra system. Slowly, all the pieces started to come together.

My counsellors did not use the term *Big Brain* like I do now to describe my body's intimate knowledge and inextricable connection to my mind, heart, and Spirit. I came to learn that my Big Brain had complex intelligence and would communicate with me. I learned to look for cues as I rebuilt trust in myself following trauma. Later, during and after my bio-energetic training, I monitored my visceral (physical) reactions to the energy vibrations I encountered in visits with family and friends, with particular individuals in my psychotherapy practice, and with clients in my Reiki and Healing Touch practices. Perhaps you are like me, and you are sensitive to the energy vibrations of those around you. It is selfish to complain about this and not protect yourself. Taking responsibility for protecting myself while still being open in agape love was a process that took some time and attention for me to figure out. I learned to shield, to detach with compassion, and to get out of my own way when helping someone heal themselves. I learned how to ground myself in the face of emotional upheaval or trauma drama and to self-regulate so I would not get in the way of another person's healing process.

Parts work changed my life. Understanding the False Self, Ego, or the illusory self as a social construction was delicious freedom. Understanding Ego's glee with triangulation helped me understand why my mom used to say, "Two's company; three's a crowd." Finally, my relationships to trees, plants, prairie grasses, beaches, deserts, mountain meadows and notches, rivers, and oceans are personal relationships that have, without exception, healed me.

Congruence Moment – Addiction and Compulsion (from Chapter Eight)

Terry'ism: "Who is master? Who is slave?"

When I overcame my first addiction many, many years ago, I had an excellent therapist who walked me through the journey. More recently, quitting smoking after several decades of using nicotine gave me extraordinary insight into the detox and recovery process. I know how excruciatingly difficult withdrawal can be. I have profound respect for anyone who chooses to reclaim mastery over this particular part of their life. I burned a package of cigarettes, one cigarette at a time, in a hibachi barbecue as part of my ritual. It was very moving when a barred owl showed up not far away and called out to me. The symbolism of the barred owl is associated with death and rebirth, a complete and total turnaround, wisdom, and mystery. I felt supernaturally supported in one of my most important spiritual journeys to date. I understood in a very personal way that ending any addiction was a grief process with all of the recursive back and forth feelings that characterize any loss—denial, fear, shame, guilt, anger, sadness, relapse, release, freedom. I was very thankful to have Allen Carr's *Easy Way to Stop Smoking* as one of my many tools.

Congruence Moment – Abundance and Gratitude (from Chapter Nine)

Terry'ism: "What you attend to grows."

I have been working *The Abundance Book* by John Randolph Price for over a decade. This is hilarious because he invites readers to try the 40-Day Prosperity Plan for... well... 40 days. However, I discovered that I like meditating on his unorthodox view of cause and effect, and this view has enlivened my spiritual practice. In addition, I can tell you that my life has radically changed since I started playing and working with his ideas. What I have learned from my success is that we need to enliven the shift by acting from our bodies. In other words, we actually have to 'do' something with the change in consciousness if we want to see results. In addition, my gratitude practice has changed completely in a way that gratitude is now a lived experience rather than a simple list of three things I am grateful for. I have been so moved by the notion of reciprocity that I have instituted it into my life every day.

A story is warranted here. Years ago, I had a huge, gorgeous, rust-coloured Laughing Buddha statue in front of my home. I was quite attached to this figure. He was holding a removable, gold, Tibetan, Om cosmic egg in his palm. One day, as I was heading out for my morning walk, I noticed he had been stolen. At first, I was in shock. How had this happened? He was huge! It would have taken a wheelbarrow to remove him or someone with long strong arms to lift and carry him away. The symbolism of a stolen Buddha statue eventually had me in stitches of laughter! Gradually and with intention, I came to a place where I understood that this was a beautiful learning opportunity for me. My attachment fell away. Of course, I was gifted with another beautiful piece of garden art within a week, a flowery piece that held much detail for contemplation and meditation. I was so grateful. Another hilarious part of this story is that the thief left the Om egg behind. Just sitting there. I still have that egg on my house altar. It is a gentle reminder of the incredible abundance I am so grateful for in my life.

Practising What I Preach: Summer Moments
Earth-based Spiritual Practices
Summer Solstice (Litha), Lammas (Lughnasadh)

In my house, I celebrate Mother Earth at this time by acknowledging the turning of the wheel from late spring to early summer. Again, the following spiritual practices and seasonal ceremonies emerge naturally from the Archetypal Human Year as our bodies note the energetic changes in the air. We search our big ritual box for ideas then head out into the forest to look for our Mother Earth's late spring and early summer love offerings. As always, please harvest mindfully and with great respect, choosing carefully from windfall. You can remind yourself of the spiritual laws of harvesting that I borrowed from Robin Kimmerer in last chapter of ***Spring*** above. As with the previous wheel's turning, our practices come mainly from the Old Religion (Pagan), Celtic practices, and Earth-based Spirituality.

Summer Solstice (Litha) June 20, 21, or 22 – The longest day (most hours of sunlight) and the shortest night of the year in our part of the world, Summer Solstice marks the beginning of summer even though the days will now get progressively shorter as we head toward Winter Solstice on December 21. We honour our connection to the sun, and how She dictates our seasons. For example, at Litha, the north pole is at its greatest tilt toward the sun, so the sun's rays touch our Mother Earth most directly.

My friends and neighbours love it when Summer Solstice comes around on the wheel because I create an opportunity for everyone to gather outside, and I have annual rituals all enjoy. I invite my guests to gather outside and feast on shared goodies, playing garden and grass games like bocce, croquet, grass badminton, or kubb. From my ritual box I pull out our fabric ribbons for messages of light on our Solstice tree branches. At some point in the festivities, my ritual partner and I hand out fabric ribbons and ask my guests to write down what brings them light. These ribbons are gently tied to my solstice tree where they flutter in the wind over the year, manifesting even more of what brings my guests light. Some of the words that people write include family, friends, my partner, my children, togetherness, pets, hope, gardens, festivals, music, art, memories, hopes, and dreams.

Lammas (Lughnasadh) August 1 – Approximately six weeks after Summer Solstice, I celebrate Lammas and begin thinking about what I can harvest early. Once again, borrowing respectfully from Earth-based Spirituality, I honour the Earth, The Great Turning of the Wheel, and my own human responses to the energetic shifts of the seasons.

This day reminds us to check in on the ripeness or fullness of particular fruits and vegetables for the first early harvest. At Lammas, we are also reminded that what was planted in the springtime—whether it be ideas, hopes, projects, or other plantings—is now up for review at this time of year. I bake bread and mindfully gather early harvest produce like hazelnuts and berries for a wee feast. I decorate the altar with wheat, bread, and apple cider.

I find Lammas a liminal time. It is a betwixt and between time. I am drawing on the Old Religion here, which was inextricably tied to the growing season. As a result, this time of year is like standing between hope (for a good crop) and fear (something could damage the crop at this vulnerable time). Of course, I am talking symbolically here. My ritual partner and I ask each other "What do you fear?" then we write it on a piece of paper and sacrifice that fear by burning it. Then we ask each other "What is it you wish to harvest?" We share bread and beverage.

Autumn

Grief, Change, and Loss
Partnerships, Trust, and Anxiety
Guidance and Intuition

Chapter Ten

grief, change, and loss

Dear Ms. Terry,

When I had to put my dog, Prince, down, I knew I was doing the right thing because he was suffering, but I am unnerved by the fact that I have cried more over him than I ever did over the death of my Gram last year, and even my divorce seven years ago. What's wrong with me?

- Sad over a dog, Bonnie

Even though Prince had been ill for most of the year prior to his death, and Bonnie herself had chosen to euthanize Prince out of respect for him, she was still bereft. There is nothing *wrong* with Bonnie's feelings of profound grief for her dog. My felt sense was that Bonnie had not completely grieved some historical losses, and these were magnifying her current loss. Additionally, pets carry many of our projections and illusions—the most common being our deep desire for unconditional love. This kind of love is rare from other humans. Losing this projection is painful. Finally, sometimes pets represent an aspect of ourselves. Prince may have represented an innocence Bonnie was losing along with him. If you relate to Bonnie's grief, fellow traveller, I invite you to consider the possibility of unresolved griefs in your own history, or that you yourself have an unfulfilled longing, or that a symbolic part of you may have died along with whatever or whoever you lost.

Grief is fundamentally a process of accepting the new reality, the physical space or emptiness created by the loss, death, or change. Initial grief sometimes presents as staring off into space, numbness, a spaced out or dazed feeling. People may feel physically exhausted at the beginning of their process. Practise exquisite self-compassion. Take your time. I never push for acceptance of the new physical empty space unless this initial resistance goes on so long that it negatively impacts daily life.

Grief can feel episodic. Early in the process, a grief episode can begin with an inability to focus and then, seemingly out of nowhere, snapping out of it. As time passes, episodes may come less often, be less intense, or intermittently cluster again, harder for a time. Bonnie learned to imagine the process of grieving as ocean waves building, growing, surging, cresting, crashing, rolling, and finally quieting to lap at the shore. Does this image work for you in your grief?

Grief can be a rare opportunity to create, question, or add to your personal cosmology (your own system of beliefs), your own thealogy. Are you clinging to conventional wisdom or someone else's? This is not always helpful. One common myth is the stage theory of grief. When the renowned Elisabeth Kubler-Ross shared her famous five stage grief process,[1] she was actually referring to the *dying* individual, coming to terms with their *own* impending death, not to the person left behind. What difference does this make? If you follow a stage model, you may feel you *should* be moving through particular stages when you are grieving the loss of a loved one or trying to accept a new reality. This is neither realistic nor compassionate.

My adaptation of the dual process model of grief (as postulated by

Margaret Stroebe and Henk Schut)[2] helps the grieving person naturally move back and forth between grief work and distraction. I emphasize that it is totally normal to move through a variety of feelings in a short period of time. A person accepts that she might laugh at a social media post one minute and burst into tears the next. She might feel anger, sadness, relief, guilt, appreciation, then back to anger, all in a half hour span. This oscillation of what I call *grief events* or *feeling events* can be unnerving so it is very helpful to normalize it. The body, mind, and Spirit want to heal, and these staccato-like occurrences of disparate feeling events generally become less intense and further apart, and with more frequent, longer-lasting neutral or positive feeling events in between. This is hopeful when you feel like the sadness will never end.

During the client's grief process, I model the softness and gentleness that I ask them to give to themselves and help them prepare for the first anniversaries of losses—the first Solstice without their loved one, the first birthday, the first hot summer day. Making self-compassion plans helps the griever ride the sometimes-debilitating waves of feeling. This process can start before death for many palliative individuals and their family members, often immediately following a sobering diagnosis. I ask everyone involved in the process, including all family members and friends, to think about this question: What part of you is eternal? This question helps the transitioning individual think about her own cosmology, her own thealogy, her own belief system. When sitting and being with people facing end of life in their current form, we talk together about the curious expansion of Spirit as form diminishes. We consider, what part of anyone is eternal? It is truly an honour for me to do this work.

Nuts and Bolts

Loss-Gift Line

It is impossible to heal what you have yet to acknowledge, so cataloguing losses and the self-compassion that accompanies this awareness are crucial steps of healing. To get you started, we are going to create a Loss-Gift Line. Turn your page sideways and draw a line horizontally across the middle for your chronology. Begin with the losses you are aware of in your ancestral line prior to your birth date. Put a dot on the horizontal line before your birth date. Draw a line vertically *down* from that dot and write the losses of your ancestors in a sentence or two. These might be war time experiences, famine, exile, immigration, or community or cultural trauma. You may wish to write what your relatives might have felt. Now put your own birth date as a dot on the horizontal line. Consider your own early losses. Drop a line down from the horizontal line for each loss by noting the year. Take this process all the way up to the present.

Now, look at the gifts of each loss. We are mining for gold here. For each loss, draw a line *up* from the dot on the horizontal line, and write a possible gift that came from this trauma or loss. You may not see the gift of a particular loss, especially if it occurred prior to your birth, but use your creative powers to imagine what was meant to be learned from the loss. This is not to take away from the sadness or tragedy of a particular loss, but to help you imagine for a moment that the Universe is for you, not against you, and that tragedy can have meaning, even if we are making it up. Giving meaning to a loss in this way is a Spiritually Integrated practice combining logotherapy and meaning making.

If you are not ready to find meaning in a recent loss, please be gentle with yourself, allowing the Universe to compassionately bring you to a place where you can at the very least, thank the person or animal or experience or relationship for the gift of their presence in your life.

Crying is incredibly healing; it is very much like detoxing. Tears of joy have a different chemical composition than tears of sadness, or even onion tears. Cry as much as you feel the need to.

One emotion that is tempting to hold on to because it feels so energizing is anger. However, anger is a secondary emotion. The primary emotion under anger is sadness. Many people actively avoid feeling sadness, as if fearing they will be unable to ever escape it once they are down. When you resist these primary feelings, your anger continues and can affect your physical health. Resistance to feeling, and the inevitable negative somatic or physical symptoms resulting from resisting, bring many people to therapy.

It takes great courage to admit that you might be using anger to avoid feeling the underlying sadness, loss, or deep disappointment. Yet there is no 'sad mess' that we cannot navigate cleaning up when we have support and acceptance from ourselves, and others if we risk vulnerability and invite them in. Remember, the goal of creating a Loss-Gift Line (or Meaning Line) is to first acknowledge how many losses you (and possibly your family across time) have endured. As you look at your Loss-Gift Line, you learn deep compassion for yourself and for your family.

When you are working on your Loss-Gift/Meaning Line, you will notice the essence of the book you are holding in your hands: *Another Spring* eventually always comes. The natural rhythms of our earth teach us this fundamental reality: death and rebirth are constant cycles everywhere, always. You can trust this cycle. Your personal transformation can be a conscious evolution if you can look at each loss and consider what obvious, and less obvious, life-changing shifts occurred for you with each loss. When you look for meaning in a loss, you are honoring it.

Spiritual Practice – Logotherapy

Viktor Frankl's belief that our primary motivation is to find meaning in our life experiences underlies all my work.[3] Over three years during World War Two, he endured four different concentration camps, including Auschwitz. He lost his wife, his mother and father, and his brother in the camps. The Nazis were unable to take away his Spirit, his free will, and that of fellow prisoners to be kind to one another in the camps, to find meaning there in the horror, to offer the last of their bread to each other. He called his model logotherapy, which is essentially finding meaning in suffering. Mining for the gold in a tragedy can help you see how growth can come from seemingly senseless tragic events. Upon completion of your Loss-Gift Line, write a gratitude letter to the event for what it taught you. This will help clear the residual grief glue still sticking. If you cannot perceive a gift, ask to be shown the gift and be open to receiving the answer.

Another psychotherapist who survived Auschwitz, Dr. Edith Eva Eger, wrote *The Choice*, detailing how she accepted Carl Jung's challenge of "saying yea to oneself" and considered personal evolution a worthy task, if not the most important task of her life.[4] She believed our most catastrophic life events serve to help us see our own resilience, to make necessary life saving decisions, and ultimately to reclaim our desire to live. I confess to cringing at Eger's challenge to acknowledge both my inner evil potential as well as my inner capacity for good. I make different choices than those who choose evil, but it is truly humbling to realize that those choices are really the only pieces that separate us.

For your spiritual practice, meditate on Edith Eger and Viktor Frankl's contributions to our notions of suffering. Suspend your automatic judgment or preconceived ideas on why bad things happen to good people, why tragedy sometimes feels meaningless or makes no sense, why change seems inevitable, or why we have to face loss in our lives. Instead, consider this: Everything happens for a reason. We are meant to evolve and grow and learn from each loss, tragedy, or change we are asked to endure and overcome.

Like anger, hidden secondary gains can be obstacles to your healing. A secondary gain is a benefit you may feel like you get from holding on to the pain of a loss. It may be that you identify as "someone who has an inconsolable loss" or as "someone who other people must feel sorry for".

If you hold on to the sadness of the loss, change, or tragedy, you are being loyal to the person, animal, or historical event, and loyalty is good, right? You may feel that moving through the grief process will somehow make it okay that this awful thing happened in the first place, or that the persecutor (if there is one) is off the hook. It takes a great deal of energy to maintain this level of resistance. I am not for a minute suggesting that we make ourselves sick by resisting what is, or by resisting healing, but I do know that when we stop allowing Ego to cling to an old narrative and allow the natural process of healing to happen, the body responds in positive, healing ways. Are you willing now to let go of a story? Are you willing to write a new one?

After meditating on Eger's and Frankl's experiences, get vulnerable and honest with yourself in your therapy journal, or with a safe friend or therapist, by answering these questions:

- *Are there secondary gains for me in my loss stories?*
- *Does my healing from tragedy feel like an act of treason?*
- *If I stop being angry, am I letting those responsible go unpunished forever?*

Soul Work (Homework or Heartwork)

Grief is the great equalizer and one of our most powerful spiritual initiations. In her beautiful book *Broken Open*, Elizabeth Lesser calls the entire grief/change process the Phoenix Process.[5] Here, we blend the ancient myth of the phoenix rising from the ashes with the natural rhythm of the seasons. This Archetypal Human Year traces the life-death cycle of summer into autumn, through the dormancy of winter to spring's fresh rebirth, and once again to the maturation of summer. Whether your losses were beyond your control—the death of a loved one, a sudden catastrophe, an unexpected medical diagnosis, empty nest, retirement, losing an adult child to addiction or overdose, the end of a marriage, aging, or whether the losses were brought on by choices you made—spring always comes again, and with it new blossoming. It is sometimes hard to believe this when you are in the beginning time of grief. Individuals in the Pagan, Celtic, or Gaia Earth-based Spiritual traditions call this natural cycle *The Great Turning of the Wheel.* Please know that the pain you are feeling will gradually subside if you allow it to. Spring always comes again.

For your Soul Work, catalogue the annual seasonal changes in the natural world that happen without your permission. Do some natural seasonal shifts resonate with the changes in your own grief process? Do you feel more hopeful that the horrific pain will pass... that spring will come again... that healing is inevitable?

Spiritual Journal Stems and Prompts

1. Choose your image for this month's work and write about it in your journal. It might be a landscape like crossing a desert, or a hike alongside a river, or a trek up a mountain. You may recall that Bonnie and I used the image of a wave. Each grief episode can feel like an ocean wave building, growing, surging, cresting, crashing, rolling, and finally quieting to lapping the shoreline. Rest assured that each grief event will definitely end, eventually. It may also be comforting to know that the 'waves' will get further and further apart. You will always carry this person, relationship, or pet in your heart, but it will not hurt as much over time.

2. As you examine and reflect on the losses and gifts on your Meaning Line, determine where you are stuck. Reflect in your journal on these questions:

- *If I were to heal from this particular grief, what might that look like on one of my typical days?*
- *How would I know I had healed?*
- *How is all change a kind of grief or a letting go?*
- *How does it feel to let go of what I never thought possible to let go of?*

3. The worst loss to endure is the loss of illusion. The hardest thing to give up is a fantasy or hope that you have held on to for so long it has become part of your bones. Letting go of illusions is excruciating. The best way I have found for healing deep pain of this kind is through repeated ritual and ceremony. Reflect on the illusions you have had to give up in the past. Remember how difficult each letting go was at the beginning. Record the gradual acceptance you experienced over time. Ask yourself if there are any residual illusions or fantasies you carry that may need to be released. Believe that you are strong enough to do this.

4. Write a dialogue with Grief. Give it a different name, if you like. Ask Grief questions. You will be surprised at the healing that can come from this very simple journal exercise.

Spiritual Inspiration

Grieving individuals may find comfort in knowing that people have been grieving and trying to explain loss and the inevitable return of hope for millenniums. The myth of Demeter and Persephone was used by our ancestors as an explanation for the changing seasons: The mother Demeter loses her daughter, Persephone, to the underworld, and as she mourns this loss, she takes away warmth and light, which we experience as winter. The old myths do not just help us understand the seasons; they also give us a template for moving through loss. More importantly... they help us feel that we are part of all the billions of people who have experienced loss before us. We are not alone. More importantly, spring always returns.

Dismantling Social Constructions and Unlearning Familial Patterns

In North American culture, we rarely welcome conversations about death or allow for grief responses outside a formal ceremony like a funeral, memorial service, or celebration of life. We do not teach our children to look at the inevitable seasonal changes as normalizing the sadness that surrounds change. It is important to ritualize loss. The funeral, the memorial service, the grave marker, or the urn for ashes are all concrete signifiers for people to be able to return to for memory and grief clearing. There is comfort in acknowledging the love you felt, possibly still feel, for this person, pet, experience, relationship, identity stage, role, health status, or job. A ritual can be as simple as lighting a candle or as complex as planning a longer ceremony. Rituals and ceremonies are meant to be repeated, at intervals or whenever you feel the desire to do so.

Once again, I remind you to always ground yourself before and after any ritual. Grounding simply means you deliberately visualize yourself connected to the Earth in some specific way. Imagine roots growing out of the bottom of your feet, or do two or three sun salutations with the intention of connecting with Mother Earth.

If you are designing your own ritual, the basic outline is:

1. Create sacred space by turning to the four directions and inviting the gifts of the four corresponding elements to infuse the ritual.
2. Cleanse yourself up and down then back and front of your body with a feather, branch, or incense.
3. Set your intention for the ritual.
4. Invoke or ask a guide, ancestor, or Goddess figure to support the healing or release.
5. Chant, read sacred text, make a testament ("I hereby now release..." or "I hereby now choose to heal from..."), and/or meditate on your intention.
6. With environmental awareness around materials and method used, burn or bury letters or talismans, set something free in the ocean or sky, drum or dance the release, or choose another way to symbolically complete your intention.
7. Sit or journal quietly to assimilate the newness, the healing.

8. When you feel ready, give thanks for supernatural support and its continued assistance in the future.

9. Reverse directions in the circle of the sacred space, giving thanks for the elements and directions. Blessed be.

Self Therapy Tools, Rituals, and Practices for Grief, Change, and Loss

Your Grief Journey as a Heroine's Journey

Recall the steps of the Heroine's Journey that I offered you in ***Chapter Eight: Addiction and Compulsion***. As you grieve, you may see yourself as a Heroine moving through the phases of the Heroine's journey, thereby elevating your struggle to the spiritual realm and receiving spiritual support as a result.

Gift Meditation

Participate in my Gift Meditation, which is readily available on my YouTube channel or through my website. This is a powerful meditation where you receive a gift from your lost loved one (person or animal) or your lost dream, relationship, place, condition, or health status. Losses have so much to teach us. Perhaps that is the gift.

Aging with Grace

If you are grieving the inevitability of aging, try ritualizing the stages you are moving through. Ritualizing elevates your process to the spiritual level and gives it reverence and meaning. To help you feel divinely supported into and through inevitable aging with grace and acceptance, Pagan spirituality offers celebration of the stages of a woman's life: Maiden, Mother, Crone. In my Sophia Women's Wisdom Spirituality Groups, I add the *Wise One/Goddess* as a marker after Mother, followed by the *Freed One* before Crone. These additions have us moving from Mother to Wise One/Goddess to Freed One then on to the Crone (or Sage).

A Personal Cosmology

In my work, I am often surprised to learn that many people feel the same way that I do—that those who have transitioned are more accessible to us now and easier to talk to. Only you will know when it feels comfortable to attempt to connect with your lost one, or what that might look like. Some people feel that every time they see a ladybug, a hummingbird, cricket, tulip, or eagle soaring that this is their loved one making themselves known. This is one piece of a personal cosmology or thealogy that you are responsible for creating for yourself. Other women I have served have literally felt themselves absorbing the positive qualities and Spirit of the person or pet crossing over at the moment of their loved one's transition. I offer these perspectives so you know that you have choices.

Many spiritual (and religious) traditions teach that a part of us lives on when the body becomes "unmanifest," or the person leaves their bodily form. Those who have survived near-death experiences have uncannily similar descriptions, and most survivors are convinced that some part of us lives on. What are your thoughts about this? Are your thoughts your own, or borrowed from someone else? If you have no personal experience, it can be difficult to formulate your own authentic opinion until proven otherwise. It might feel easier to borrow an already formulated opinion. I gently challenge you to create your own spirituality, your own cosmology, your own thealogy. Who decides?

A Ritual for Clearing a Layer of Grief

In my world, Samhain is the time when I take a special bowl of stones from my altar, remove my ancestor rocks, and display them. Each stone represents an individual who has left her or his body, someone I have known and loved. I hold the rock to my heart and sing repeatedly one line from a beautiful hymn by Gregory Norbet. The hymn's refrain insists that the departed simply want to be lovingly remembered as being loving beings. You will experience heart-fullness if you try this ritual any time you feel moved to do so. You do not have to wait until Hallowe'en. You can do it on the anniversary of a loved one's passing, or on their birthday, or whenever you are yearning to connect.

Service to the Planet and Connecting with Others

Volunteering with hospice or offering to hold vigil with a transitioning individual has potential for profound personal insights. Receiving training on how to support children as they grieve the loss of a parent has deep and lasting effects on your own growing compassion and evolution. Consider how you can support grieving individuals in non-invasive, non-intrusive ways by simply asking what would be most genuinely helpful. Listen. Listen some more. Then... listen.

When you find yourself immersed in a different kind of grief, grief for our planet, lend a hand. Embody your spirituality in your actions. Allow your body to be a conduit for evolving consciousness. If you cannot help in physical ways, remember, your prayers—focused healing energy—make a real difference. Monks and nuns whose Soul purpose is deep sustained prayer for the health of our planet are making a genuine difference in healing Mother Earth and in bringing hope and recovery to all of us.

Follow Up with Bonnie

Fellow traveller, I hope that as you worked alongside Bonnie in this chapter, you were able to heal layers of grief. Bonnie uncovered several unresolved losses that needed to be considered, cleared in the ways described in this chapter and transmuted to wisdom. Each loss had its own characteristic wave pattern, and as she allowed herself to finally feel the sadness and pain, she discovered the peace and calm that followed. She learned to honour each loss with a talisman of some sort—a photo, a stone, a prized treasure. While the work we did together helped her clear historical grief, the losses remain part of her life. However, she has metamorphosed these losses into wisdom.

Biblio-Therapy for Chapter Ten

Books and Resources to Support Your Work with Grief, Change, and Loss

- *The Grieving Brain,* Mary-Frances O'Conner
- *It's OK That You're Not OK: Meeting Grief and Loss in a Culture That Doesn't Understand,* Megan Devine
- *A Grief Observed*, C.S. Lewis
- *Man's Search for Meaning,* Viktor Frankl
- *The Choice*, Dr. Edith Eva Eger
- *Broken Open*, Elizabeth Lesser

Chapter Eleven

partnerships, trust, & anxiety

Dear Ms. Terry,

It's been seventeen months since I learned of my partner's affair. I actually knew about the affair deep down for quite a long time. Why didn't I trust myself? People keep telling me that it's time to get out there and have some fun dating. I am terrified. My trust has been brutally taken away from me. How will I ever trust another person enough to even consider dating again? I have always been an anxious person, but it feels worse than ever now.

- In Need of Restoration, Simone

Simone was heartbroken. A year and a half ago, she discovered her partner of fifteen years was in a long-term affair. Her partner moved into the lover's apartment. In the months following, she slipped into a state of shock and paralysis, unable to move forward. Her self-confidence was shattered, and she was questioning everything she thought she knew. Much to her astonishment, her ex-partner continued to reach out to her for life advice. Friends she assumed she could rely on ghosted her, but she received unexpected support from others. Her teenaged son and daughter kept encouraging her to socialize. Yet Simone felt like doing nothing most evenings. Devastated, confused, and uncharacteristically anxious, she became concerned about her mental health.

The metaphor for our work together was the image of a phoenix rising from the ashes. This image is a cliche now, but it so perfectly captures the notion that some things must die before something new can be born. It is a hopeful positive image, following our perpetual natural Earth cycle of birth, death, regeneration.

Nuts and Bolts

Perfect Partner Strategy

This activity is not about finding the perfect partner *out there* but discovering your own inner soul mate. The irony, of course, is that once you fall in love with yourself, a lovely candidate for your heart often miraculously appears! When I ask my clients how they would feel if they knew there were three-thousand soul mates for every individual, they look at me in disbelief, and yes, with a curious sense of relief.

This marriage to self is not encouragement to any latent narcissistic tendencies lying within but is actually the integration of our own inner feminine and masculine energies. The goal of Spiritually Integrated therapy is... well... integration! Whether we are considering Carl Jung's *anima* and *animus*, Shakti Gawain's masculine and feminine energies, or acknowledging the metaphorical divine union wedding stories of many religious and spiritual traditions, we are really talking about the same thing: the integration of our energies as we move toward wholeness within ourselves. Many spiritual explorers reference yin and yang as masculine and feminine within each of us. I do not, but I do consider our yin aspect to share much of what our culture describes as feminine traits—yielding, open, receptive, cooperative—while our yang aspect holds what we have been conditioned to believe are masculine features—rational, structured, active, and competitive. Many men's yin aspect is strongly developed. Many women have a yang aspect that is wonderful to behold. Think of this Perfect Partner strategy as the marriage of your inner male and female energies, your healing toward wholeness. When you are whole, you might be ready to meet another whole person. What you create with each other is a completely separate entity—the relationship. You remain whole. So do they. The relationship itself is another 'whole' that is only possible with two whole people.

First, you must fall in love with yourself and know that you set the standard for how another treats you. It sounds so trite to suggest you become your own best friend but cliches are cliches because there is something inherently true about them.

The following strategy is in four parts, and *all* must be completed for potential success.

Part One – The Crush List

Pretend you are back in middle school making your 'crush list'. You will make an exhaustive list of all of the qualities you would ever want in your perfect partner. Consider all four domains: physical, intellectual, emotional, and spiritual. You might want to download a blank Wellness Wheel from my website and fill in each quadrant to come up with a comprehensive list. Be honest. Nobody is judging you for the qualities you want.

Under the physical realm, remember to include overall health, height, weight, addictions, self-care, biorhythms, activity levels, sleep hygiene, financial stability, and comfort in their own skin. People often overlook a potential partner's attitude toward animals and pets. If pets are important to you, this is essential information. When considering the intellectual domain, think about crystallized and fluid intelligence. The former is subject or world knowledge while the latter is the ability to reason quickly and with flexibility. If your perfect partner has earned a degree, say so. If that does not matter to you, say that. If you want to share intellectual discussions about shared readings with your partner, do crosswords, carry on an intelligent conversation, say so.

Under the emotional realm, think about your potential partner's connection to self first, then the quality of their connections to family, friends, coworkers, and even their ex-partners. Include interest in personal growth, family of origin work, or exposure to therapy or recovery programs. Consider their willingness to be vulnerable, and therefore intimate. Is emotional intelligence essential, or at least enough emotional vocabulary to communicate their feelings? Another piece I encourage you to consider under the emotional realm is to revisit the introversion/extroversion work we did together in ***Chapter Two: Stillness***. It is helpful to be able to meet somewhere near the center of the continuum. Characteristics in the spiritual domain might include openness to exploring the non-physical realm, beliefs about Source and the afterlife, core values, religious upbringing and whether they still practise it, notions about spirituality, political leanings, environmental responsibilities, service to the community and our planet, and beliefs about women, ethnicity, ableism, classicism, ageism, and other human rights issues.

Part Two – The Challenge

Many spiritual traditions echo the same teaching: if you cannot find what you seek within yourself, no partner will be able to supply it for you.

For each characteristic or quality on your completed list, ask yourself, "Do I have this quality?" If the answer is no, ask yourself whether you are looking for someone to do for you what you are unable, or unwilling, to do for yourself. Be honest. For example, if you want a partner who understands you, ask how well you understand yourself, or how committed you are to learning. If you dream of a financially stable partner, ask whether your own financial ducks are in a row.

Yes, there may be skills your ideal partner has that you lack, and that is acceptable in some areas. For example, they might be an exceptional cook while you are better at darning socks. Your goal here is to balance and appreciate these superficial differences. If you expect someone else to love you in ways you do not love yourself, you are putting unfair expectations on your partner. This imbalance accounts for many failed relationships. Loving yourself is your job first.

Women in our culture are often overtly and subtly encouraged to emulate the female characters in famous made-for-children films. The message being conveyed is that a partner completes you, makes you whole. This message does great disservice to our understanding of wholeness and weighs heavily on our partners. After all, what is more romantic than being complete onto yourself? I like to say, "You are the cake, and your relationship is the icing." You are enough.

Through your work on your attachment style in ***Chapter Six: Overly Responsive to Others' Needs (Codependence)***, you may have learned you have an anxious attachment style. What the Perfect Partner challenge brings is attachment to yourself, developing personal growth goals that bring you closer to seeing yourself as ideal. The work of Part Two here invites you to commit to developing the desired partner qualities in yourself. Acknowledge that you will never be with someone "perfect." When you commit to yourself in this way, your expectations of a partner become more realistic. You know you are more than fine alone. I have officiated for a number of women who designed weddings to ritualize their commitment to themselves, complete with wedding ring and flowers. You are choosing you... first. Your plan should include your goals, your actions steps, timelines, and personal commitments.

Part Three – Non-negotiables (Core Values)

The common myth that opposites attract has led to polarization, projections, unrealistic expectations, and attempts to change our partners. As we evolve and grow, we realize that having values in common can help us remain friends through difficulties. This section distills down to seven or eight key qualities, your "must haves" for a life partner; your bottom line for the relationship you dream of. You may end up with qualities like compassion, self-awareness, prioritizes family, or openness. These values are the beliefs you hold about what is most deeply important in life, they are your non-negotiables for a spiritual partnership.

By now, you can probably predict the next important step: Give three examples of how you live out these values every day. In other words, check your congruence. Are you expecting to share a life with someone who will have values you wish you had? Develop these values in yourself by acting on them, not just speaking about them.

A partner who challenges you to be your best self is part of the fresh spiritual model of marriage taught by the wise Gary Zukav in his famous treatment of this new paradigm in *Spiritual Partnership.*[1] Two whole people who find each other are amazing in their personal power and individual autonomy. Together they are a force to be reckoned with, especially if they challenge each other to grow spiritually. I encourage people to try replacing the outdated and unhealthy romantic expression, "You complete me" with the healthier, spiritually evolved and more realistic expression, "You challenge me to become a better version of my authentic self."

For a revealing Values Clarification exercise, go to ***Self Therapy Tools, Rituals, and Practices for Partnerships, Trust, and Anxiety*** later in this chapter.

Part Four – The Body Never Lies

Here is where you spend some quiet, mindful, meditative time checking in with your body. Where specifically do you feel resonance when you are connecting with someone who shares your core values? For example, if one value is a similar sense of humour, where do you feel that in your body when someone shares your laughter? If your bottom-line value is service to the planet, when you work alongside someone who shares your love of service, where is that resonating in your body? Often your Big Brain will cue you to a spiritual partner's presence. Pay attention. The body does not know how to lie. An important note here is that the bodily sensations popular culture attributes to being 'in love', such as pounding heart, breathlessness, and sweaty palms are also the signs of your body's awareness of danger. So, it is doubly important to be sure you are not allowing your yearning for partnership to cause you to misinterpret your body's cues.

When you have completed this Perfect Partner strategy, spend some quality retreat time reflecting in your journal on all that you have learned about yourself. Ask yourself: What does any of this work have to do with trusting yourself? What does this have to do with Simone's wish to trust someone again?

The Wedding Ceremony

You may decide to marry yourself. These can be beautiful ceremonies, complete with ring and attire, flowers and vows. Your commitment to yourself is solemn and fun, serious and poignant. You are setting the standard for how to treat yourself, and no lesser treatment by a potential partner is welcome. You are already wed to yourself; any other relationship is icing. You choose. Hold fast to your commitment to yourself.

Spiritual Practice – Anxiety

What does anxiety have to do with partnerships and trust? Anxiety can be read as the erosion of trust in yourself. You lose, or never learned, to trust your own intuitive abilities or your ability to make sound decisions on your own behalf. How did you lose your trust in yourself? Where did this first occur? How can we heal an eroded trust in the self? Building, or rebuilding, your trust in yourself will deepen your intuition so that you will make choices in partners and in life from a healthy, wise, deeper core.

Usually when a child knows something to be true but the adults in her life tell the child she is mistaken, she experiences the first undermining of her trust in herself. She is told that what she knows is not true. How can what you *know* to be true be *not* true? If she is rewarded for giving up her truth (or her intuitive knowing) this becomes positive reinforcement by those in authority or those in charge of feeding her (or not). Her path to being loved and accepted as a member of the family, culture, classroom, or colony is built on lying to herself. If she is punished for holding fast to what she intuitively knows is true, punishment becomes a deterrent for integrity. What is she to do? I theorize that this slow erosion of confidence in your inner knowing causes anxiety because you eventually stop trusting yourself.

In your journal, write and process your feelings about my general theory of anxiety described above. After you have written out your thoughts, work out a visualization in which you go into a childhood memory as your now adult self (perhaps your own inner spiritual parent) and tell your little self that she was absolutely correct in what she perceived to be true. Tell her you believe her. Reassure her that her sense of what was true, was indeed true. If you are an adult child of an alcoholic, you might find yourself doubting yourself on a regular basis in adulthood or feeling anxious when you are required to confront the truth. This may be because as a child, you knew something was wrong but were told to stop being so melodramatic. You may have been told you were imagining things or that you were too sensitive. Your sense of yourself knowing truths would have been eroded in this way.

The same process can sometimes happen with children of a parent who is mentally ill. Gas lighting (the effect of someone who psychologically has you second guessing your accurate perception of reality) is a very real phenomenon for children and adult children of narcissists. Again, challenge yourself to go into a visualization where you scoop up your little self and tell her you believe her. Gradually over time, your confidence in yourself will improve. Learning to trust yourself as your own steadfast partner significantly reduces anxiety. There is a beautiful, calm confidence in those who have connected with their Deep Self as their true spiritual partner.

Trusting your own intuition can literally save your life, especially as a woman in the patriarchal culture. In T*he Gift of Fear*[2], Gavin de Becker expresses shock that a woman who always wants to be perceived as kind or polite will actually be 'nice' to a man holding a knife to her throat! I believe this need to be nice comes out of fear of disapproval. In the context of anxiety, disapproval feels like punishment. The *reward and punishment mindset* is the basis for many religious doctrines, striking fear into community members, congregants, or believers, making them afraid to disobey the rules. This system is very effective because it capitalizes on another fear: the fear of being abandoned, shunned, or outcast. So-called heretics have been murdered, burned, or cast out as examples of what happens when your attempt to honour your own beliefs and experiences goes against the dominant culture's expectations of you. In addition, over time, the reward and punishment mindset becomes personalized or internalized. Everything that happens is personal—it is a reward or it is a punishment, directly targeted at you. Sound familiar? The anxiety that many women feel is in direct proportion to their risk of losing approval, acceptance, or any little remaining power they possess. It takes great courage to withstand the threat of abandonment.

Write and process your feelings about the reward and punishment mindset as it has affected your life up to this point. How can you become your own, internal, unconditionally loving, compassionate, sovereign authority? How can you decide what is actually a life-and-death situation that merits such anxiety, and what is only a possibly unrealistic fear of punishment? Set up a system of healthy rewards for yourself every time you act or speak from your authentic, intuitive, knowing self. Build your confidence in this way by noticing how your tolerance for the anxiety you experience when you disappoint others rises. You actually have larger capacity for this tolerance than you might realize but you may not have tested it. Try it. If you are working with a partner, offer a vulnerability script. These scripts were taught in ***Chapters Five and Six***.

Other Ways to Reduce Anxiety

When individuals first come to see me for work on anxiety, I always ask, "How do you do your anxiety?" This may seem like a strange question if you believe you are the only one who suffers, that you have no control over it, or that everyone and everything around you should change so you no longer have to experience anxiety. Everyone has experienced anxiety, some of us on a regular basis. However, each of us *does* our anxiety differently. Some people pace the floor, wring their hands, hyperventilate, perseverate, self-medicate, or engage in compulsive behaviours like shopping or gambling. Everyone's treatment plan is different, unique to them. Managing anxiety is like managing diabetes. Both are serious life challenges. Both require management, since we cannot eliminate them from our lives completely. Both belong to the person who has the life challenge. This is the beginning of healing. However, it is important to remember that some treatment plans are healthier than others.

Remind yourself that anxiety is not necessarily stress. Positive stress in small doses can provide the level of energy needed for that new job, that creative project, that physical challenge. Another way to frame it is, anxiety can be to see as Ego's tool to keep you fear-based, keep you in its control. Ego craves drama. It wants to keep you wondering if you will be punished for following your own internal teacher. Ego makes every event or incident into a personal story about you. Ego wants you to forget that you are Spirit First. Externalizing Ego like we did in the Parts and Positions strategy in ***Chapter Seven*** can dramatically reduce anxiety.

My theory of anxiety along with my method of going in and telling your little self you believe her may provide enough insight and correction to move you out of anxiety on a regular basis. When you are challenged by generalized anxiety, I also recommend drawing or colouring mandalas or meditating on *yantras* (patterned images for contemplation) for calming your nervous system. The Sri Yantra, sacred geometric symbols of the Divine Mother (Sri Vigda) is calming whether you create one yourself or meditate on one prepared by someone else. The great psychoanalyst Carl Jung suggested that playing or working with mandalas helped people integrate their psychological work toward wholeness and was effective in calming individuals when they were feeling distressed or anxious. I also offer some other effective ways to reduce anxiety in ***Chapter Two: Stillness***.

Finally, I invite you to consider whether the anxiety you are experiencing is actually yours. We turn here to the work of Mark Wolynn. In his book, *It Didn't Start with You: How Inherited Family Trauma Shapes Who We Are and How to End the Cycle,* Wolynn helps us see that we may have inherited anxiety, or may be re-experiencing trauma, or "remembering" it as though it actually happened to us.[3] He offers techniques for clearing what does not actually belong to us. I have found this clearing very effective in my work. If this work interests you, go to ***Nuts and Bolts*** section of ***Chapter Twelve: Guidance and Intuition – Personal Power: The Genogram, Family Mythology, and Historical Family Trauma***. I have watched many individuals experience profound relief when they have "given" back trauma that was never theirs to begin with. Remember, the goal is to develop trust in yourself and reclaim your intuition so that you will make wiser, healthier choices in partners and in life.

Soul Work (Homework or Heartwork)

Your Circle of Support

You get to choose who supports your healing journey and those who are in your inner circle. Simone discovered, much to her dismay, that some people she expected to support her rapidly became too busy for her. Others came through for her in unexpected ways.

Create your Circle of Support. On a blank page in your journal, put a little circle in the centre of the page. Write your name in it. You are the center, the calm pool. Your relationship with yourself is the most important relationship, and you are responsible for it. Now imagine dropping a stone from directly above into this still pond. The concentric circles around the centre where the stone sank are almost perfect rings. This is your universe. At various points on these rings, place dots that represent people in your life. Consider each one before placing the person on a ring close to you or further away from the center. Does this person add to your feelings of self-acceptance? Does that person challenge you to be your best self? Which of them celebrate your achievements with you? Who shares your core values? Who is allowed to be on the rings closest to you. Who lives on rings further away from you? Which people are on the outer edges?

You are actually in charge of your Circle of Support. It is organic and changes over time. Sometimes it is appropriate to move people closer if they are supporting your journey (even if they are challenging you!). Sometimes it is imperative that you move people further away, if they are draining your energy and bringing nothing good into the relationship. Change the dosage with some people. People I call "dose" friends are those I can manage their energy for a limited time. Do you have people in your life like that? You know... *doze* friends.

I sometimes call your Circle of Support, your *Panel*. Your Panel is not a bench of judges criticizing your choices or your behaviour. Rather, when you find yourself wondering if a particular decision is right for you, imagine bringing it to this caring Panel of your closest allies and asking for their honest loving feedback. Choose *only* individuals for your Panel who you know have your best interests at heart, are aware of your Johari Window Blind Spot (see ***Chapter Six: Overly Responsive to Others' Needs***), and who can challenge you in loving ways to examine all angles when discerning a particular life decision. You are very blessed if you have a trustworthy Panel. Build one.

Managing your energy, plugging holes if you are leaking your energy to particular people who would suck you dry given the chance, or changing how much time and space you give—these are all tasks that fall into your responsibility. Take some time to journal about your discoveries.

Spiritual Journal Stems and Prompts

Choose your image for this month's work, whether a particular landscape or element of nature like a volcano or a meandering river, or an action, like hiking through a dense forest where you are bushwhacking your path. You could choose, like Simone, the image of a phoenix rising from the ashes. Whatever symbol, metaphor, or archetype you choose, journal about why you feel it is effective.

Revisit your spiritual autobiography from ***Chapter Three: Spirituality***. Begin to reframe betrayals: your work now is not about trusting others but about rebuilding your trust in yourself, confirming that you can handle anything life throws at you. Whether or not you choose to trust another human, you must first trust yourself to not only survive another betrayal, but to flourish... after the grief has run its course. Ideally, the person you feel betrayed by will eventually transform into what I like to call your *unlikely teacher*. This person has no idea how much they have helped you evolve. Paradoxically, you may never have learned so much about yourself if this person had not come into your life. The spiritual autobiography traces your unfolding understanding of your deepest connection to your Soul or Deep Self, the Self that would never betray you. Choosing never to betray yourself again is an important decision. It means you create boundaries around your values. If you recheck Part Three of the Perfect Partner strategy above, you now know what your evolving values are.

Spiritual Inspiration

Complete this journal prompt: *If I believe that I am responsible for my own happiness, I will have to give up the illusion or fantasy that someone out there will ride to my rescue, meet my needs, understand me completely, offer me the ultimate distraction, or make up for all my shortcomings. The grief I feel about giving up this fantasy makes me...*

Dismantling Social Constructions and Unlearning Familial Patterns

There are so many unrealistic and unhealthy expectations that we need to unlearn and dismantle if we are to re-vision love and have a chance at successful partnerships.

Spiritual Partnership as the New Paradigm

As I referenced briefly under ***Nuts and Bolts***, the renowned Gary Zukav encourages us to consider a new paradigm for marriage. I describe it this way as I understand him, and I invite you to journal your thoughts about this idea. The old paradigm of marriage was the joining of two people for economic reasons, for convenience, or to procreate. Recall that the expression I used for the old way of looking at marriage is: "You complete me." The new paradigm of marriage is two autonomous individuals who choose to be together to evolve and grow as spiritual companions. Each challenges the other to stretch, develop, and be vulnerable. The expression I use for this coupling is: "You inspire me to grow into a more authentic version of myself."

Some of my best inspiration comes from *Anam Cara*[4] by John Donaghue and *Embracing the Beloved*[5] by Steven and Ondrea Levine. The words *anam cara* loosely translate as 'soul friend' so you may find an *anam cara* in yourself, a romantic partner, a good friend, a sibling, or another person. I would add that you might find an *anam cara* in the natural world as a tree, a pet, or a sacred space. Recall that I invited you to consider that there might be three-thousand soul mates for each person and to reflect on what that might mean in the search for love. This consideration can help you see that your first soul mate is the Friend within. In *Embracing the Beloved,* the Levines speak to my belief that it is only through vulnerability that we find intimacy. They invite us to challenge ourselves and each other in relationship by being assailable, defenceless, compassionate, and accepting.

In terms of my theory of anxiety, reclaiming your felt sense of what is true for you may be the hardest unlearning of your family pattern. Your intuition is one of your greatest gifts. Reclaim it. As Gavin de Becker warns, not honouring and acting on this felt sense can endanger you. As women exiled in the patriarchy, daily moment-by-moment statistics on violence, assault, rape, and murder against females are our lived reality worldwide. It is imperative that we reclaim our intuition.

Self Therapy Tools, Rituals, and Practices for Partnerships, Trust, and Anxiety

Values Clarification

Values clarification activities can be fun, challenging, revealing. They help you learn what mountain you are willing to stand on. What does this have to do with Partnerships and Trust? Once you can trust yourself enough to know what your bottom lines are, the hills you will stand on, these core values help you weed out contenders for your heart. This is an especially useful tool if you are dating or what I call "friend-shipping." You need to sense and trust your body's response to this person.

Values Clarification Strategy – She's Alive!

This is my modified version of a similar strategy from Stephen Covey's *7 Habits of Highly Effective People*.[6] Imagine that your plane went down at sea. At your memorial service, people get up to talk about you: what you meant to them, what you stood for, what you could be counted on for. What will each person say? Are you happy with your legacy?

Now, imagine you did not die after all. You are alive! You now have many years left to change what people might say about you at your *eventual* funeral. Did anyone from the previous step say, "She was always true to herself"? Did anyone say, "She was honest with herself and me, and even though it hurt sometimes, I could always trust her to challenge me in the same way she challenged herself"? Would you change anything? What legacy would you like to leave?

By now you may be able to predict the next step: connecting your actual behaviours to the values you claim to have. Give examples of each. If you cannot think of any values activities, consider making it a personal goal to take some action on each of the values you profess to have. Congruency and authenticity are built by living your values, not by talking or thinking or journaling about them. Combine the above strategy with Part Three of my Perfect Partner strategy. If your values are your non-negotiables, you will want to make sure you stand by them. Your values can also help you set and maintain significant personal boundaries as you learned in ***Chapter Six: Overly Responsive to Other's Needs (Codependence)***.

Managing Expectations

Melody Beattie is such an amazing gift to the planet. She wrote excellent resources that I use and share with my clients. In her amazing perpetual daily reader, *More Language of Letting Go: 366 New Daily Meditations*, look for her reading for December 22. You will be surprised and enlightened when she teaches you how to manage your expectations of your romantic partner by applying the same expectations you might have of friends.

Service to the Planet and Connecting with Others

When we do our personal work and become the partner we seek, we actually serve the planet. We are no longer putting unrealistic expectations on others, dissolving marriages, and disappointing children. We are modelling what it looks like to be true to yourself first. It can take generations to change the way cultures colonize, indoctrinate, or socially condition their children. If we continue to encourage our children to buy into the romantic media notion of "You complete me", we are setting them up for disappointment and marital failure. Can you think of ways that we might begin to change the ways we teach our children to seek their life partner within themselves first? Can you think of ways we can encourage our children to seek out their spiritual partner rather than their 'other half'?

An environment where you will certainly find yourself as your own spiritual partner is in the service you offer to your community. You might meet your outer spiritual partner there, as well. What a way to share core values! Service to others might also come in the form of modelling or teaching your process of self-realization to others. If you are one of the fortunate who have learned how to regain your trust in your own intuition, please go out and share this with other women. Share your personal work with your daughters, your mothers, your sisters, and your girlfriends.

Follow Up with Simone

Simone learned so much about herself in her work with trust. She realized she was expecting her life partner to complete her and how unrealistic this was. She learned that trust was not about other people, and she would never betray herself. In other words, she learned that it was not about trusting others; it was about trusting herself to handle any betrayal of trust by others because she trusted herself first.

Her wedding ceremony to herself was beautiful, and the ring was perfect. She found parts of herself she did not even know existed as she worked through the Perfect Partner strategy and the Values Clarification work. Developing this relationship with herself was so moving to behold. She knew she deserved a spiritual partner who could be challenged to grow, and she felt courageous enough to be challenged with this person. They would grow together. She knew that she had all the time in the world.

As for her anxiety, it gradually dissipated as she rebuilt her trust in herself, in her intuition, and in her decisions. Simone realized that her trust in herself had been undermined most of her life, and that she was always waiting to be 'punished' or for 'the other shoe to drop'. Her greatest victory after our time together? She came to believe, to actually know, that she belonged to herself.

Biblio-Therapy for Chapter Eleven

Books and Resources to Support Your Work with Partnerships, Trust, and Anxiety

- *How to Be Adult in Relationship*, David Richo
- *When the Past is Present*, David Richo
- *Embracing the Beloved*, Stephen and Ondrea Levine
- *Anam Cara*, John Donohue
- *Spiritual Companions*, Gary Zukav
- *More Language of Letting Go*, Melody Beattie

- *Living in the Light*, Shakti Gawain
- *7 Habits of Highly Effective People*, Stephen Covey
- *It Didn't Start with You: How Inherited Family Trauma Shapes Who We Are and How to End the Cycle*, Mark Wolynn
- *The Gift of Fear*, Gavin de Becker

Chapter Twelve

guidance and intuition

Dear Ms. Terry,

I read my horoscope faithfully each day and have had my natal chart prepared based on the date and time of my birth. I've consulted psychics and mediums in my community, and in the cities closest to me based on the recommendations of others. I have so many oracle decks of cards that I have to choose a different deck each day to draw from. I've had tarot card readings and taught myself how to read them for myself and others. I have consulted runes and had my tea leaves read. I know my numbers, my colours, and most of the classic dream interpretation symbols. With all of this guidance, why is it that I still feel unsure of how to move forward with several major decisions in my life?

- Seeking answers, Tammy

Tammy suffers from a misunderstanding of the purpose of *tools* and a lack of confidence in her own intuitive powers. There is nothing inherently mystical or magical about any one of these tools. Horoscopes, oracles, psychics, Tarot cards, divination cards, runes and other instruments are simply ways for Ego to connect with the unconscious in a way that allows your intuition or Source to guide you. A wand, a paten, a chalice, or an athame is a dead thing until you enliven it. The power lies in you. You can interpret any card if your question is at the forefront of your mind and if you allow your intuition to reveal patterns and connections. I suggested that Tammy visualize herself as Dorothy in *The Wizard of Oz*[1], pulling back the curtain on the wizard only to discover someone pretending to be all-powerful. With this image, my hope was that Dorothy would recognize that true power came from within herself. I hope, dear sojourner, that you discover the same truth as you work through this chapter with Tammy.

No one can tell Tammy how to move forward in her life except Tammy. No one can tell her what decisions to make. Even her intuition, once trained, developed, and cultivated, can only point to personal life patterns that, unless consciously interrupted, will continue to manifest in her life. The voice of your Deep Self, your Essence, your True Self, Spirit, or Source guides your intuitive response to these tools. You enliven whatever tools you choose to use. You imbue objects, cards, implements, and psychic readings with your energy and vibration, your inner wisdom.

The tools are bridges between the inner and outer worlds. For example, the purpose of a horoscope reading for a particular day is not to make you behave a certain way, but to help you to be conscious or aware during your daily round. A reading may inform your intention for the day and, as long as it is empowering for you and helps you draw more heavily on your intuition, what harm is there?

In a similar way, ancestors, Spirit guides, and angels are aspects of ourselves projected outward, helping the Ego to grasp the inner guidance of your Higher Self. These guides are extremely powerful because *you are* incredibly powerful. The guides are aspects of you. Across her lifetime, Anandamayi Ma would refer to *kheyal* or inspired *mood* to explain why and how she acted on the world. She attributed this inspired thought to

Source or Divine Will[2]. I would call it intuition. She also taught that it made no difference which deity we called upon or worshipped; all were equally powerful if we were steadfast in our process or practice. This Source is your power. Consult it. Get quiet. Listen.

Remember, your best guide is your body, what I call your Big Brain. Listen more to it than to anyone or anything else. Review ***Chapter Seven: Feeling and Emotional Self-regulation*** for more ideas about how to listen to your Big Brain. Your dreams are also excellent guides, if you pay attention, as are messages from your ancestors if you are open to them.

Nuts and Bolts

Personal Power: The Genogram, Family Mythology, and Historical Family Trauma

I invite you to own your power and to take responsibility for it. You can stop giving it away or looking for answers outside yourself. You can discover your noticeable patterns and default positions in relationships.

How? Create a genogram. Unless you have a real penchant for genealogy or ancestry research, this need not be an extensive family tree. I apologize in advance for giving gendered instructions here. You will use matrilineal and patrilineal lines if there are two female parents or two male parents. Your genogram can be a simple visual diagram with circles for females and squares for males, and with birthplaces, birthdates, deathplaces, and death dates written beside their names. Your mom (or moms), a circle (or circles), is shown below a "T" that connects their mom and dad (your maternal grandparents) and your dad (or dads), a square (or squares), lies below the "T" connecting their mom and dad (your paternal grandparents). You are represented by a circle or square below the "T" between your mom (circle) and your dad (square). Other circles and squares on your level are your siblings. If you can, go back three or four generations above your parents. Go back as far as you reasonably can. Put an "X" through any circle or square representing someone who has transitioned, noting the reason, date, and place of death. There is a point to this work, but we want to get the genogram set up first.

For self therapy purposes, you will create your own legend or key, using your own symbols for specific life circumstances you know of, secrets you suspect, or patterns you notice during the work. For example, you may decide a squiggly line between two family members indicates their conflicted relationship, or you may cut a line between people who have cut each other off. You might use an "s" for suicide or an "a" for addiction beside a name. A capital "S" could mark strong women in your family lineage, a "D" for any divorce. If there is a pattern of abuse, choose a symbol for the perpetrator and one for the victim. Creating this legend will be therapeutic as you notice patterns surfacing. Reflect on these discoveries in your journal.

You are likely to notice a family story or mythology running back generations. It might be, "We always triangulate against a third person as a way of bonding. We do this even if the person is in our own family. We seem to need an 'outsider' for us to bond with each other," or "We never talk about Great Aunty Betty's mental illness" or "Our family believes in lifelong learning, so we are always sharing our latest passion with each other." Once you see these family myths and truths, you can choose to continue living some, to strengthen some, or to break free of those that are not helping you live with congruence now. Ancestors can become unlikely teachers, the negative example you decline to copy or the positive you choose to emulate. Have any of them worked to break patterns? Were they ostracized? Have they paved the way for you by positive example? Again, consider your discoveries in your journal.

Awareness brings power and choice. However, it is not always easy to unlearn a way of being in the world. You must be vigilant and correct your course gently, without shaming yourself, until the new way becomes your habitual way. If you discover a pattern of woman martyrdom in your genogram, you may want to consult ***Chapter Six: Overly Responsive to Others' Needs (Codependence)*** for help with unlearning, then replacing, a pattern. Yours is the power, regardless of what tools like tarot cards or psychics tell you. Once you are conscious of a pattern, you have the personal power to change it. Use tools to point to the work left to do.

Accepting and Returning Gifts Ritual

Recall the shoe box ritual from ***Chapter Five: Freedom*** where you listed the rules and expectations you were taught in your early life, dividing them by which ones worked and might continue to work for you and which ones did not. The rules no longer serving you were written on slips of paper, put in a box, and ceremoniously destroyed or buried. For your work in this particular chapter, consider the patterns from your parents and their ancestors. Write these on pieces of paper. Examples of such ancestor gifts might be martyrdom or frugality or stoicism. Decide which you wish to keep and which ones you want to give back. Put the latter in a box and bury or burn it. This ritual adds weight and finality. As you evolve on the spiral of self-realization, you might want to repeat the ritual later on in your journey. Remember to respect our Earth and perform your ceremonial disposal in a way that does not hurt Her.

Inherited Family Trauma

You may be carrying inherited trauma, a response to an event that happened to one or more of your ancestors and influenced how they raised their children You may sense this as a dislocated melancholy or anxiety that seems to surface from nowhere in particular. It might require personal research, archival investigation, or gently interviewing family members for stories to emerge and reveal cross-generational or inter-generational trauma.

One way to dissipate the energy of an historical event that is not yours is to honour the memory of the person or people that underwent the tragedy. Mark Wolynn, one of my teachers I introduced in the last chapter, uses ritual and ceremony to guide individuals in clearing an inherited family trauma response to an historical event[3]. You can do the same for yourself. Is there a relative whose story resonates for you? Do you intuitively know this person's life experience is affecting your present life? How can you honour their experience in a ritual or ceremonial way? When you do this, the healing is phenomenal.

You could write a therapeutic letter to an ancestor. This will honour what they went through and provide release for you. You could acknowledge ancestors' trauma by researching their traumatic event, whether an immigration experience, war atrocities, or a horrific crime against humanity like the Holocaust or other genocide. One of my own favourite ways to acknowledge my ancestors, or those who have transitioned, is to sing a song I feel intuitively they would like me to sing for them, or to recite a poem I think they might like. This is especially poignant when I am honouring my mom. We sang together every Saturday in our weekly phone calls, and now she often plants songs in my mind while I'm dreaming. I feel very connected to her through music.

On the positive side of inter-generational legacy work, you may also discover that gifts or blessings received by your ancestors are just waiting for you to accept them. You can access the wisdom, support, and guidance of those loved and loving ancestors who have transitioned.

Sometimes all you really need or want is a sense of connection with a beloved ancestor. Know in your heart that this Spirit is ultimately respectful and will never intrude in your life in negative way. If it feels wrong or 'evil' then it is not real. It is not for you. If it feels loving and trustworthy, it is authentic. You can honour the blessings and gifts by creating a gratitude ritual, giving ancestors deep thanks. You will be pleasantly surprised how this honouring will heal you.

When you explore your inheritance through your genogram and become aware of patterns in your genetic line, you are no longer giving your power to someone else or to a tool. You are taking responsibility for your own investigations, research, and life changes. You are becoming empowered to make changes for yourself, changes that will flow through you to future generations.

Spiritual Practice – Connecting with your Greatest Guides: Your Own Intuition and Your Body

Part way through our work together, I invited Tammy to imagine herself as a tree whose roots go deep into our Mother Earth. I invite you to do the same now. Visualize yourself accepting life-giving assistance from the trees around you, from the soil, fungal network, sunshine, rain, and natural nutrients. Recognize yourself as part of all that is. This connective vision reinforces the wisdom that answers to your deepest questions come from inside yourself. Become familiar with this sensation in your body so you will recognize when you have stopped. It will feel as though you are split off from the natural world.

Maintaining this sense of yourself as a tree, stand before your altar or sit/lie in meditation. Ask yourself an important life question, then quietly, receptively listen for information from your Deep Self. Note any body sensations you feel. Is the felt sense comfortable, calming, expansive, spacious, and peaceful? You may find yourself smiling and nodding knowingly. You may feel like you have received a positive confirmation for something you know in your heart is true.

On the other hand, you may not like what you hear or receive. You may notice a tightening in your stomach, or tension in your throat, or an impulse to cry. Remember, you do not have to act on the information but *know* it. If you did not like what your True Self told you, be very gentle with yourself. Practice self-compassion. Give yourself a future date when you will return to what you have heard and consider it more thoroughly then. Ask your Source, guides, inner teachers, and Deep Self to gently bring you to a way of moving forward with the information. Ask for awareness and soft kindness.

One of my favourite intuition teachers, Tina Zion, encourages us to be selective in who we choose to call upon as sacred guides via the intuitive process.[4] Two other teachers you may wish to explore as you practise accessing your intuition are Shakti Gawain and Enid Hoffman. Shakti Gawain was a pioneer in the art of creative visualization[5]. Enid Hoffman, a no-nonsense psychic from the early 19th century, freely shared how to acquire and improve intuition and psychic skills.[6]

Soul Work (Homework or Heartwork)

Play with tools like tarot cards, oracle decks, runes, the I Ching, pendulums, numerology, astrology, or tea leaves. The colonial mindset of reward and punishment may have you experiencing spiritual fear to even think about playing with tools. It might be helpful for you to ask your Source to speak to you through the tools. Be compassionate with yourself as you work through any personal fear or challenge. It might be that you are giving the tools too much power. Tools are only tools. You yourself have the power. Note in your journal not only your experiences with the tools, but also your process of believing that they are dead things until you enliven them with your intuition, creativity, reverence, and intention.

Spiritual Journal Stems and Prompts

Recall that Tammy imagined herself as a tree whose roots go deep into the Earth and visualized herself accepting life-giving assistance from her natural environment. The goal was to help her know her connection to all that is. Is this an image that works for you? If not, does the image of the man pretending to be a wizard behind the curtain make you chuckle? Does it lighten your journey and help you draw aside your own inner curtains? Choose a metaphor, symbol, image, or visualization that will help you in your work with developing your intuition. Write about why this image works for you.

The archetypal characteristics of the Greek Goddess Hestia (Vesta to the Romans) may hold appeal for you. Jean Shinoda Bolen's *Goddesses in Every Woman* pays particular attention to the "virgin" Goddesses – Artemis, Athena, and especially Hestia.[7] The term *virgin* is used here in its original intended meaning: one who is complete unto herself, untainted, untouched, intact, and complete unto herself. I am not talking about 'virginal' in the sense of never having experienced sexual intercourse, but rather about the beautiful, carefree confidence that comes with seeing yourself as whole unto yourself, self-contained. This joyful, quiet knowledge of Self will guide you to the answers you seek.

Spiritual Inspiration

Historically, we have always consulted some form of divination or another, looking for signs or messages to reassure us, guide us, or forewarn us. Yet the simple fact of the matter is, dear reader, you really do already know. Hearing what you know deep inside spoken aloud by someone else feels magical. You know you can change a pattern, and therefore change your future, by yourself (or perhaps with a little guidance and truth-telling with a qualified therapist). Be very careful what, or who, you give your power to. You are your own guru. Consult Her.

When you read my gentle challenge to save your own life this way, how does it make you feel?

Dismantling Social Constructions and Unlearning Familial Patterns

No matter what source we choose, our culture judges how we seek guidance. Our family may do the same. If we consult a psychic or prophesier, we are accused of being gullible or desperate. If we seek guidance from oracle cards, the tarot, runes, or horoscopes, we are deemed flaky or foolish.

You might even be judged or criticized for seeking guidance from a therapist or counsellor. Families, friends, and partners can still be Ego Forward, fearing you might grow away from them as you evolve and heal yourself. You can reassure them that your spiritual and mental health improvements will help you be a better friend, spouse, daughter, or sibling to them. You can also gently remind them that you know deep down they only want you to be well. Friends and family members may also feel pressured to do their own personal work by your modelling. They may feel threatened by your modelling instead of beautifully inspired. Their journey (and defensiveness) is not your journey. Even your inner critic may resist your developing trust in your intuition. Revisit the rituals around burying or burning learned rules that are not working for you.

We can counter all these judgments with the following script:

"I know that guidance in any form is simply a projection of my Deep Self in the outer world, which is precisely how they assist my intuition, and give me different perspectives on my current situation. I can think for myself, so you don't have to worry about me. I know you love me, and I love you. I want to use these tools to guide my strengthening intuition, and to take my time thinking things through. Would you be more supportive of my process if I posted a query on social media?"

Self Therapy Tools, Rituals, and Practices for Guidance and Intuition

Sacred Spaces

Many people have received guidance or have had their intuitive powers strengthened by visiting sacred spaces. These may be local areas in and around your communities that have special energy that others also notice, or they may be spaces that you sanctify. Spend some time thinking and writing about sacred or special spaces from your own personal history or in your current living environment. Where do you feel a special kinship with the land? Do you remember when the land around you claimed you?

When I visited the vortices[8] in Sedona, Arizona, I was given exactly what I needed. The land there, the rock formations, the energy was, for me, a spiritual experience of sacred space. Meditations in sacred spaces can be life changing, provided you set your intention for a positive, transformative experience for yourself. I have also been deeply affected during visits to old sites in Germany, the Yucatan Peninsula, Northern Canada, and Panama. When I participated in Carol Christ's legacy Ariadne Institute's Goddess Pilgrimage on Crete[9], so profound was my experience of "homecoming" that I felt it in my blood and bones. The pilgrimage was not at all what I expected but exactly what I needed. I am also anticipating trans-formative experiences when I visit at least two megaliths in the next five years, Newgrange and Stonehenge.

You need not travel around the world to receive guidance or enhance your intuition in sacred spaces. In ***Chapter Two: Stillness***, I referenced our *Shinrin-yoku* practice and my noticing that it takes at least twelve minutes of stillness for nature's elements to settle in around me. You might be surprised at the guidance you receive from the natural elements once you are in stillness with them. Any space can be a sacred space if you choose to sanctify it.

Totems/Earth-based Spirituality

Make a habit of noticing any recurring animal, bird, or insect sightings, natural landscapes, and vegetation or floral imagery in your daily life, your dreams, or your meditative visualizations. These are important symbolic representations of your inner psychic (nature) life, invitations to a Sacred Pause. Use them to reflect on their current meaning in your journey. These totems are organic and evolve over time. Each may become relevant at different periods in your life. Remember that the meanings of your Earth-based symbols are unique to you, and to your life experiences.

Some clients, about to experience a major change in their life such a serious death/rebirth process (total change in vocation, relationship, life passage, transition, or other complete turnaround) experience owl sightings. I have had many owl sightings at pivotal points in my life journey. When I was a single mom and run off my feet, I saw great blue herons many times. I interpreted them as reminders to stop, be still, enjoy my daughter before she grew up and away from me. Some power animals show up in dreams when you are facing challenges to own your power or when you are being invited to stop leaking energy or power to others. Power animals may show up as cougars, bears, wolves, or snakes. Our psyche (nature) self connects us to these creatures to guide our journeys.

You may notice that a recurring dream or dream imagery from long ago surfaces again after being absent for years, even decades. Some recurring dreams or images are comforting, but only you can determine the meaning based on your evolving healing. Remember, your intuition is a beautiful gift from your own psyche. The power does not lie in the totem, the dream, the sightings, the animal, or the flora and fauna. These are tools or guides. You hold the power to interpret and determine their usefulness.

Service to the Planet and Connecting with Others

Developing your intuition can assist those closest to you. They learn to trust that you will be considering many angles, looking for patterns, and synthesizing many pieces of information when they come to you for guidance. The *best* gift you can give them is to help them *trust themselves* and their own intuitive knowing.

Developing your trust in yourself and your intuition reduces anxiety (see ***Chapter Eleven: Partnerships, Trust, and Anxiety***) and increases self-confidence and self-esteem. When you heal yourself, you are healing the planet. Mother Earth needs individuals who are self aware, psychically strong, and open to the teachings of the Universe. As we grow in our service to Mother Earth, we find each other as kindred spirits, and we work together to save Her.

Herein lies the hope for a better world. Save yourself. Save the planet.

Follow Up with Tammy

Tammy worked at making connections between guidance *out there* and her own internal intuitive voice that was nudging her along her path to wholeness. She practised and experimented, noting her body's messages to her mind and heart. Her Big Brain became a reliable source. Her work with her genogram revealed many patterns in the matriarchal line. Some she wished to hone and others she chose to discard or change for herself. This took great courage. She realized that she was also intimately connected to the rhythms of the Earth and the phases of the moon. Tammy came to understand that all she needed was inside her, and that any and all guidance was a mirror reflection of her thoughts, feelings, and ideas. As within, so without.

Biblio-Therapy for Chapter Twelve

Books and Resources to Support Your Work with Guidance and Intuition

- *Develop Your Psychic Skills,* Enid Hoffman
- *Living in the Light: Follow Your Inner Guidance to Create a New Life and a New World,* Shakti Gawain
- *Animal-Speak: The Spiritual & Magical Powers of Creatures Great & Small,* Ted Andrews

- *Be Your Own Medical Intuitive: Healing Your Body and Soul*, Tina Zion
- *Anatomy of the Spirit: The Seven Stages of Power and Healing*, Caroline Myss
- *The Earth Path: Grounding Your Spirit in the Rhythms of Nature*, Starhawk
- *Goddess Companion*, Patricia Monaghan
- *It Didn't Start with You: How Inherited Family Trauma Shapes Who We Are and How to End the Cycle*, Mark Wolynn
- *Goddesses in Every Woman*, Jean Shinoda Bolen

Risking Vulnerability, Walking the Talk, and Keeping it Real

Congruence Moment: Grief, Change, and Loss

Terry'ism: "People are so much more accessible and easier to forgive after they have transitioned... but why wait?"

Some might say I have had more than my share of change, loss, trauma, and tragedy. It is true I have lost many family members and friends to death and to the effects of addiction. I faced an inordinate number of moves with my military family of origin, both overseas and within Canada, as well as moves in adulthood either by choice or by circumstance. And yes, I chose to face the grief of ending unhealthy, even abusive relationships. Still, I continue my recovery from codependence, even as I witness, with horror and heartbreak, the ongoing loss of those close to me. Positive psychology does not sugar-coat my losses or justify them. Their pain has been excruciating. Yet I am blessed to have had a mother who lived, breathed, and taught: "Everything happens for a reason. We are meant to evolve and grow and learn from each loss, tragedy, or change we are asked to endure and overcome." I also had excellent therapists who guided me through these losses. Any residual pain is now transmuted to wisdom.

I still carry these losses and changes. We all do. However, they have moved to a different part of my awareness, and they are no longer the filter or lens through which I frame my life. My losses make me more deeply human but also more Spiritually Integrated in my practice. I bring this learned empathy and understanding to my service to others.

My compassion comes from personal experience, but it also comes from my decision to treat all change as a grief process. If you are changing, you are, by definition, letting go of a way of being in the world or at least a piece of the way. In our work together in the therapy room, people make choices. Each choice means we let go of one or more other possible paths; this, too, is a grieving. It takes great courage to choose change, deliberately and with intention, especially when we fear that which is beyond our control. My heartfelt congratulations to you if you are choosing positive change, on purpose.

Congruence Moment: Partnerships, Trust and Anxiety (from Chapter Eleven)

Terry'ism: "I have a centre that vibrates even when I am alone."

My resistance to taking responsibility for my own life had its roots in movies, fairy tales, and a vivid fantasy life. My resistance was very strong. I became quite angry that I alone was responsible for my life. I felt that I had been sold a bill of goods, that I had been duped. I had grown quite fond of the idea of relinquishing all control and abdicating my birthright: responsibility for my own happiness.

After I got over myself, I was humbled by the truth that *any* support I asked for, and accepted, was grace. Eleanor Roosevelt said, "You must do the thing you think you cannot do." Tentatively, but with underlying determination, I built my trust in myself by doing things I did not think I could do.

My confidence in myself grew. When I dared to be true to myself, my anxiety dissipated. I also underwent the personal work of building trust in myself, connecting my emotional responses to messages from my body. I know, for example, that a queasy tight sensation in my gut is a cue—a finger-pointing to the presence of—individuals who are consciously or unconsciously inviting me into their trauma drama. In their presence, I deliberately and with intention ground myself and focus on my own internal calm. At the same time, I offer them loving kindness. This work has required me to do the deep work of connecting psychosomatic reactions to specific individuals and life events. The somatic healing pieces I offer in ***Chapter Seven*** come from my lived experiences. I hope you find them helpful.

Congruence Moment: Guidance and Intuition (from Chapter Twelve)

Terry'ism: "All that you need is inside you. Let's mine for your gold together."

I have imbued objects with my own energy, vibration, and deep wisdom. I have sanctified rocks for loved ones and family members, then given them as gifts. The objects on my altar have all been given sacred energy by me, and sometimes by others. I have been gifted with drum skins, feathers, talismans, and other objects consecrated by my teachers and spiritual companions on this life journey.

Many people I loved have shed their bodies (returned to the unmanifested), and for each I have a special stone that I hold in the palm of my hand on my own 'remembrance' day (usually close to Samhain when the veil is said to be thinnest). I am open to and receive encouragement and psychic assistance from my ancestors this way.

I have had intense, persistent, recurring, archetypal dreams that dissolved as I have moved through great personal transformation. I remember them being so very important at particular phases of my life, and I look back on them with a smile as I would a wonderful old book I read long ago. I invite you to consider your own archetypal dream imagery.

I have been gifted with the ability to say "Yes" to the guidance offered from my intuition, from my ancestors, from Source, and from my guides and deities as I serve the women in my practice. My rigorous training and my years of experience coalesce with this Source guidance to offer something unique to those I serve. I am deeply grateful. What do I do with the gratitude? I share with the women in my Sophia Women's Wisdom Spirituality Groups that our wisdom lies in our intuition, our bodies, and the sacred whisperings from within.

Practising What I Preach: Autumn Moments
Earth-based Spiritual Practices
Autumnal Equinox or Mabon, Samhain or Halloween

Autumnal Equinox or Mabon (around September 22) – Day and night are equal in length. This natural balance of light invites us to explore what is *not* in balance in our lives. We may have overindulged during the summer months, and it may be time to rein it in, to begin preparations for the stillness and more introspective qualities of late fall and early winter. I celebrate the harvest with root vegetable recipes: soups, tomato sauces, canning, and preserving. My favourites are squash dishes and carrot soup with ginger.

At Mabon, I also explore the symbolic meaning of the Greek myth of Demeter and Persephone, which for millennia has been used to explain the death of summer and the birth of winter. Harvest deity Demeter's daughter Persephone is said to have been kidnapped by Hades, the king of the underworld. Demeter ultimately got her daughter back. However, every year Persephone goes to visit Hades for three months, during which time Demeter refuses to allow plants to grow.

Using the Demeter Persephone myth again as inspiration, I reflect on the natural cycle of loss, the void, and eventual rebirth that Mother Earth continually tries to teach us. While we are not privileged to experience the original Eleusinian Mysteries, we can allow our active imagination to recreate this most ancient mystical ceremony wherever we happen to find ourselves. One year I was in the Redwood forests of Northern California for Mabon, the perfect setting for a memorable Eleusinian ceremony. It was a wonder to take in the obvious natural signs of life and death in these great forests. Mabon is the perfect time to experience firsthand this ultimate necessary cycle of our planet, indeed a cycle that is inevitable for all of us.

I find it meaningful to remember my lived experiences echoing this natural cycle, times when I faced losses, the betwixt and between time (the void), and the eventual rebirth I experienced. Sometimes I represent this with a ritual death—harvesting beets, carrots, onions, and potatoes—followed by quiet reflection, and then a rebirthing ritual like planting garlic or spring bulbs.

Samhain or Hallowe'en (October 31/November 1) – This is New Year in the Pagan or Old Religion. It is said that the veil between the physical world and the spiritual world is thinnest at this season, and that those who have transitioned from physical form are more accessible. There are mediums for whom this accessibility is not only true at Samhain. In Chapter Ten, under *A Ritual for Clearing a Layer of Grief*, I shared my personal ritual for remembering loved ones who have transitioned. Remember that the main purposes of any grief ritual or ancestor-honouring practice are to clear a layer of grief and to make connections to those who have left their bodily form, yet remain in our hearts.

I referenced this beautiful chant earlier in this book, as it is actually the chorus from a hymn written by Gregory Norbet who was a Benedictine monk at Weston Priory in Vermont. If you choose to remember your loved ones who have transitioned by using this chant, you will experience heart-fullness.

Coming Full Circle

So here we are again. The Great Wheel turns. Steadfast and dependable. Samhain passes again, and we begin preparing for Winter Solstice. I invite you to embrace the nostalgic bittersweetness that characterizes our autumn journey. Begin again, dear reader. Begin again.

Afterword

During the first years of COVID, and those immediately following, I faced several traumatizing personal and family crises. Eventually, and after painstaking resistance, I decided I wanted to live. I moved through the great death/rebirth cycle over and over (and over), knowing in my heart of hearts that there is always Another Spring.

What saved me? My spiritual practices, courageous personal work, my guides and ancestors, my mom, my friends and family, my own therapist, my daughter, who was returned to me, and my twin granddaughters, Grace and Hope—these were all pivotal in my journey back to wholeness.

Service to women is my passion, and this continued throughout those challenging years. Providing professional support to others gave me a reason to wake up every morning and challenged me to improve my practice. My trauma has made me a better therapist. I have deep empathy, yet I carry respectful compassion so I can truly be of service.

As a member of the LGBTQ community, and as an eco-feminist, spiritually integrated psychotherapist with a thriving private practice on Vancouver Island, Canada, I challenge many social constructions that limit women's spiritual, emotional, intellectual, and physical freedoms, and I draw correlations between how we treat women and how we treat the Earth.

I hope this book helped you see those important connections. Please consider returning to it over and over again each year, knowing that there is always Another Spring for you as well. I have a special rock I keep on my altar, engraved with the words "Begin Again." May that be your inspiration.

So, I bring us full circle, dear reader. This book was meant to empower you. I wish for you ever-increasing levels of liberation as you continue to discover the beautiful layers of your True Self. May you also find the courage to extend healing to our beautiful home, Mother Planet Earth.

Once again, I am genuinely humbled by my relationship with you, dear reader, throughout our journey together in the pages of this book.

Blessed be.
Terry Folks,
Spring 2026

Appendix

HOW TO CHOOSE A THERAPIST

Since your relationship with your therapist is so important, a brief note on how to choose a therapist is relevant here. I want you to feel empowered. Since I often have to put individuals on a cancellation or wait list, I offer the following direction so they can find another therapist who might be a good match and who has the education, credentials, ethical knowledge, and professional qualifications required for public safety in general, and your personal safety, specifically.

1. Yes, a good match is important, but it makes no sense to seek a match without first checking her credentials and professional status. When you are vulnerable, you may feel that you can trust someone who calls herself a "counsellor" or a "coach" or a "therapist" to have the professional requirements to give themselves these titles. However, this is simply not always true. It is up to you to check her credentials. Your counsellor or therapist should have a minimum of a master of arts degree or equivalent in counselling psychology. She should be able to discuss her thesis, course work, and practicum experiences in detail. Do not feel you have to give your personal power away just because someone gives themselves a title or has a piece of paper framed on their wall.

2. Check her registration. It requires time, effort, financial investment, and maintenance to become registered with professional licensing bodies. Your counsellor or therapist should be able to provide you with her registration numbers and relevant professional associations. Belonging to a professional organization or college requires the counsellor to agree to abide by a Code of Ethics and particular Standards of Practice. Finally, ask her directly how she participates in continuing competence and stays current on the latest research regarding mental health.

3. Ask her for her professional disclosure statement. This statement outlines the conditions of confidentiality in therapy along with her fee schedule. The informed consent you must be asked to review and sign should be comprehensive, and you must be allowed to review it and ask questions. Always look for the limitations of confidentiality as therapists are required by law to break confidentiality if they learn that a child may be at risk of abuse or neglect, or in need of protection, or if they believe you or another person is a clear risk of imminent harm. The payment agreement shows you how transparent she is, and it will also help you avoid awkward misunderstandings around late arrivals, no-shows, and outstanding invoices. These are ethical pieces, and if she cannot provide these documents, you have the personal right and responsibility to decline her services.

4. Ask her if she maintains a personal protection and policy information page. It is your right to know how she protects your privacy in her practice. She should be able to provide you with this if you ask for it.

5. Without asking for details, inquire if she participates in her own personal growth and self-care regimen, or if she has her own therapist, or if personal therapy was a requirement of her training or educational program. You are looking for congruence here—actions that match professed values. You may feel reassured if you know that your therapist has another professional she goes to for personal, ethical, or professional consultation. You will feel safer knowing she has her own care in place.

6. Once you feel satisfied with her credentials, professional status, and self-care, you will want to make sure you and she are a match. You need to feel safe and comfortable with your therapist. She should be non-judgmental and professional. A piece of paper in a frame on a wall does not guarantee the personal qualities, active listening skills, demeanour, tone of voice, or feeling of safety you will need to make personal progress. She should ask you what your goals are for therapy, and she should offer you useful tools and strategies for moving forward. If you feel there is not a match, move on. If you do choose to allow her to work with you and you encounter a problem, try to find the courage to speak openly about it. If you cannot, I recommend you communicate with her governing body. You will *not* hurt her feelings, and it is actually your responsibility to keep yourself safe.

Acknowledgements

First and foremost, I thank Teena Clipston for her compassion and professionalism, and editor extraordinaire, Jessica Kirby. Thank you Alyssa, Elaine, Joyce, and Cathy for your gracious graphic artistry. I thank Jayne Barnard for her early general manuscript editing, along with my first reader and “first” sister, Patti Potvin. I thank my sisters in Sophia Women’s Wisdom Circles who offered feedback on early drafts, especially Diane, Carol, Caroline, Wendy, Heather, Kate, Helena, Joyce, Jessie, Katie, Flo, Lenore, Barb, Melanie, Melissa, and Deb. I owe a debt of gratitude to the thousands of women who tried the strategies and practices in this book as they sought to empower themselves and save their own lives.

For allowing me to incorporate their unique wisdom during our time together on our Goddess Pilgrimage at Zaros, Crete, thank you Summer, Doreen, and Faye. Thank you Robynn for sharing your Qi Gong knowledge, and for always welcoming me to circle.

Thank you to Artemis and Sophia, my loyal felines who witnessed the unfolding from their yoga positions in my home office.

My gratitude would not be complete without my deepest, heartfelt thanks to my mom, Marjorie Geneva Folks (1930–2024), who always, and still, believes in me. Finally, my daughter’s courageous inspiration pushed me to bring this book of empowerment to women all over the world. Thank you from my heart, my girl, Somer Folks-McNeil. I am so very proud of you. I hope one day that my granddaughter twins, Hope and Grace, will be inspired by my belief in the extraordinary global change that comes from empowered women.

Chapter Notes

Introduction

1. Miller, Scott; Duncan, Barry; and Hubble, Mark (1997). *Escape from Babel: Toward a unifying language for psychotherapy practice* (New York: W.W. Norton).

2. Glauser, A.S., & Bozarth, J.D. (2001). *Person-centered Counseling: The Culture Within. Journal of Counseling & Development*, 79, 142-147. According to the research, third in order of importance to your successful therapy experience is your counsellor's theoretical model and her techniques. Interestingly enough, in 2001, researchers Ann Glauser and Jerold Bozarth blew the specificity myth out of the water. The specificity myth says that there are specific techniques for specific groups of people. These researchers found that it is *still actually* our relationship and your own resources combined with chance events that account for a whopping 70% of your success in therapy. So, what about the last 30% of influence on your success? Glauser and Bozarth actually found that this last bit was an equal combination of techniques and placebo. Again, in plain language, this means that a mere 15% of success in therapy can be attributed to technique. The final 15%, the placebo effect—or hope—is crucial in good therapy. For success, you need to believe there is hope for improve-

ment, and you must believe at some level that the work you are doing will lead to improved mental health.
3. Kimmerer, Robin W. (2013). *Braiding Sweetgrass: Indigenous Wisdom, Scientific Knowledge, and the Teachings of Plants*. First edition. (Minneapolis, Minnesota: Milkweed Editions), p. 214; 377.
4. Eisler, Riane (1987). *The Chalice and the Blade: Our History, Our Future*. (San Francisco: Harper & Row). p. 9.
5. Folks, Theresa (Terry) (2009). *Counselling Approaches to Spiritual Issues: A Course Proposal*. (A thesis submitted to the Faculty of the Graduate School of City University of Seattle, Division of Arts and Sciences, in partial fulfillment of the requirements for the degree of Master of Arts in Counselling Psychology, 2009). Folks' dissertation resulted in a training manual. Her curriculum invites MA candidates to explore the world's wisdom literature, global spiritual traditions, their own biases, and core values. "Spiritual" in this context is not necessarily connected to "religion," although it can be. The curriculum uses the American Counselling Association's competencies in four major areas: knowledge of spiritual phenomena, awareness of one's own spiritual perspective, understanding clients' spiritual perspectives, and spirituality-related interventions and strategies (Hage et al., 2006). These competencies are ecumenical and not specific to any one spiritual tradition.

Chapter One: Reverence

1. Hay, Louise L. (1984). *You Can Heal Your Life*. (Santa Monica, CA: Hay House, Inc.).
2. Hay, Louise L. (2016). *Mirror Work: 21 Days to Heal Your Life*. (Carlsbad, CA: Hay House, Inc.).
3. Starhawk (2004). *The Earth Path: Grounding Your Spirit in the Rhythms of Nature*. (San Francisco: HarperSanFrancisco), pp. 205-209.
4. Kimmerer, Robin W. (2013). *Braiding Sweetgrass: Indigenous Wis-*

dom, Scientific Knowledge, and the Teachings of Plants. First edition. (Minneapolis, Minnesota: Milkweed Editions), p. 122.

Chapter Two: Stillness

1. Starhawk (2004). *The Earth Path: Grounding Your Spirit in the Rhythms of Nature*. (San Francisco: HarperSanFrancisco), p. 57.
2. Cain, Susan (2013). *Quiet: The power of introverts in a world that can't stop talking*. (New York: Broadway Paperbacks).

Chapter Three: Spirituality

1. Taylor, Steve (2020). *The Clear Light: Spiritual Reflections and Meditations*. (Novato, CA: New World Library), p. 70.

Chapter Four: Balance

1. Taylor, Steve (2020). *The Clear Light: Spiritual Reflections and Meditations*. (Novato, CA: New World Library), p. 68. Consider Steve Taylor's enlightened invitation to re-vision our bodies in his beautiful poem "Your Body".
2. Chia, Mantak (2008). *The Inner Smile: Increasing Chi through the Cultivation of Joy*. (Rochester, VT: Destiny Books).
3. Judith, Anodea (2004). *Eastern Body, Western Mind: Psychology and the Chakra System as a Path to the Self*. Revised. (Berkeley, CA: Celestial Arts).
4. Brennan, Barbara (2011). *Hands of Light: A Guide to Healing Through the Human Energy Field*. (New York, NY: Random House).
5. Curteis, Sister Eileen (2011). *Reiki: Universal Gift of God's Healing Love*. (Terrace, British Columbia: CCB Publishing, 2011).
6. Rosenberg, Stanley (2017). *Accessing the Healing Power of the Vagus Nerve: Self-Help Exercises for Anxiety, Depression, Trauma, and Autism*. (Berkeley, CA: North Atlantic Books).

Chapter Five: Freedom

1. Gilligan, Carol (1993). *In a Different Voice: Psychological Theory and Women's Development.* (Cambridge, MA: Harvard University Press).

2. Gilligan, Carol (1993). *In a Different Voice: Psychological Theory and Women's Development.* (Cambridge, MA: Harvard University Press). *Letter to Readers.*

3. Gimbutas, Marija (1982). *Goddesses and Gods of Old Europe, 7000 – 3500 B.C.* (Berkeley and Los Angeles: University of California Press).

4. Eisler, Riane (1987). *The Chalice and the Blade: Our History, Our Future.* (San Francisco: Harper & Row).

5. Christ, Carol (1989). *Why Women Need the Goddess: Phenomenological, Psychological, and Political Reflections.* In C.P. Christ & J. Plaskow (Eds.). *Womanspirit Rising: A Feminist Reader in Religion.* (New York: HarperCollins, 1979/1989), pp. 273-287. See also: Carol Christ and Judith Plaskow (Eds). *Weaving the Visions: New Patterns in Feminist Spirituality.* (New York: HarperCollins, 1989).

6. Monk Kidd, Sue (1996). *The Dance of the Dissident Daughter.* (San Francisco: HarperOne).

7. Shinoda Bolen, Jean (1984). *Goddesses in Everywoman: A New Psychology of Women.* (New York: Harper & Row).

8. Marashinsky, Amy Sophia (2007). *Goddess Oracle Book and Deck Set.* (Stamford, CT: U.S. Games Systems, Inc.).

9. Wells, Theodora. (1970, 1972). *Woman – Which includes Man, of Course: An Experience in Awareness.* In English and held by 1 WorldCat member library worldwide. From ERIC - "Woman – and That Includes Man, Of Course: An Experience in Awareness," Theodora Wells. A role reversal reading concerning language and role-tasks. Copies from P.O. Box 3922, Beverly Hills, CA 90211: 1-2 copies. $1. 3-100 copies, 50¢ each. Includes postage and handling.

10. Freud, S. (1905). Three Essays on the Theory of Sexuality. Translated

by James Strachey. In The Standard Edition of the Complete Psychological Works of Sigmund Freud (Vol. 7). London: Hogarth Press.
11. Eisler, Riane (1987). *The Chalice and the Blade: Our History, Our Future.* (San Francisco: Harper & Row).
12. Christ, Carol. Reading List is Extensive: *Goddess and God in the World* with Judith Plaskow (Fortress, 2016); *Serpentine Path: Mysteries of the Goddess* (Goddess Ink, 2021, revision of *Odyssey with the Goddess* (Continuum, 1995)); *She Who Changes* (Palgrave-MacMillan, 2003); *Rebirth of the Goddess* (Routledge, 1998); *Laughter of Aphrodite: Reflections on a Journey to the Goddess* (Harper & Row, 1987); *Diving Deep and Surfacing* (Beacon Press, 1980, 1985, 1995). Carol's blogs are at https://feminismandreligion.com/
13. Gilligan, Carol (1993). *In a Different Voice: Psychological Theory and Women's Development.* (Cambridge, MA: Harvard University Press).
14. Eisler, Riane (1987). *The Chalice and the Blade: Our History, Our Future.* (San Francisco: Harper & Row), p. 192.
15. United Nations (2025). Ending Female Genital Mutilation by 2030. (International Day of Zero Tolerance for Female Genital Mutilation). URL: https://www.un.org/en/observances/female-genital-mutilation-day

Chapter Six: Codependence

1. Luft, J., & Ingham, H. (1955). The Johari Window: A graphic model of interpersonal awareness. Proceedings of the Western Training Laboratory in Group Development.
2. Byron Katie, with Stephen Mitchell, *Loving What Is: Four Questions That Can Change Your Life.* (New York: Three Rivers Press, 2003).
3. Karpman, S. B. (1968). Fairy tales and script drama analysis. Transactional Analysis Bulletin, 7(26), 39–43.
4. Karpman, Stephen (2014). *A Game Free Life.* (San Francisco, CA: Drama Triangle Publications).

5. Taylor, Steve (2020). *The Clear Light: Spiritual Reflections and Meditations*. (Novato, CA: New World Library), p. 45.
6. The Attachment Project (2025). www.attachmentproject.com
7. Reynolds, Vikki (2025). *Workshops, trainings, consultations.* https://vikkireynolds.ca/writings/workshop-exercises

Chapter Seven: Emotional Self-regulation

1. Rosenberg, Marshall (2015). *Nonviolent Communication. (*Encinitas, CA: PuddleDancer Press).
2. White, Michael and Epston, David (1990). *Narrative Means to Therapeutic Ends*. (New York: W.W. Norton & Company).
3. Berne, Eric (1996). *Games People Play: The Basic Handbook of Transactional Analysis*. (New York: Ballantine Books).
4. Jung, Carl (1968). *Man and His Symbols*. (New York: Dell).
5. Schwartz, Richard (1995). *Internal Family Systems Therapy*. (New York: Guilford Press).
6. Beresford-Kroeger, Diana. *The Medicine of Trees, Ninth Haig-Brown Lecture (transcript)*, p. 14. and p. 18.

Chapter Eight: Addiction and Compulsion

1. Prochaska, James; Norcross, John; and DiClemente, Carlo (1994). *Changing for Good: A Revolutionary Six-Stage Program for Overcoming Bad Habits and Moving Your Life Positively Forward*. (Fort Mill, SC: Quill).
2. Campbell, Joseph (1972). *The Hero With a Thousand Faces*. (Princeton, NJ: Princeton University Press).
3. Neff, Kristin (2025). Self-compassion. www.self-compassion.org
4. Covington, Stephanie (1994). *A Feminist Reinterpretation of the Twelve Steps for Women* (from *A Woman's Way Through the Twelve Steps*. (MN: Hazelden Publishing).

5. Kasl, Charlotte (1992). *Many Roads, One Journey – Moving Beyond the 12 Steps.* (New York: HarperCollins).
6. Murdoch, Maureen (1990). *The Heroine's Journey: Woman's Quest for Wholeness.* (Boulder, CO: Shambhala Publications).

Chapter Nine: Abundance and Gratitude (Reciprocity)

1. Starhawk (1999). *The Spiral Dance: A Rebirth of the Ancient Religion of the Great Goddess.* (San Francisco: HarperOne).
2. Randolph Price, John (1996). *The Abundance Book.* (Carlsbad, CA: Hay House, Inc.).
3. de Shazer, Steve and Dolan, Yvonne (2007). *More Than Miracles: The State of the Art of Solution-Focused Brief Therapy.* (Oxfordshire, UK: Routledge).
4. Randolph Price, John (1996). *The Abundance Book.* (Carlsbad, CA: Hay House, Inc.).
5. Kimmerer, Robin W. (2013). *Braiding Sweetgrass: Indigenous Wisdom, Scientific Knowledge, and the Teachings of Plants.* First edition. (Minneapolis, Minnesota: Milkweed Editions).
6. McIntosh, Peggy (2003). White Privilege: Unpacking the Invisible Knapsack. In S. Plous (Ed.), Understanding Prejudice and Discrimination. (Chicago: McGraw-Hill), pp. 191-196.
7. Rosenthal, Robert and Jacobsen, Lenore (1968). Pygmalion in the classroom: teacher expectation and pupils' intellectual development. (New York: Holt, Rinehart and Winston).

Chapter Ten: Grief, Change, and Loss

1. Kubler-Ross, Elisabeth (1969). *On Death and Dying: What the Dying Have to Teach Doctors, Nurses, Clergy and Their Own Families.* (New York: The Macmillan Company).
2. Stroebe, Margaret and Schut, Henk (1999). The dual process model of

coping with bereavement: Rationale and description. *Death Studies*, 23, 197-224.
3. Frankl, Viktor (1962). *Man's Search for Meaning: An Introduction to Logotherapy*. (Boston: Beacon Press).
4. Eger, Edith Eva (2017). *The Choice: Embrace the Possible.* (New York: Scribner), p. 162.
5. Lesser, Elizabeth (2005). *Broken Open*. (New York: Villard).

Chapter Eleven: Partnerships, Trust, and Anxiety

1. Zukav, Gary (2010). *Spiritual Partnership: The Journey to Authentic Power.* (San Francisco: HarperOne).
2. de Becker, Gavin (1999). *The Gift of Fear: Survival Signals That Protect Us from Violence*. (New York: Dell Publishing).
3. Wolynn, Mark (2016). *It Didn't Start with You: How Inherited Family Trauma Shapes Who We Are and How to End the Cycle.* (New York: Penguin Life).
4. O'Donohue, John (1998). Anam Cara: A Book of Celtic Wisdom. (New York: HarperCollins).
5. Levine, Stephen and Levine, Ondrea (1996). *Embracing the Beloved: Relationship as a Path of Awakening*. (Albany, New York: Anchor).
6. Covey, Stephen (2004). *The 7 Habits of Highly Effective People: Powerful Lessons in Personal Change.* (New York: Free Press).

Chapter Twelve: Guidance and Intuition

1. Baum, L. Frank (1900). The Wonderful Wizard of Oz. (Chicago: George M. Hill Company).
2. Mangalananda, Swami (2007). *A Goddess among us: The divine life of Anandamayi Ma*. (Mumbai: Yogi Impressions), p. 13.
3. Wolynn, Mark (2016). *It Didn't Start with You: How Inherited Fam-*

ily Trauma Shapes Who We Are and How to End the Cycle. (New York: Penguin Life).
4. Zion, Tina (2021). *Intuition Training.* The Shift Network.
5. Gawain, Shakti (1998). *Living in the Light: Follow Your Inner Guidance to create a New Life and a New World.* (Novato, CA: New World Library).
6. Hoffman, Enid (1997). *Develop Your Psychic Skills.* (Atglen, PA: Schiffer Publishing).
7. Shinoda Bolen, Jean (1984). *Goddesses in Everywoman: A New Psychology of Women.* (New York: Harper & Row).
8. Sedona Chamber of Commerce & Tourism Bureau (2025). Sedona Vortex Sites. https://visitsedona.com/spiritual-wellness/vortex-sites/
9. The Goddess Pilgrimage to Crete (2025). www.goddessariadne.org

Autumn Moments

1. Norbet, Gregory, The Monks of Western Priory (2012). *All I Ask of You.* [MP3] From: Journeysongs Third Edition CD Library.

Bibliography

Dear Reader, I learned from the following sources through written works and personal teachings, and I invite you to consult them as you deepen your personal work.

- A Course in Miracles. (2007). Combined volume (3rd ed.). Mill Valley, CA: Foundation for Inner Peace.
- Allen, R. (Ed.). (2012). SMART Recovery Family & Friends Handbook. Mentor, OH: Alcohol & Drug Abuse Self-Help Network, Inc.
- American Psychiatric Association. (2013). Diagnostic and Statistical Manual of Mental Disorders (5th ed.).
- Ariadne Institute. Goddess Ariadne. https://www.goddessariadne.org/
- Baldwin, C. (1991). Life's Companion: Journal Writing as a Spiritual Quest. New York, NY: Bantam Books.
- Beattie, M. (2000). More Language of Letting Go: 366 New Daily Meditations. Danvers, MA: Hazelden Publishing.
- Berne, E. (1996). Games People Play: The Basic Handbook of Transactional Analysis. New York, NY: Ballantine Books.
- Beresford-Kroeger, D. (n.d.). The Medicine of Trees. Ninth Haig-Brown Lecture (transcript).

– Bolen, J. S. (1985). Goddesses in Everywoman: A New Psychology of Women. New York, NY: Harper & Row.
– Bower, S. A., & Bower, G. H. (1976). Asserting Yourself: A Practical Guide for Positive Change. Reading, MA: Addison-Wesley.
– Brennan, B. (2011). Hands of Light: A Guide to Healing Through the Human Energy Field. New York, NY: Random House.
– Budapest, Z. (1989). Self-Blessing Ritual. In C. P. Christ & J. Plaskow (Eds.), Womanspirit Rising: A Feminist Reader in Religion. New York, NY: HarperCollins.
– Cain, S. (2013). Quiet: The Power of Introverts in a World That Can't Stop Talking. New York, NY: Broadway Books.
– Campbell, J. (1972). The Hero with a Thousand Faces. Princeton, NJ: Princeton University Press.
– Chia, M. (2008). The Inner Smile: Increasing Chi through the Cultivation of Joy. Rochester, VT: Destiny Books.
– Christ, C. P. (1989). Why women need the goddess. In C. P. Christ & J. Plaskow (Eds.), Womanspirit Rising: A Feminist Reader in Religion. New York, NY: HarperCollins.
– Christ, C. P., & Plaskow, J. (Eds.). (1989). Womanspirit Rising: A Feminist Reader in Religion. New York, NY: HarperCollins.
– Christ, C. P., & Plaskow, J. (Eds.). (1989). Weaving the Visions: New Patterns in Feminist Spirituality. New York, NY: HarperCollins.
– Covey, S. R. (2004). The 7 Habits of Highly Effective People. New York, NY: Free Press.
– Covington, S. (1994). A Woman's Way through the Twelve Steps. Center City, MN: Hazelden Publishing.
– Curteis, E. (2011). Reiki: Universal Gift of God's Healing Love. Terrace, BC: CCB Publishing.
– de Becker, G. (1999). The Gift of Fear. New York, NY: Dell.
– de Shazer, S., & Dolan, Y. (2007). More Than Miracles: The State of

the Art of Solution-Focused Brief Therapy. Oxfordshire, UK: Routledge.
- Dillard, A. (1990). The Writing Life. London, UK: Picador.
- Eger, E. E. (2017). The Choice: Embrace the Possible. New York, NY: Scribner.
- Eisler, R. (1987). The Chalice and the Blade. San Francisco, CA: Harper & Row.
- Feminism and Religion. Edited by J. Rudolph. https://feminismandreligion.com/
- Folks, T. M. (2009). Counselling Approaches to Spiritual Issues: A Course Proposal. Master's thesis, City University of Seattle.
- Frankl, V. (1962). Man's Search for Meaning. Boston, MA: Beacon Press.
- Gawain, S. (1998). Living in the Light. Novato, CA: New World Library.
- Gilligan, C. (1993). In a Different Voice. Cambridge, MA: Harvard University Press.
- Gimbutas, M. (1982). Goddesses and Gods of Old Europe, 7000–3500 B.C. Berkeley, CA: University of California Press.
- Glauser, A. S., & Bozarth, J. D. (2001). Person-Centered Counseling: The Culture Within. Journal of Counseling & Development, 79, 142–147.
- Gordon, J. The Attachment Project. https://www.attachmentproject.com/
- Hage, S. M. (2006). Spirituality in psychology training programs. Professional Psychology: Research and Practice, 37(3), 303–310.
- Hay, L. L. (1984). You Can Heal Your Life. Santa Monica, CA: Hay House.
- Hay, L. L. (2016). Mirror Work. Carlsbad, CA: Hay House.
- Hoffman, E. (1997). Develop Your Psychic Skills. Atglen, PA:

Schiffer Publishing.
- Hollis, J. (2005). Finding Meaning in the Second Half of Life. New York, NY: Gotham Books.
- Hollis, J. (2018). Living an Examined Life. Boulder, CO: Sounds True.
- Hollis, J. (2020). A Life of Meaning (Audio CD). Boulder, CO: Sounds True.
- Jourard, S. M. (1964). The Transparent Self. New York, NY: Van Nostrand.
- Judith, A. (2004). Eastern Body, Western Mind. Berkeley, CA: Celestial Arts.
- Jung, C. G. (1968). Man and His Symbols. New York, NY: Dell.
- Jung, C. G., & Hinkle, B. M. (2013). Introvert and Extrovert Personality Traits (Kindle ed.).
- Karpman, S. (2014). A Game-Free Life. San Francisco, CA: Drama Triangle Publications.
- Kasl, C. (1992). Many Roads, One Journey. New York, NY: HarperCollins.
- Katie, B., & Mitchell, S. (2003). Loving What Is. New York, NY: Three Rivers Press.
- Kidd, S. M. (1996). The Dance of the Dissident Daughter. San Francisco, CA: HarperOne.
- Kimmerer, R. W. (2013). Braiding Sweetgrass. Minneapolis, MN: Milkweed Editions.
- Kleiner, L. (2023). As Is Your Desire, So Is Your Destiny. Jungian lecture, Comox Valley Jung Society.
- Knudtson, P., & Suzuki, D. (1993). Wisdom of the Elders. Toronto, ON: Stoddart.
- Kübler-Ross, E. (1969). On Death and Dying. New York, NY: Macmillan.

– Levine, S., & Levine, O. (1996). Embracing the Beloved. Albany, NY: Anchor.
– Lesser, E. (2005). Broken Open. New York, NY: Villard.
– Lewis, C. S. (2001). A Grief Observed. San Francisco, CA: Harper.
– Lipski, A. (2007). The Essential Sri Anandamayi Ma. Delhi, India: Motilal Banarsidass.
– Luft, J. (1969). Of Human Interaction. Palo Alto, CA: Mayfield.
– Maharshi, R. (1989). Be As You Are. London, UK: Penguin.
– Mangalananda, S. (2007). A Goddess Among Us. Mumbai, India: Yogi Impressions.
– Marashinsky, A. S. (1997). Goddess Oracle Book and Deck. Stamford, CT: U.S. Games Systems.
– McIntosh, P. (2003). White privilege. In S. Plous (Ed.), Understanding Prejudice and Discrimination. Chicago, IL: McGraw-Hill.
– Miller, G. (2003). Incorporating Spirituality in Counseling and Psychotherapy. Hoboken, NJ: Wiley.
– Miller, S. D., Duncan, B. L., & Hubble, M. A. (1997). Escape from Babel. New York, NY: W. W. Norton.
– Miyazaki, Y. (2018). Shinrin-Yoku: The Japanese Art of Forest Bathing. London, UK: Aster.
– Monaghan, P. (1999). The Goddess Companion. St. Paul, MN: Llewellyn.
– Monaghan, P. (1999). The Goddess Path. Woodbury, MN: Llewellyn.
– Murdoch, M. (1990). The Heroine's Journey. Boulder, CO: Shambhala.
– Neff, K. Self-Compassion. https://self-compassion.org/
– Norbet, G. (2012). All I Ask of You. MP3 recording.
– O'Donohue, J. (1998). Anam Cara. New York, NY: HarperCollins.
– Price, J. R. (1996). The Abundance Book. Carlsbad, CA: Hay House.
– Prochaska, J., Norcross, J., & DiClemente, C. (1994). Changing for

Good. New York, NY: Quill.
- Restakis, J. (2021). Civilizing the State. Gabriola Island, BC: New Society Publishers.
- Reynolds, V. Workshop Exercises. https://vikkireynolds.ca/
- Rilke, R. M. (2016). Letters to a Young Poet. Chicago, IL: Penguin Classics.
- Rogers, C. R. (1951). Client-Centered Therapy. Boston, MA: Houghton Mifflin.
- Rogers, C. R. (1961). On Becoming a Person. Boston, MA: Houghton Mifflin.
- Rogers, C. R. (1978). Carl Rogers on Personal Power. London, UK: Constable.
- Rogers, C. R. (1980). A Way of Being. Boston, MA: Houghton Mifflin.
- Rosenberg, M. (2015). Nonviolent Communication. Encinitas, CA: PuddleDancer Press.
- Rosenberg, S. (2017). Accessing the Healing Power of the Vagus Nerve. Berkeley, CA: North Atlantic Books.
- Rosenthal, R., & Jacobson, L. (1968). Pygmalion in the Classroom. New York, NY: Holt, Rinehart and Winston.
- Rumi. (1997). The Illuminated Rumi (C. Barks, Trans.). New York, NY: Broadway Books.
- Rumi. (2004). The Essential Rumi (C. Barks & J. Moyne, Trans.). San Francisco, CA: HarperOne.
- Schwartz, R. C. (1995). Internal Family Systems. New York, NY: Guilford Press.
- Schwartz, R. C. (2023). Greater Than the Sum of the Parts (Audio course).
- Shange, N. (2010). For Colored Girls Who Have Considered Suicide / When the Rainbow Is Enuf. New York, NY: Scribner.

– Shunya, A. (2022). Roar Like a Goddess. Boulder, CO: Sounds True.
– SpiritFirst Counselling. https://spiritfirstcounselling.ca/
– Starhawk. (1999). The Spiral Dance. San Francisco, CA: HarperOne.
– Starhawk. (2004). The Earth Path. San Francisco, CA: HarperSanFrancisco.
– Stroebe, M., & Schut, H. (1999). Dual process model of coping with bereavement. Death Studies, 23, 197–224.
– Taylor, S. (2020). The Clear Light. Novato, CA: New World Library.
– Thich Nhat Hanh. (1998). The Heart of the Buddha's Teaching. Berkeley, CA: Parallax Press.
– Thoreau, H. D. (2016). Walden. Chicago, IL: Macmillan Collector's Library.
– Tolle, E. (2005). A New Earth. London, UK: Penguin.
– Tolle, E. (2019). The Power of Now Journal. Novato, CA: New World Library.
– Truss, D. Interview with Roy Henry Vickers. https://pairadimes.davidtruss.com/
– Weil, S. (2012). Gravity and Grace. Abingdon, UK: Routledge.
– White, M., & Epston, D. (1990). Narrative Means to Therapeutic Ends. New York, NY: W. W. Norton.
– Wolynn, M. (2016). It Didn't Start with You. New York, NY: Penguin Life.
– World Health Organization. International Day of Zero Tolerance for Female Genital Mutilation. https://www.un.org/en/observances/female-genital-mutilation-day
– Zion, T. (2021). Intuition Training. The Shift Network.
– Zukav, G. (2010). Spiritual Partnership. San Francisco, CA: HarperOne

About the Author

Terry Folks (Theresa Folks), MA, RCC, CCC (Ms. Terry) is an eco-feminist, spiritually integrated psychotherapist, educator, and author with a thriving private practice on Vancouver Island, Canada. She serves women through SpiritFirst Counselling in Comox, British Columbia, supporting clients in their personal, emotional, and spiritual growth.

Terry believes we can help heal the planet by attending to our own conscious evolution. She facilitates Sophia Women's Wisdom groups and leads workshops focused on women's empowerment. Through her work, she shares self-therapy strategies and spiritual practices in support of her life's mission: helping women reclaim their inner authority and wisdom.

She is also the author of *Counselling Approaches to Spiritual Issues,* a master's-level curriculum for MA candidates interested in integrating spiritual resources into therapeutic practice. Terry feels deeply grateful for her publishing relationship with Teena Clipston.

Learn more at: www.spiritfirstcounselling.ca

www.ingramcontent.com/pod-product-compliance
Lightning Source LLC
LaVergne TN
LVHW090313210926
848480LV00001B/234
9781738170562